I Want to Be a Wall

Honami Shirono

Contents

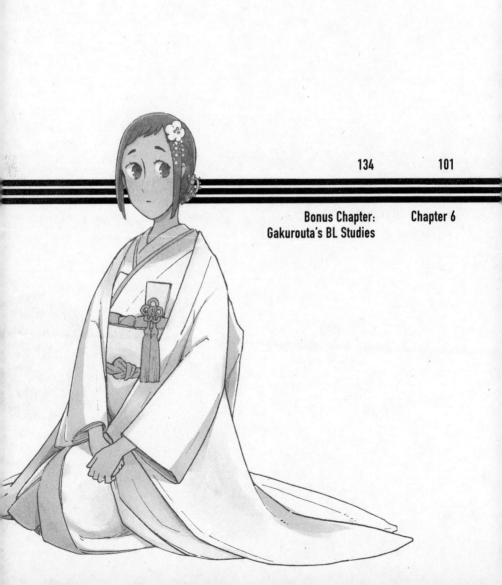

I Want
to Be a
Wall

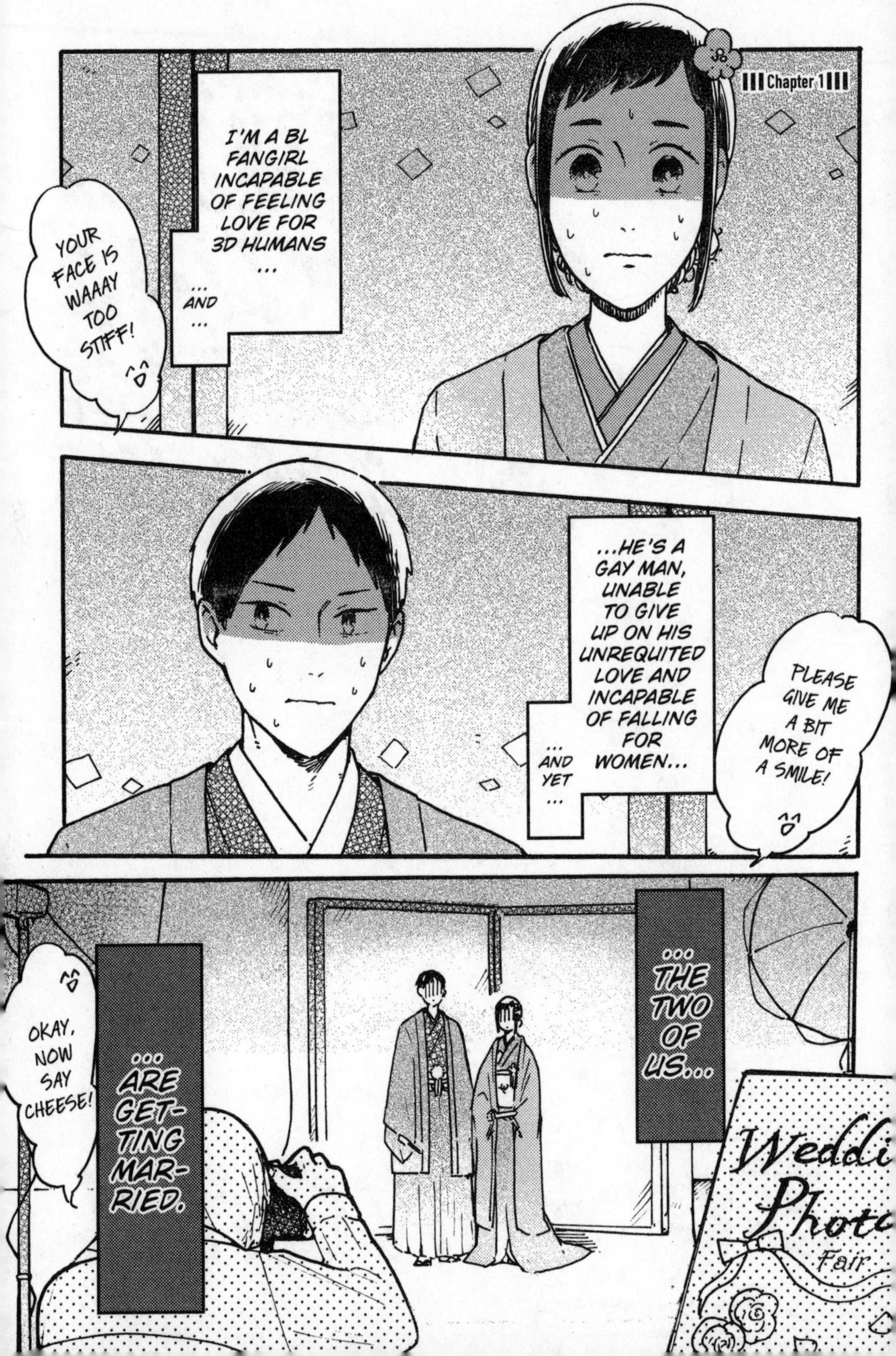
Chapter 1
I'M A BL FANGIRL INCAPABLE OF FEELING LOVE FOR 3D HUMANS ...
... AND ...
YOUR FACE IS WAAAY TOO STIFF!
...HE'S A GAY MAN, UNABLE TO GIVE UP ON HIS UNREQUITED LOVE AND INCAPABLE OF FALLING FOR WOMEN...
... AND YET ...
PLEASE GIVE ME A BIT MORE OF A SMILE!
...THE TWO OF US...
...ARE GETTING MARRIED.
OKAY, NOW SAY CHEESE!
Fair

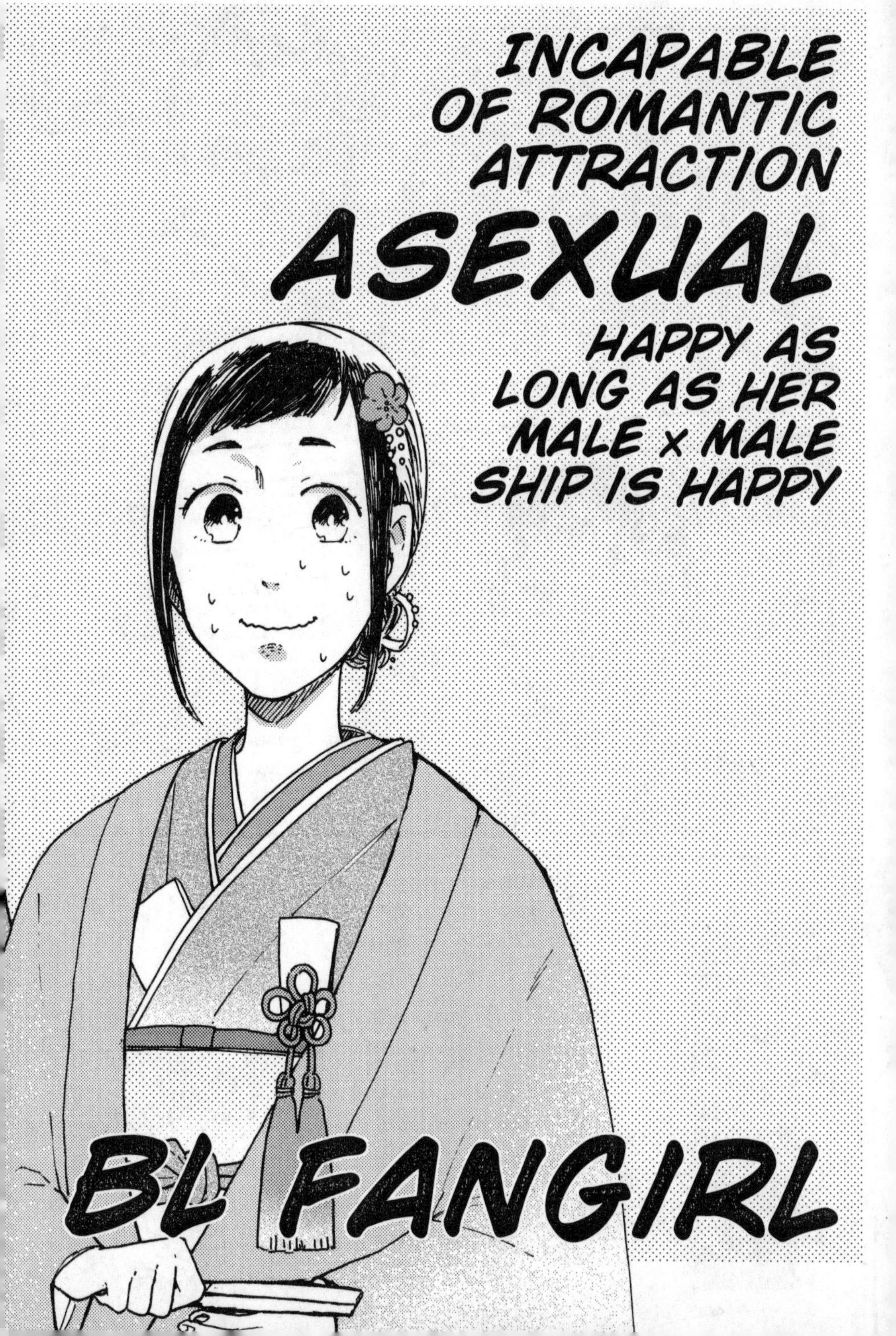
INCAPABLE OF ROMANTIC ATTRACTION
ASEXUAL
HAPPY AS LONG AS HER MALE x MALE SHIP IS HAPPY
BL FANGIRL

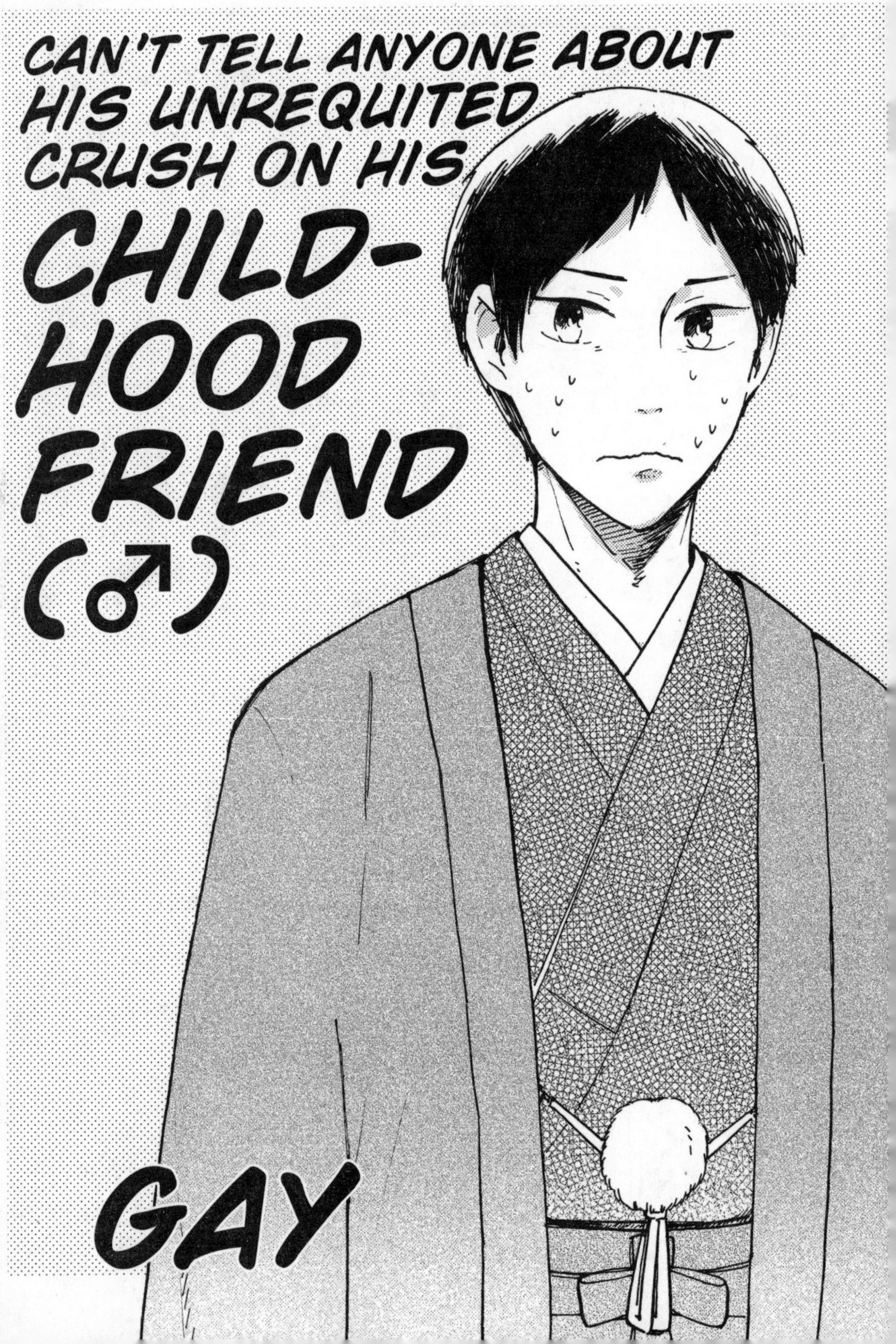
CAN'T TELL ANYONE ABOUT HIS UNREQUITED CRUSH ON HIS
CHILD-HOOD FRIEND (♂)
GAY

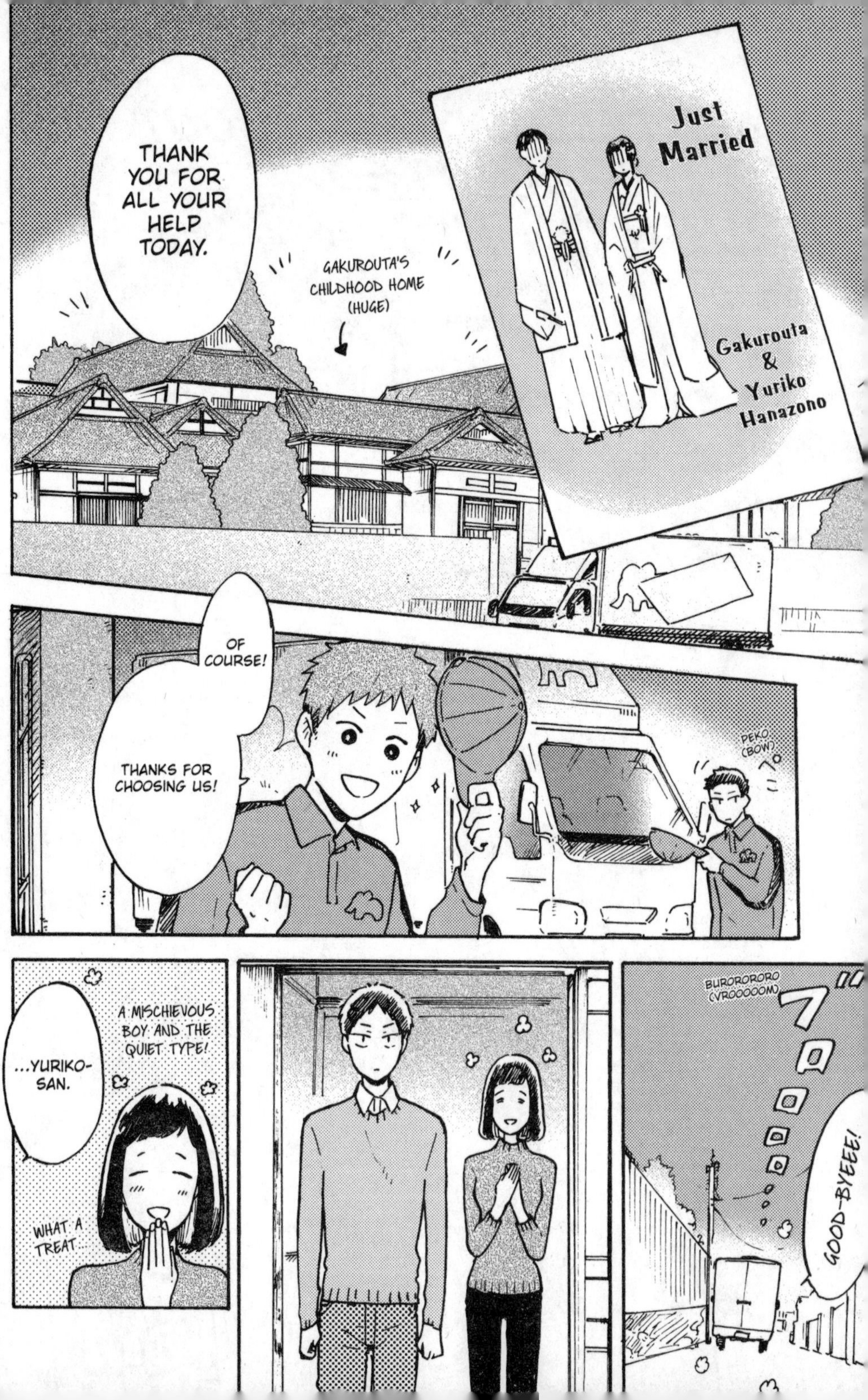
Just Married
Gakurouta & Yuriko Hanazono
GAKUROUTA'S CHILDHOOD HOME (HUGE)
THANK YOU FOR ALL YOUR HELP TODAY.
PEKO (BOW)
OF COURSE!
THANKS FOR CHOOSING US!
BURORORORO (VROOOOOM)
GOOD-BYEEE!
A MISCHIEVOUS BOY AND THE QUIET TYPE!
...YURIKO-SAN.
WHAT A TREAT...

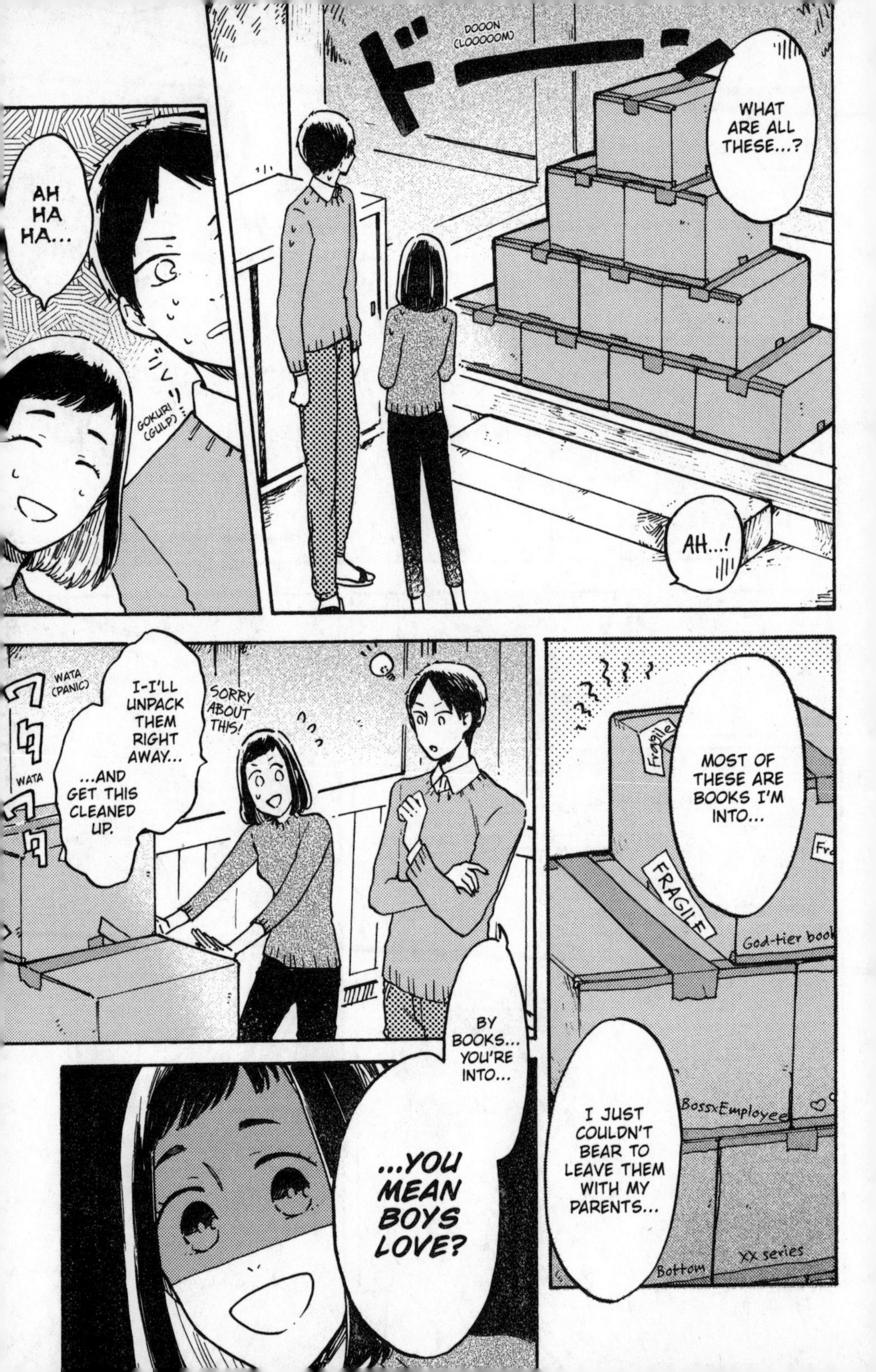
DOOON (LOOOOOM)
WHAT ARE ALL THESE...?
AH...!
GOKURI (GULP)
AH HA HA...
MOST OF THESE ARE BOOKS I'M INTO...
Fragile
FRAGILE
God-tier book
BossxEmployee
XX series
Bottom
I JUST COULDN'T BEAR TO LEAVE THEM WITH MY PARENTS...
SORRY ABOUT THIS!
I-I'LL UNPACK THEM RIGHT AWAY...
...AND GET THIS CLEANED UP.
WATA (PANIC)
WATA
BY BOOKS... YOU'RE INTO...
...YOU MEAN BOYS LOVE?

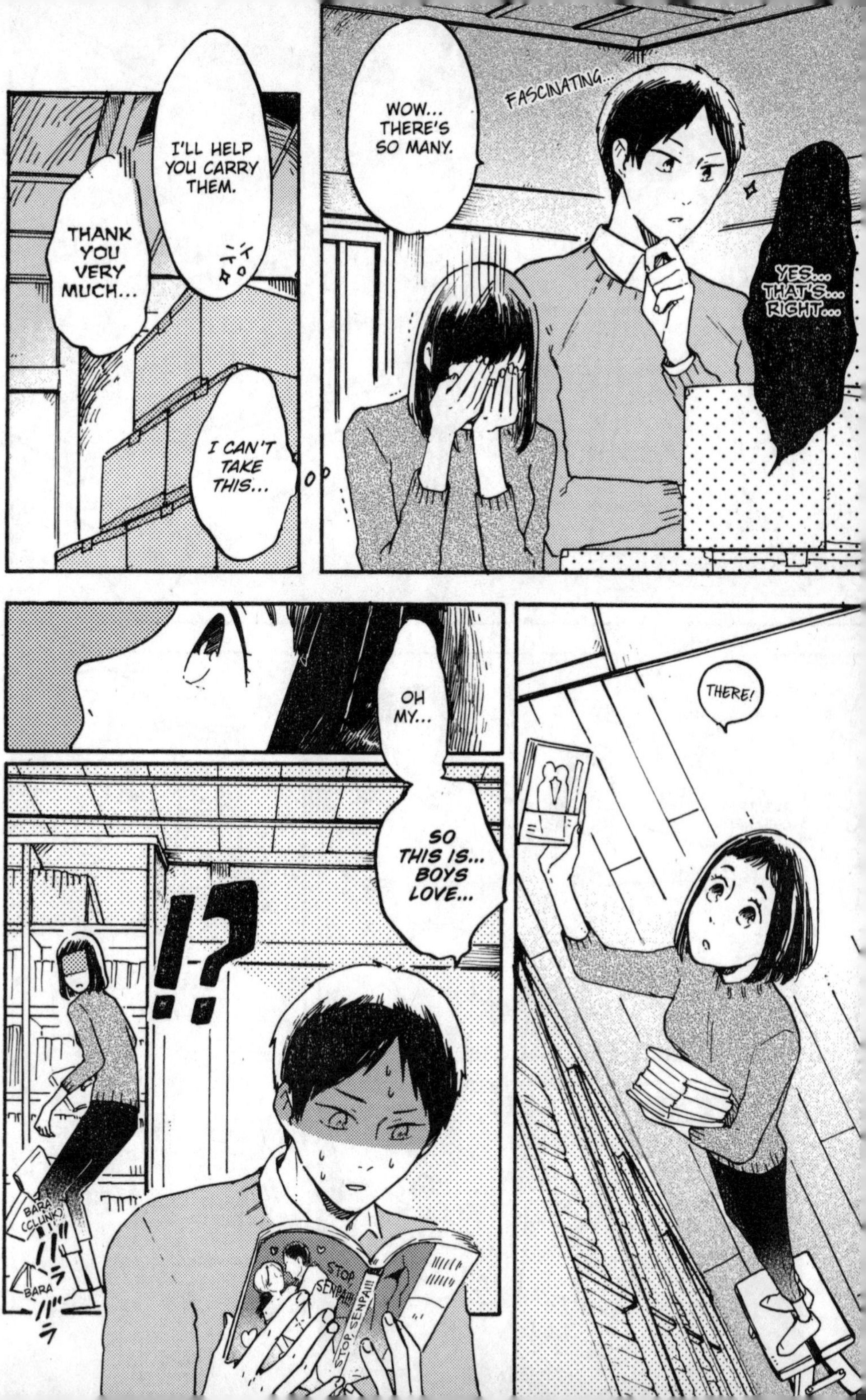
FASCINATING...
WOW... THERE'S SO MANY.
YES... THAT'S... RIGHT...
I'LL HELP YOU CARRY THEM.
THANK YOU VERY MUCH...
I CAN'T TAKE THIS...
THERE!
OH MY...
SO THIS IS... BOYS LOVE...
!?
STOP SENPAI!!!
STOP SENPAI!!!
BARA (CLUNK)
BARA

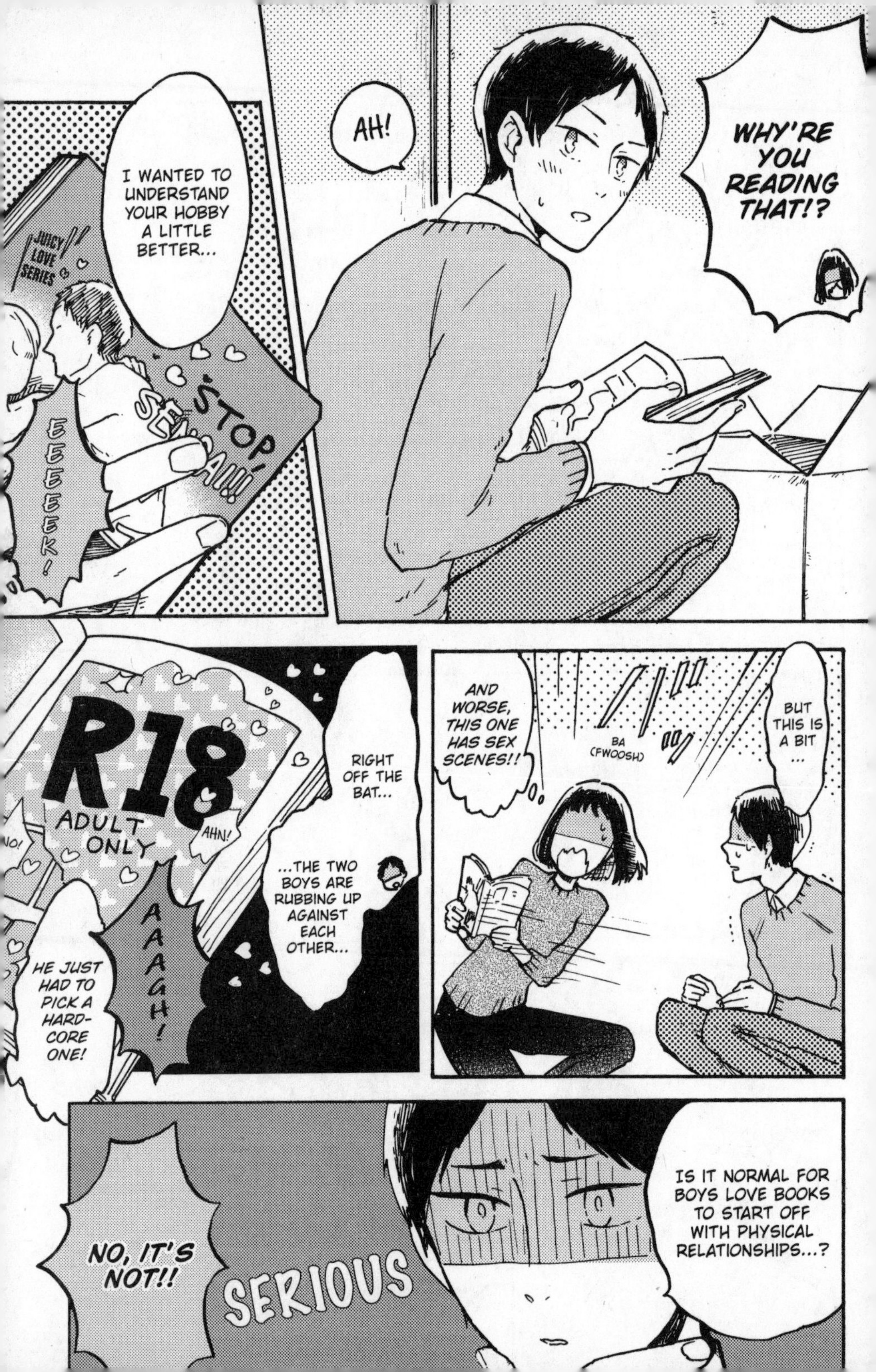
WHY'RE YOU READING THAT!?
AH!
I WANTED TO UNDERSTAND YOUR HOBBY A LITTLE BETTER...
JUICY LOVE SERIES
STOP
EEEEEEK!
BUT THIS IS A BIT ...
AND WORSE, THIS ONE HAS SEX SCENES!!
BA (FWOOSH)
RIGHT OFF THE BAT...
...THE TWO BOYS ARE RUBBING UP AGAINST EACH OTHER...
R18
ADULT ONLY
AHN!
NO!
AAAAGH!
HE JUST HAD TO PICK A HARD-CORE ONE!
IS IT NORMAL FOR BOYS LOVE BOOKS TO START OFF WITH PHYSICAL RELATIONSHIPS...?
SERIOUS
NO, IT'S NOT!!

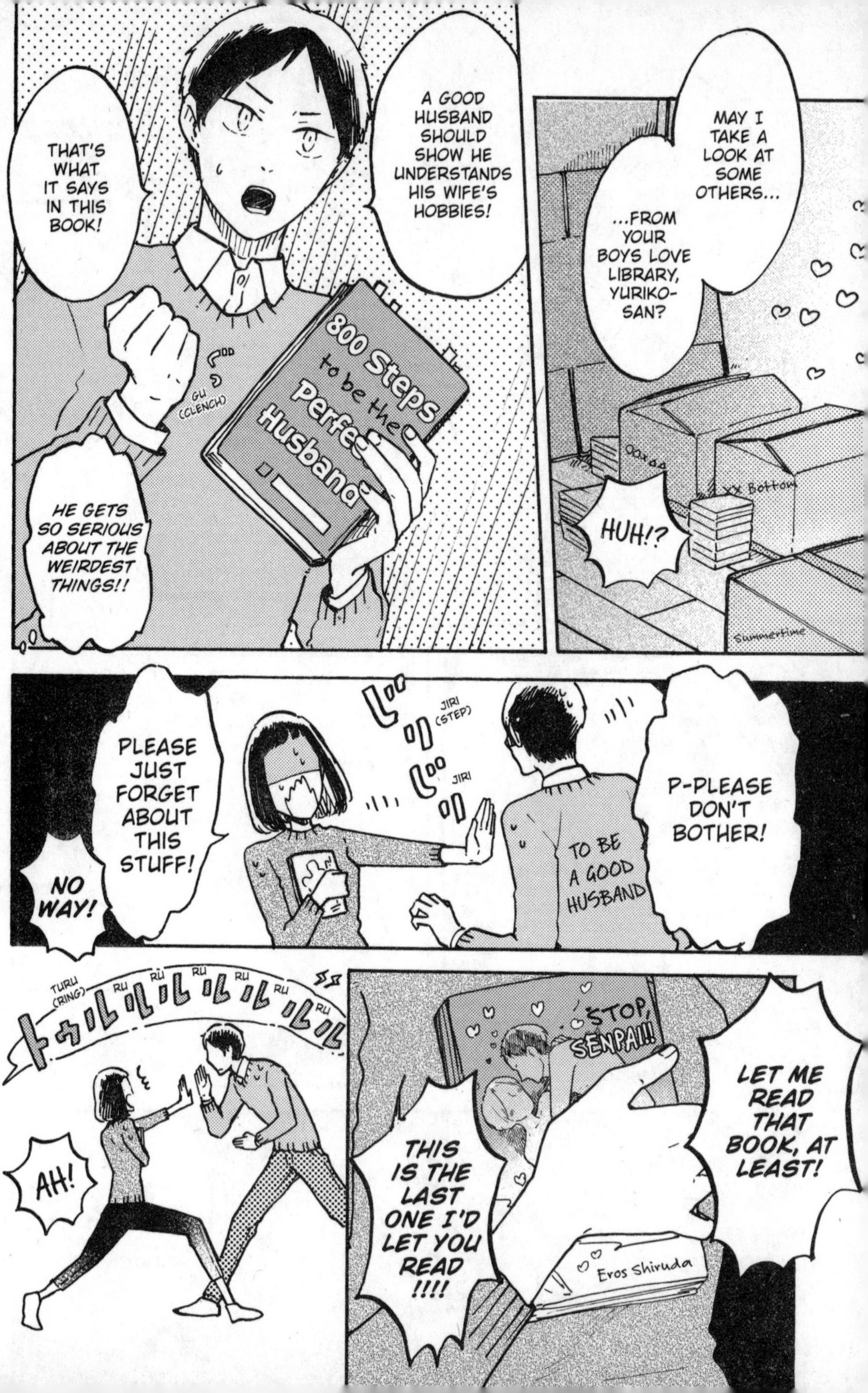
MAY I TAKE A LOOK AT SOME OTHERS...
...FROM YOUR BOYS LOVE LIBRARY, YURIKO-SAN?
xx Bottom
Summertime
HUH!?
A GOOD HUSBAND SHOULD SHOW HE UNDERSTANDS HIS WIFE'S HOBBIES!
THAT'S WHAT IT SAYS IN THIS BOOK!
GU (CLENCH)
800 Steps to be the Perfe Husband
HE GETS SO SERIOUS ABOUT THE WEIRDEST THINGS!!
P-PLEASE DON'T BOTHER!
TO BE A GOOD HUSBAND
JIRI (STEP)
JIRI
PLEASE JUST FORGET ABOUT THIS STUFF!
NO WAY!
LET ME READ THAT BOOK, AT LEAST!
STOP, SENPAI!!!
THIS IS THE LAST ONE I'D LET YOU READ!!!!
Eros Shiruda
TURU (RING) RU RU RU RU RU
AH!

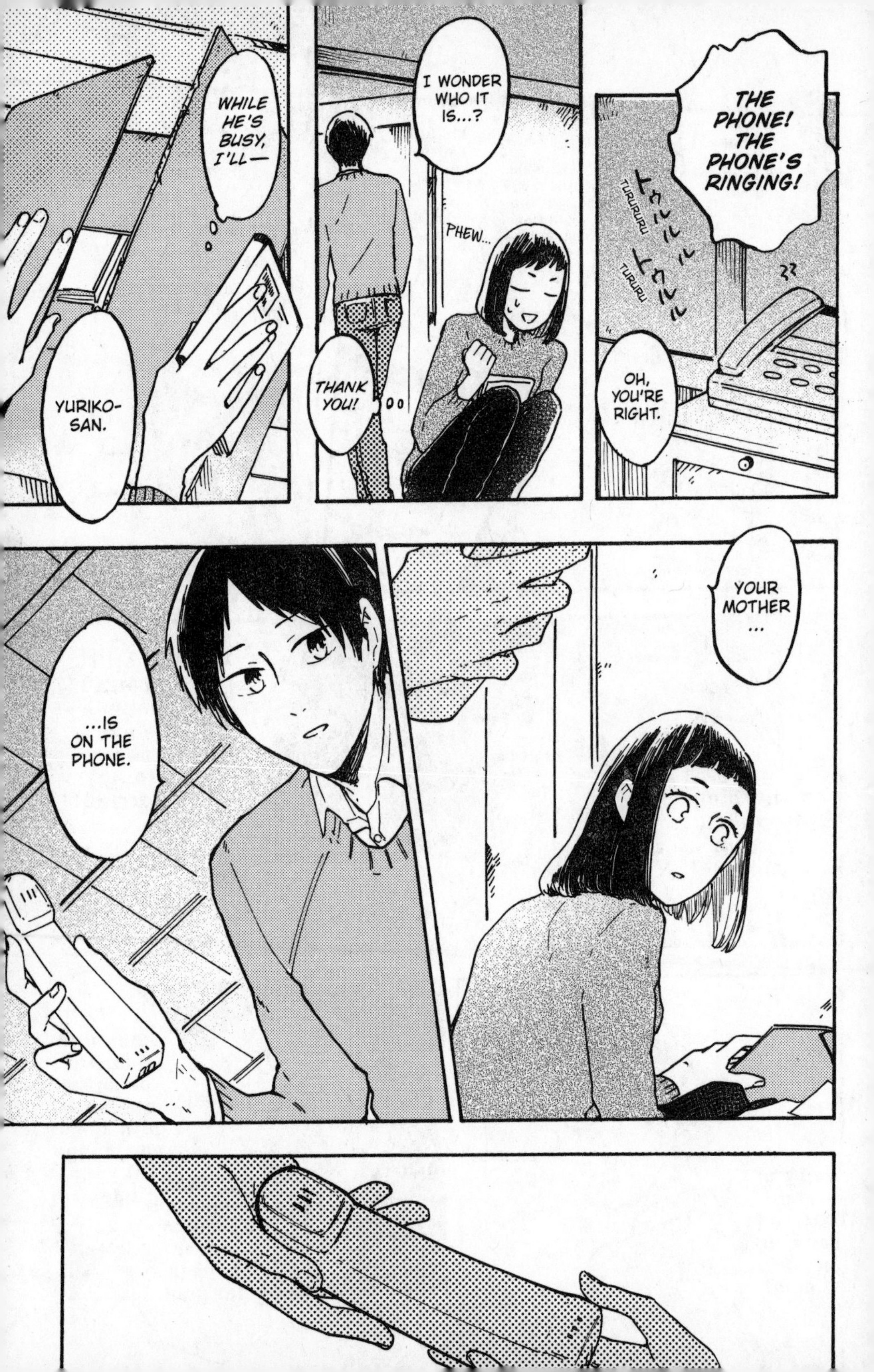
THE PHONE! THE PHONE'S RINGING!
TURURURU
TURURU
OH, YOU'RE RIGHT.
I WONDER WHO IT IS...?
PHEW...
THANK YOU!
WHILE HE'S BUSY, I'LL—
YURIKO-SAN.
YOUR MOTHER ...
...IS ON THE PHONE.

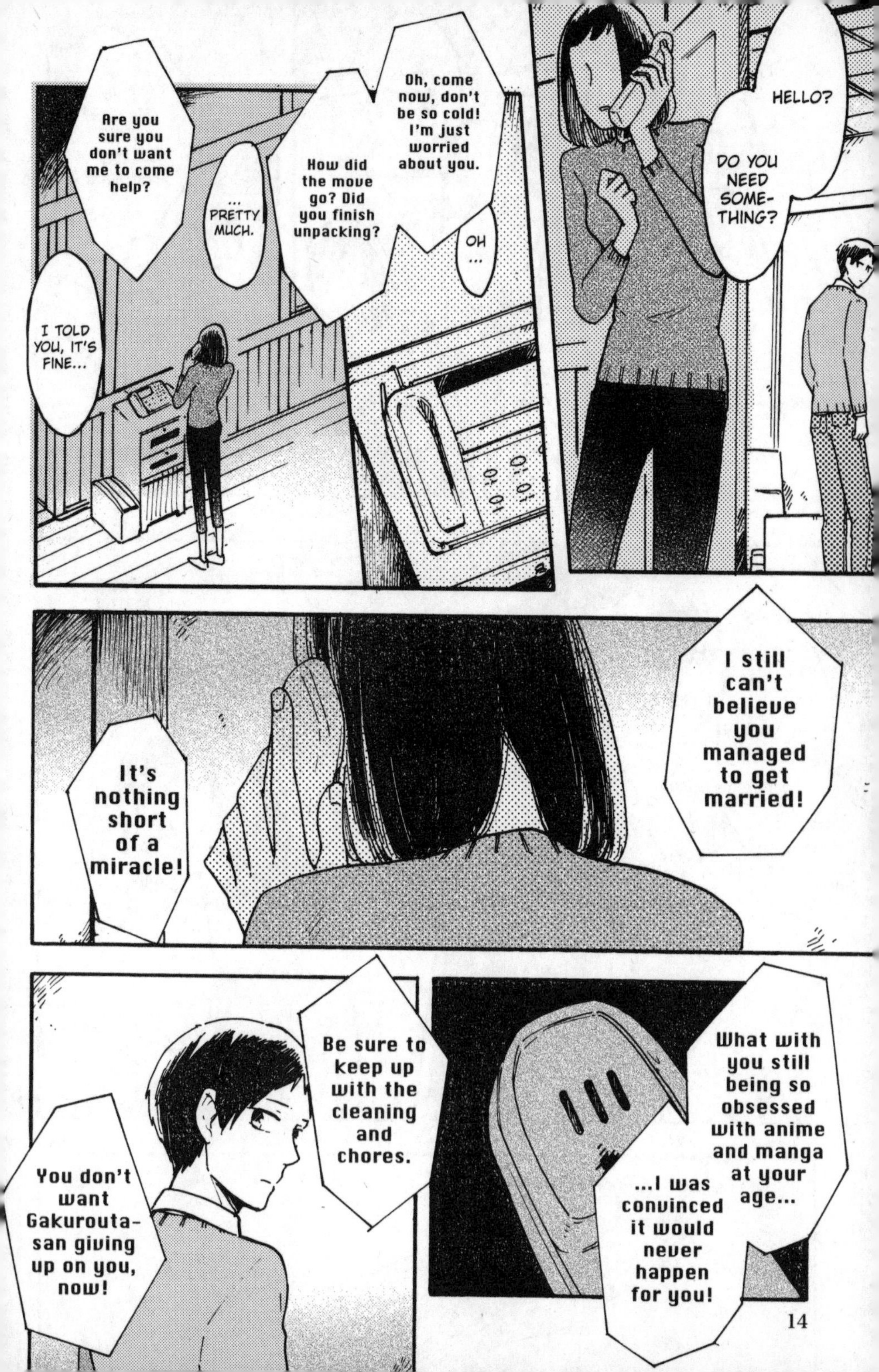
HELLO?
DO YOU NEED SOMETHING?
Oh, come now, don't be so cold! I'm just worried about you.
OH ...
How did the move go? Did you finish unpacking?
... PRETTY MUCH.
Are you sure you don't want me to come help?
I TOLD YOU, IT'S FINE...
I still can't believe you managed to get married!
It's nothing short of a miracle!
What with you still being so obsessed with anime and manga at your age...
...I was convinced it would never happen for you!
Be sure to keep up with the cleaning and chores.
You don't want Gakurouta-san giving up on you, now!

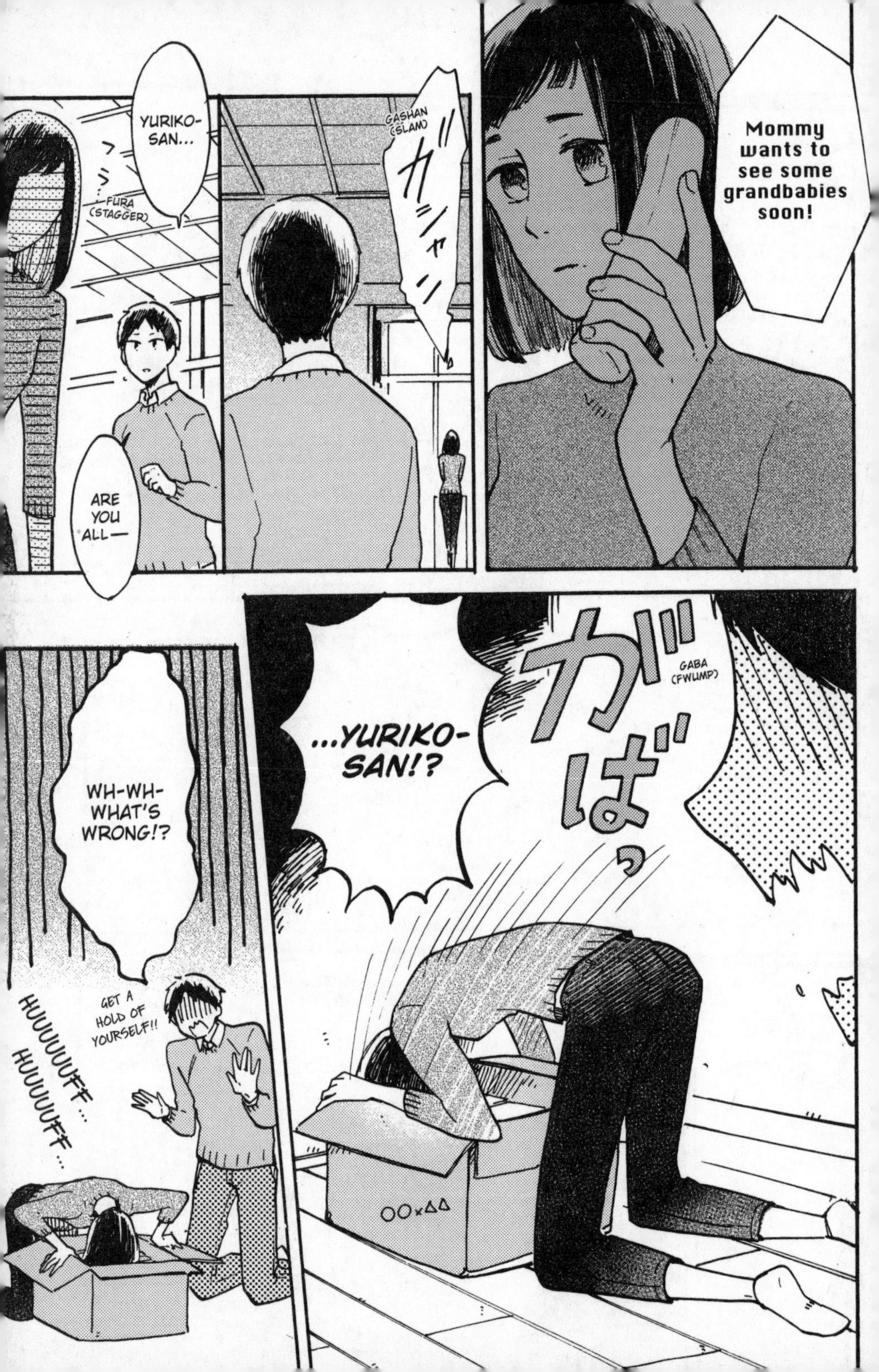
Mommy wants to see some grandbabies soon!
GASHAN (SLAM)
YURIKO-SAN...
FURA (STAGGER)
ARE YOU ALL—
GABA (FWUMP)
...YURIKO-SAN!?
WH-WH-WHAT'S WRONG!?
GET A HOLD OF YOURSELF!!
HUUUUUFF... HUUUUUFF...

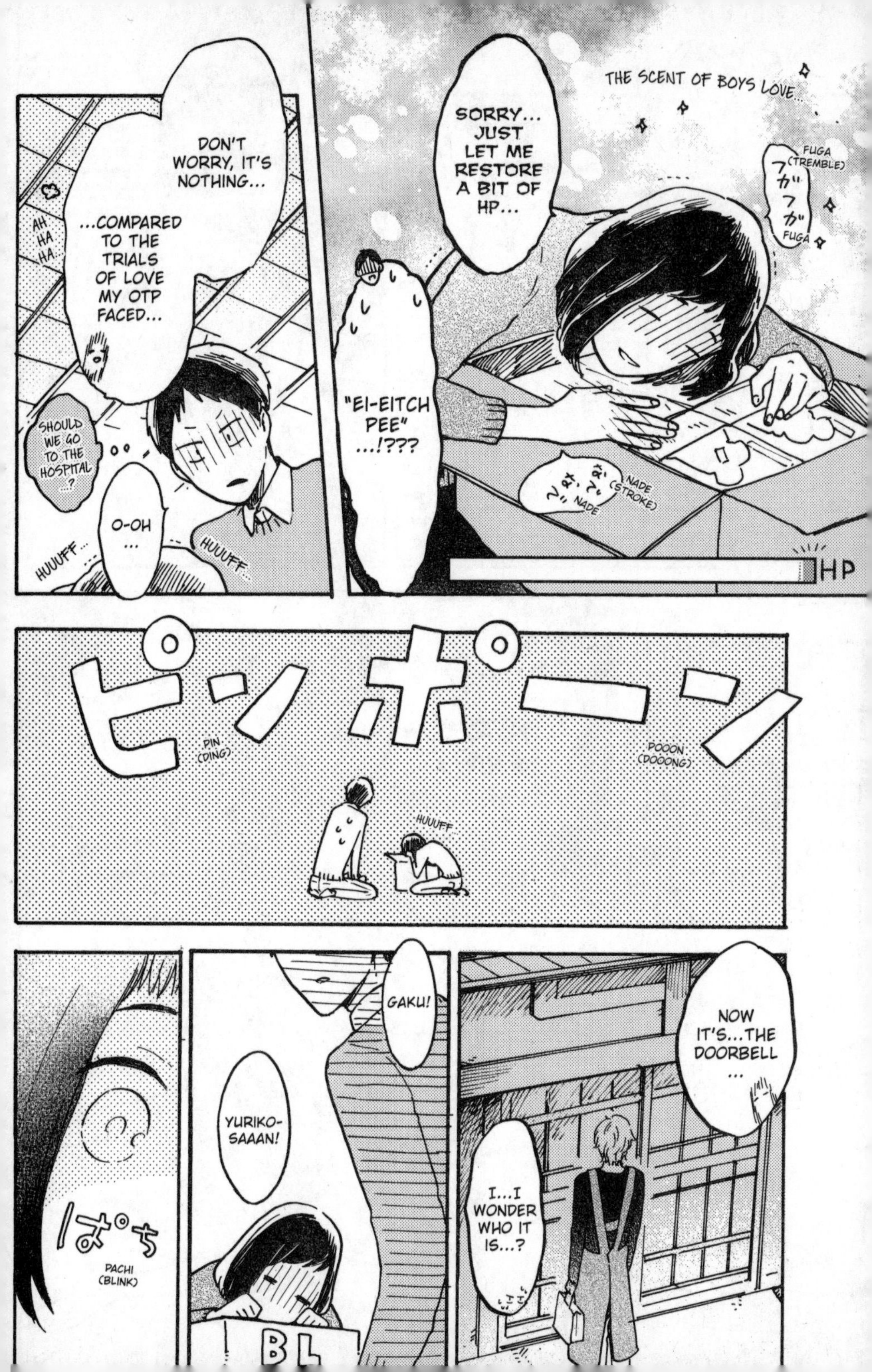
THE SCENT OF BOYS LOVE...
SORRY... JUST LET ME RESTORE A BIT OF HP...
フガフガ
FUGA (TREMBLE) FUGA
"EI-EITCH PEE" ...!???
なで なで
NADE (STROKE) NADE
HP
DON'T WORRY, IT'S NOTHING...
...COMPARED TO THE TRIALS OF LOVE MY OTP FACED...
AH HA HA
SHOULD WE GO TO THE HOSPITAL ...?
O-OH ...
HUUUFF...
HUUUFF
ピンポーン
PIN (DING)
POOON (DOOONG)
HUUUFF
NOW IT'S...THE DOORBELL ...
I...I WONDER WHO IT IS...?
GAKU!
YURIKO-SAAAN!
BL
ぱち
PACHI (BLINK)

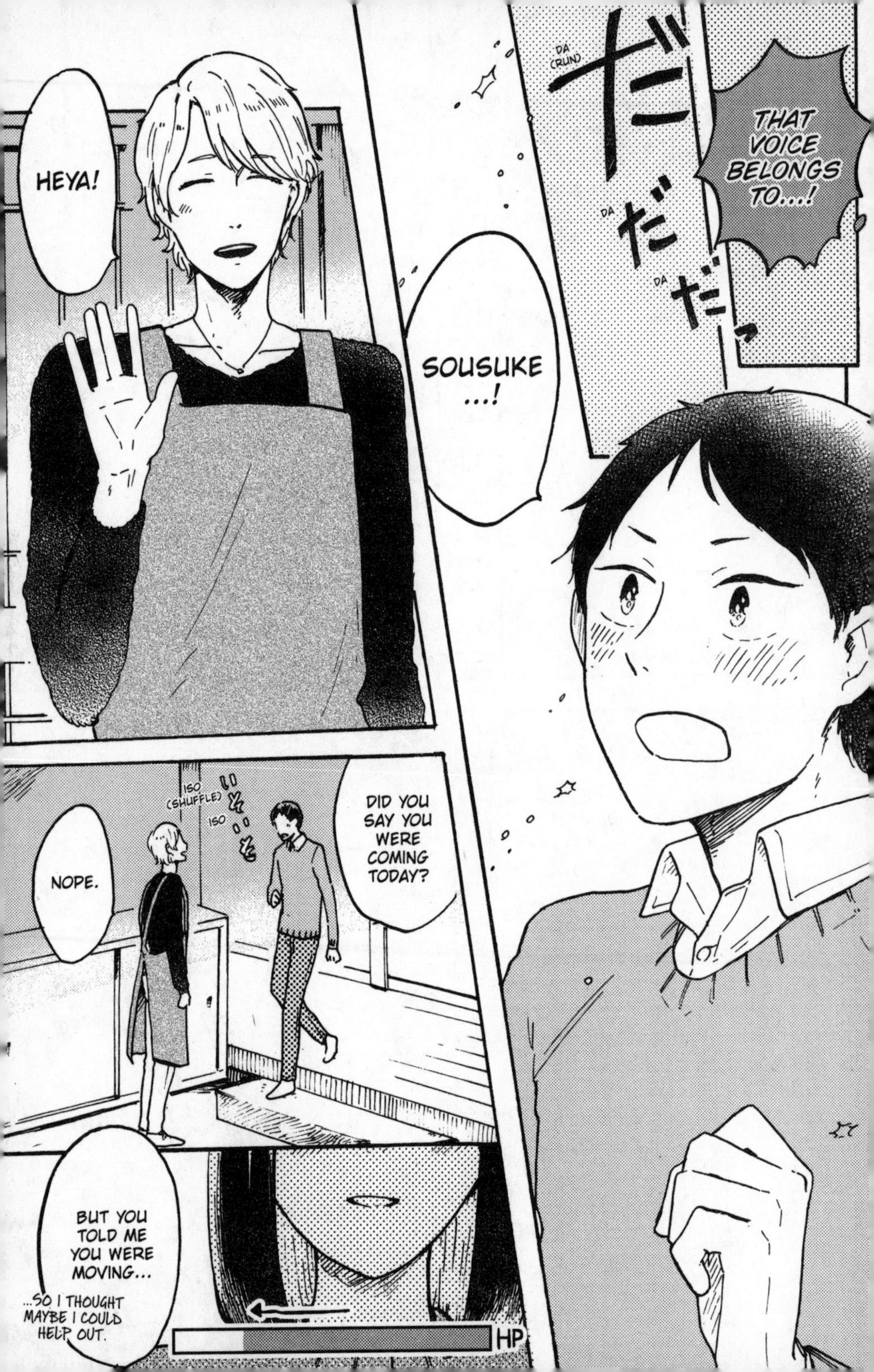
THAT VOICE BELONGS TO...!
DA (RUN)
DA
DA
SOUSUKE ...!
HEYA!
DID YOU SAY YOU WERE COMING TODAY?
ISO (SHUFFLE)
ISO
NOPE.
BUT YOU TOLD ME YOU WERE MOVING...
...SO I THOUGHT MAYBE I COULD HELP OUT.
HP

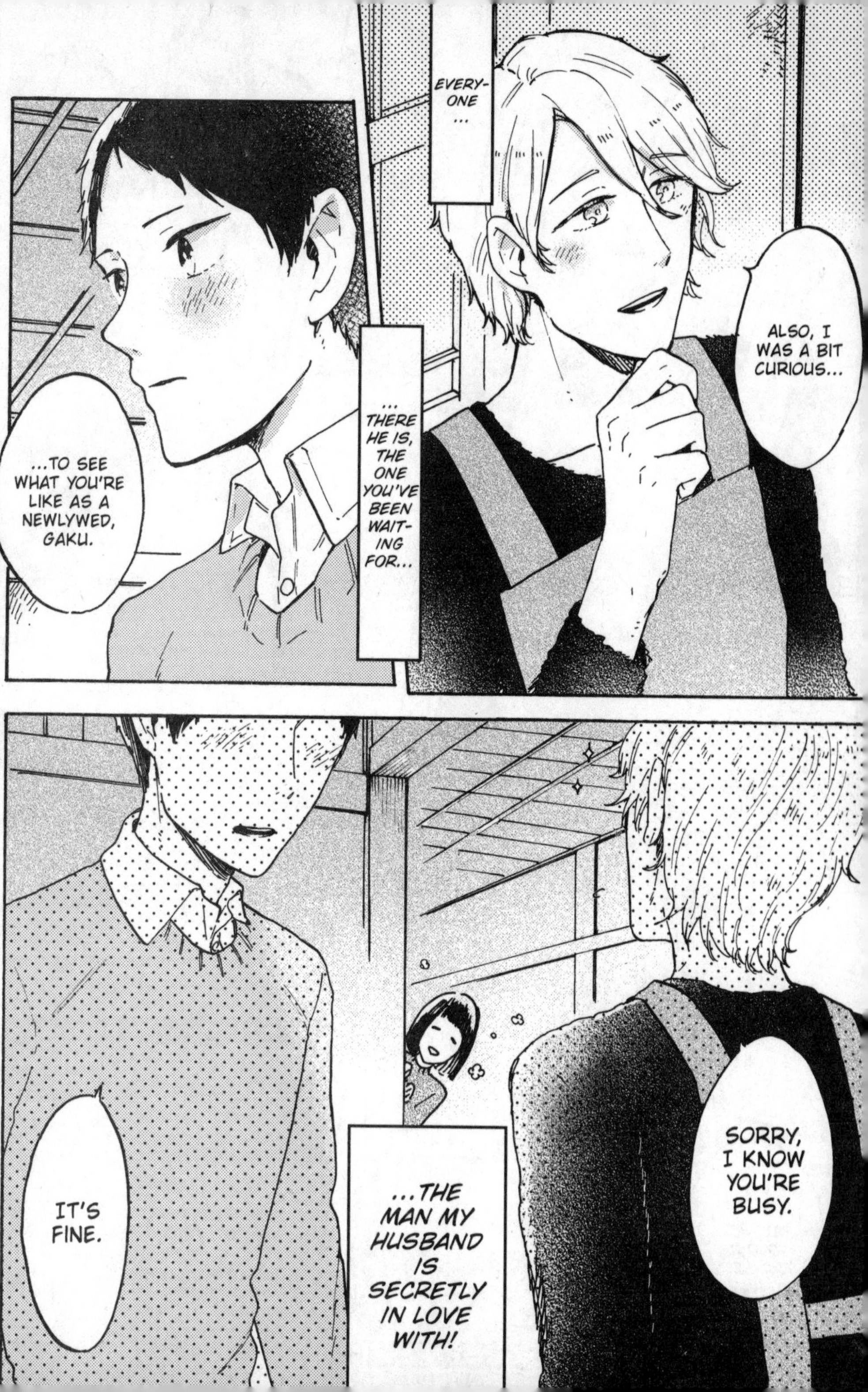
EVERY-ONE...
ALSO, I WAS A BIT CURIOUS...
...THERE HE IS, THE ONE YOU'VE BEEN WAITING FOR...
...TO SEE WHAT YOU'RE LIKE AS A NEWLYWED, GAKU.
SORRY, I KNOW YOU'RE BUSY.
...THE MAN MY HUSBAND IS SECRETLY IN LOVE WITH!
IT'S FINE.

I Want
to Be a
Wall

I Want
to Be a
Wall

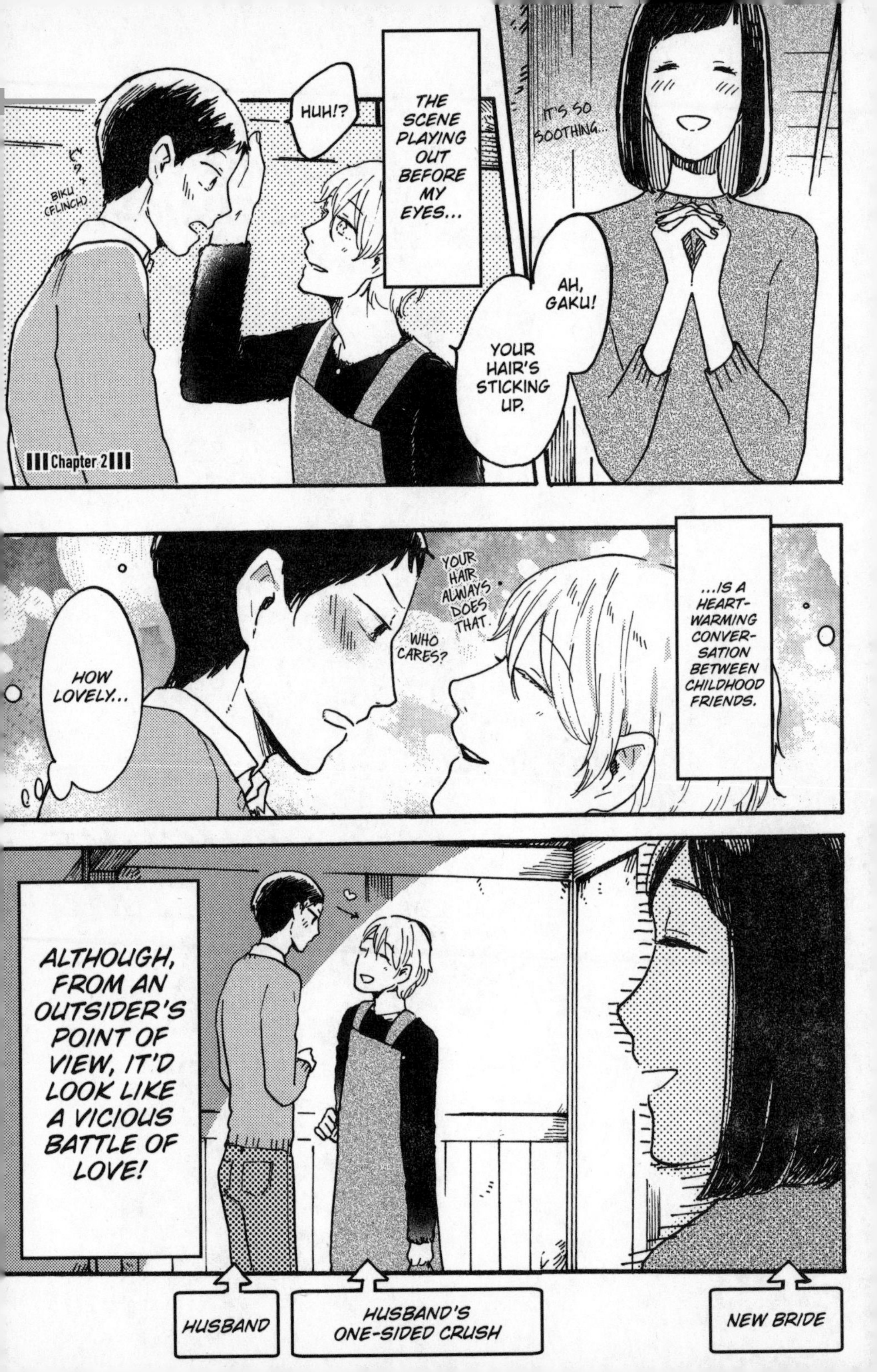
IT'S SO SOOTHING...
THE SCENE PLAYING OUT BEFORE MY EYES...
AH, GAKU!
YOUR HAIR'S STICKING UP.
HUH!?
BIKU (FLINCH)
Chapter 2
...IS A HEART-WARMING CONVER-SATION BETWEEN CHILDHOOD FRIENDS.
YOUR HAIR ALWAYS DOES THAT.
WHO CARES?
HOW LOVELY...
ALTHOUGH, FROM AN OUTSIDER'S POINT OF VIEW, IT'D LOOK LIKE A VICIOUS BATTLE OF LOVE!
NEW BRIDE
HUSBAND'S ONE-SIDED CRUSH
HUSBAND

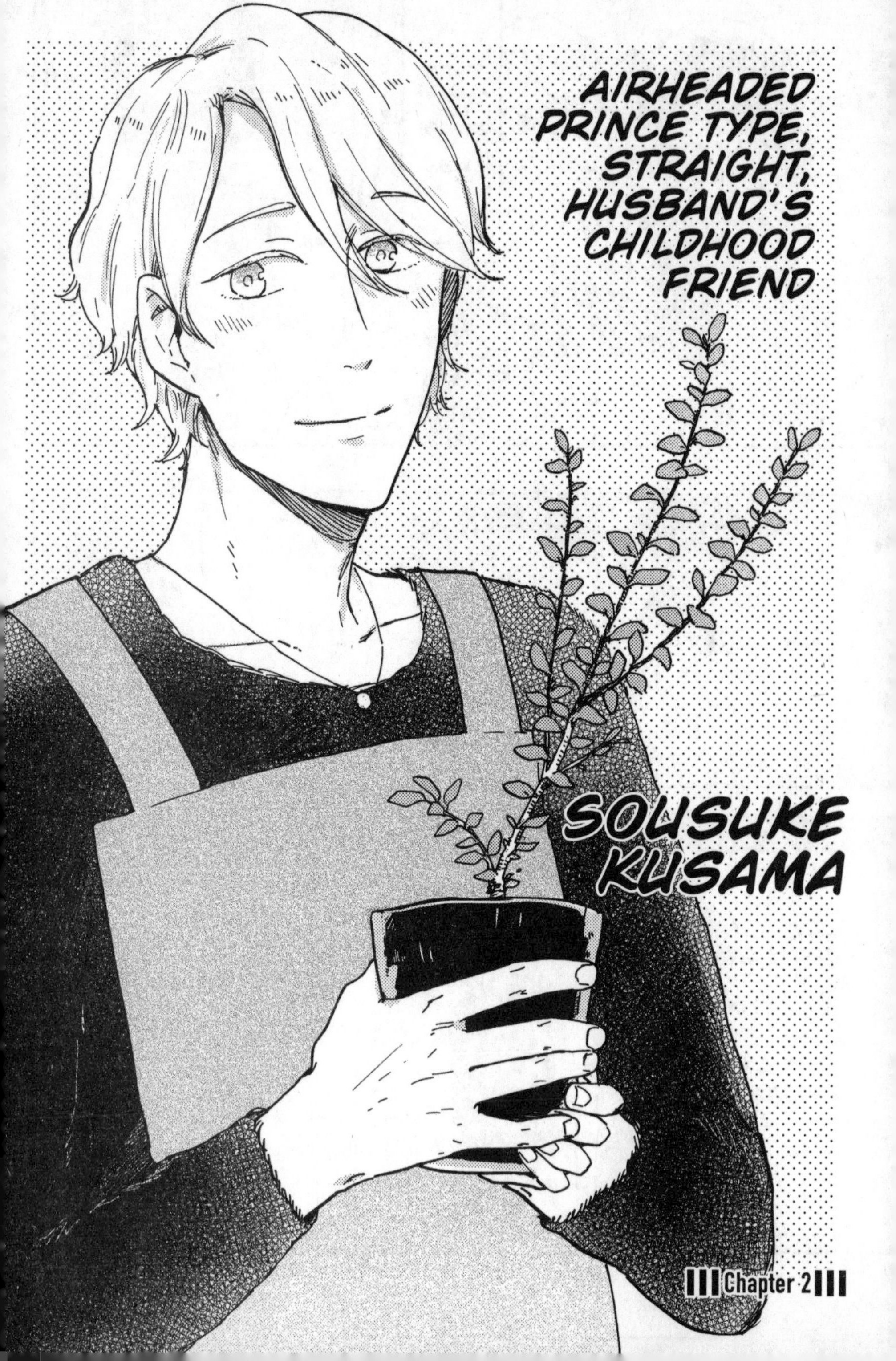
AIRHEADED PRINCE TYPE, STRAIGHT, HUSBAND'S CHILDHOOD FRIEND
SOUSUKE KUSAMA
Chapter 2

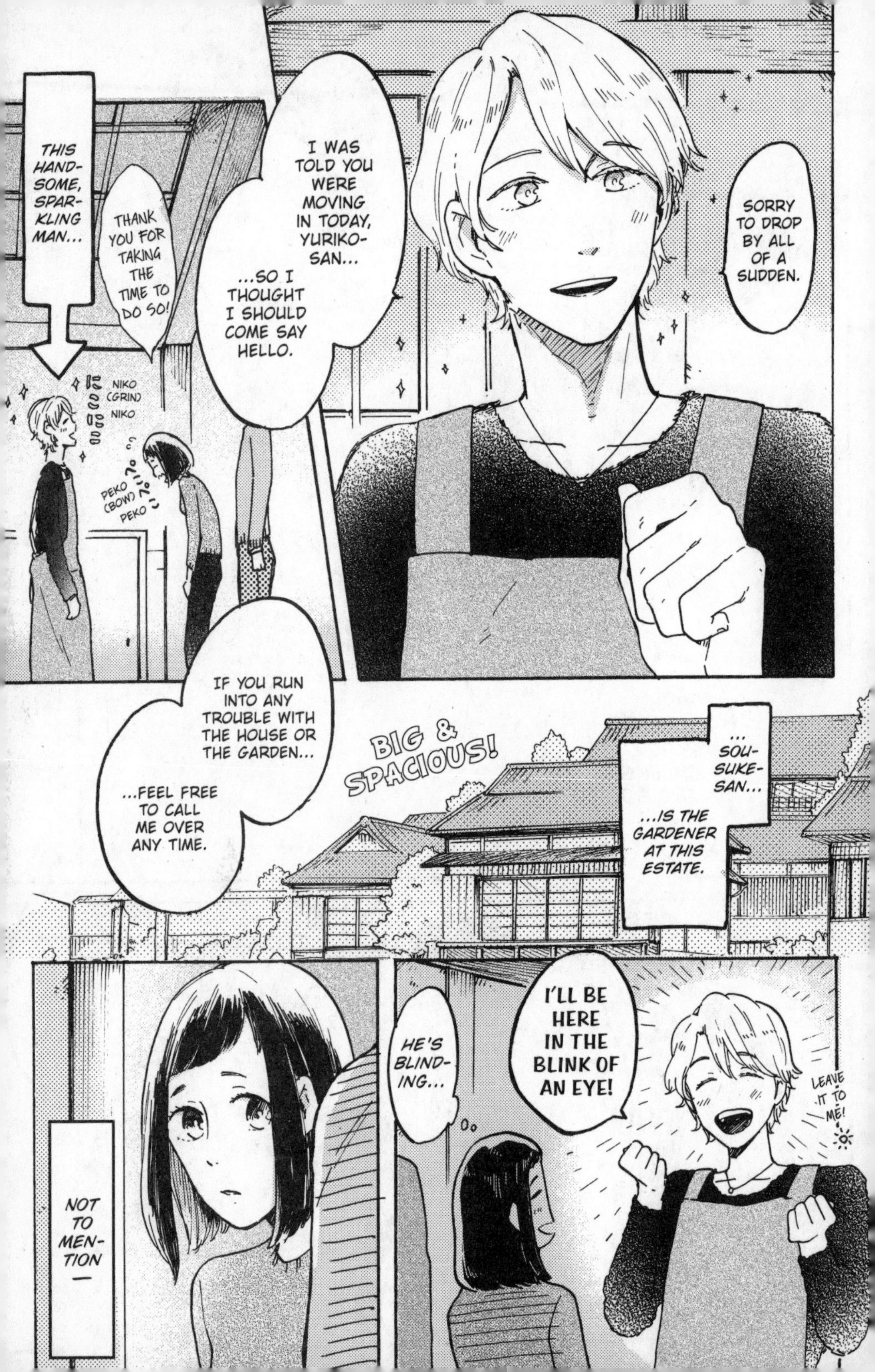
SORRY TO DROP BY ALL OF A SUDDEN.
I WAS TOLD YOU WERE MOVING IN TODAY, YURIKO-SAN...
...SO I THOUGHT I SHOULD COME SAY HELLO.
THIS HANDSOME, SPARKLING MAN...
THANK YOU FOR TAKING THE TIME TO DO SO!
NIKO (GRIN) NIKO
PEKO (BOW) PEKO
...SOUSUKE-SAN...
...IS THE GARDENER AT THIS ESTATE.
BIG & SPACIOUS!
IF YOU RUN INTO ANY TROUBLE WITH THE HOUSE OR THE GARDEN...
...FEEL FREE TO CALL ME OVER ANY TIME.
I'LL BE HERE IN THE BLINK OF AN EYE!
LEAVE IT TO ME!
HE'S BLINDING...
NOT TO MENTION—

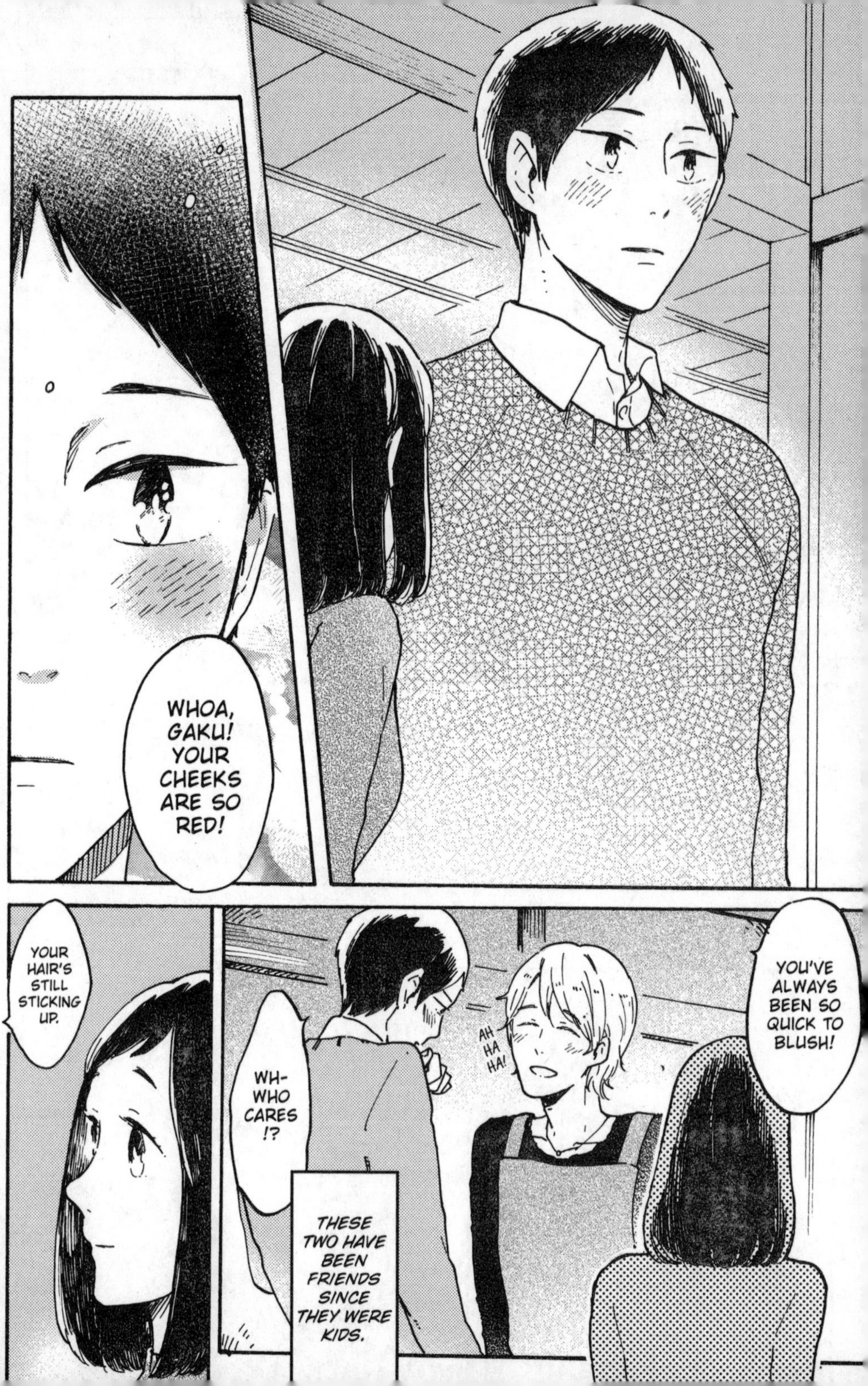
WHOA, GAKU! YOUR CHEEKS ARE SO RED!
YOU'VE ALWAYS BEEN SO QUICK TO BLUSH!
AH HA HA!
WH-WHO CARES!?
THESE TWO HAVE BEEN FRIENDS SINCE THEY WERE KIDS.
YOUR HAIR'S STILL STICKING UP.

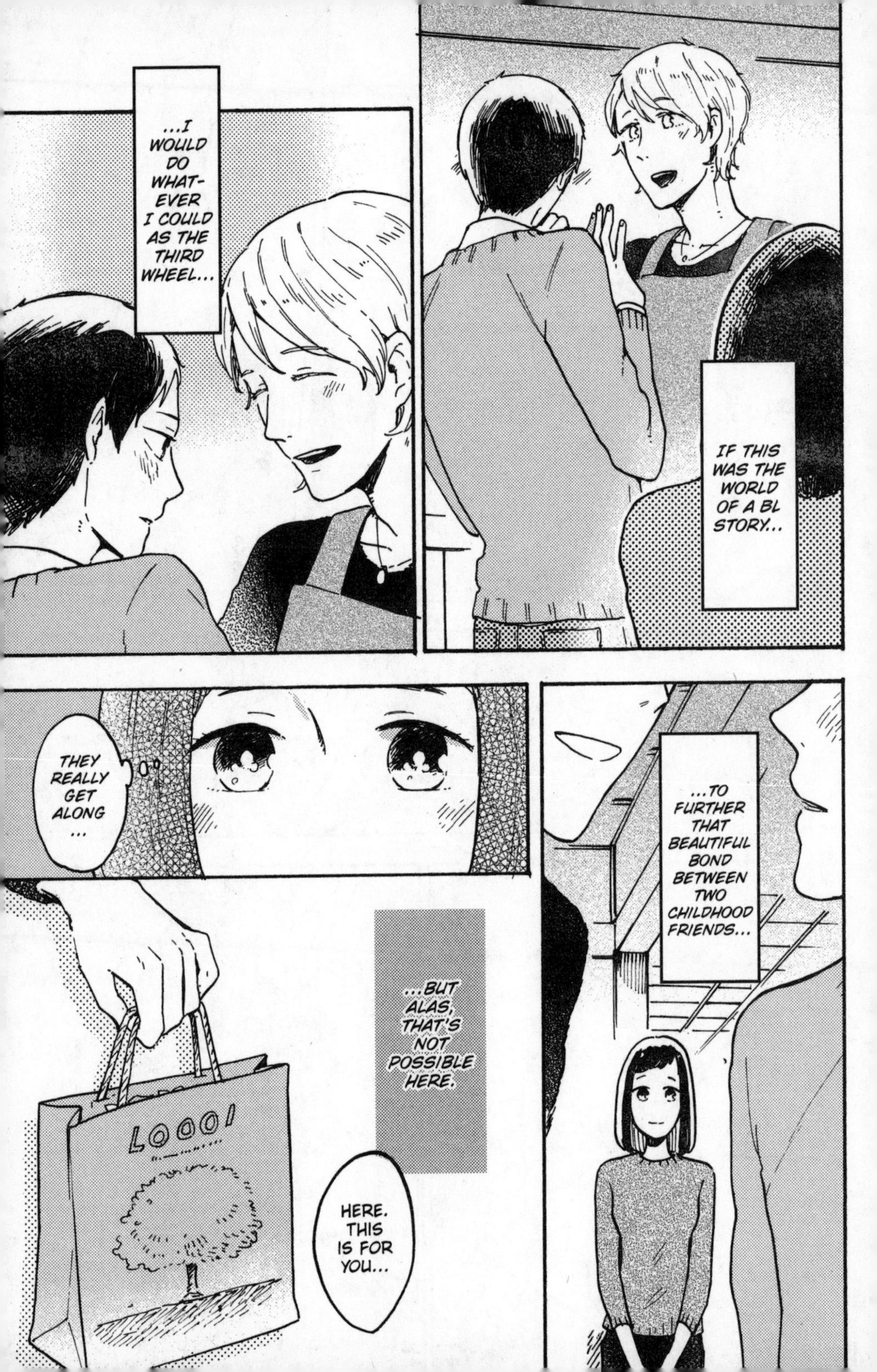
IF THIS WAS THE WORLD OF A BL STORY...
...I WOULD DO WHATEVER I COULD AS THE THIRD WHEEL...
...TO FURTHER THAT BEAUTIFUL BOND BETWEEN TWO CHILDHOOD FRIENDS...
THEY REALLY GET ALONG...
...BUT ALAS, THAT'S NOT POSSIBLE HERE.
HERE. THIS IS FOR YOU...

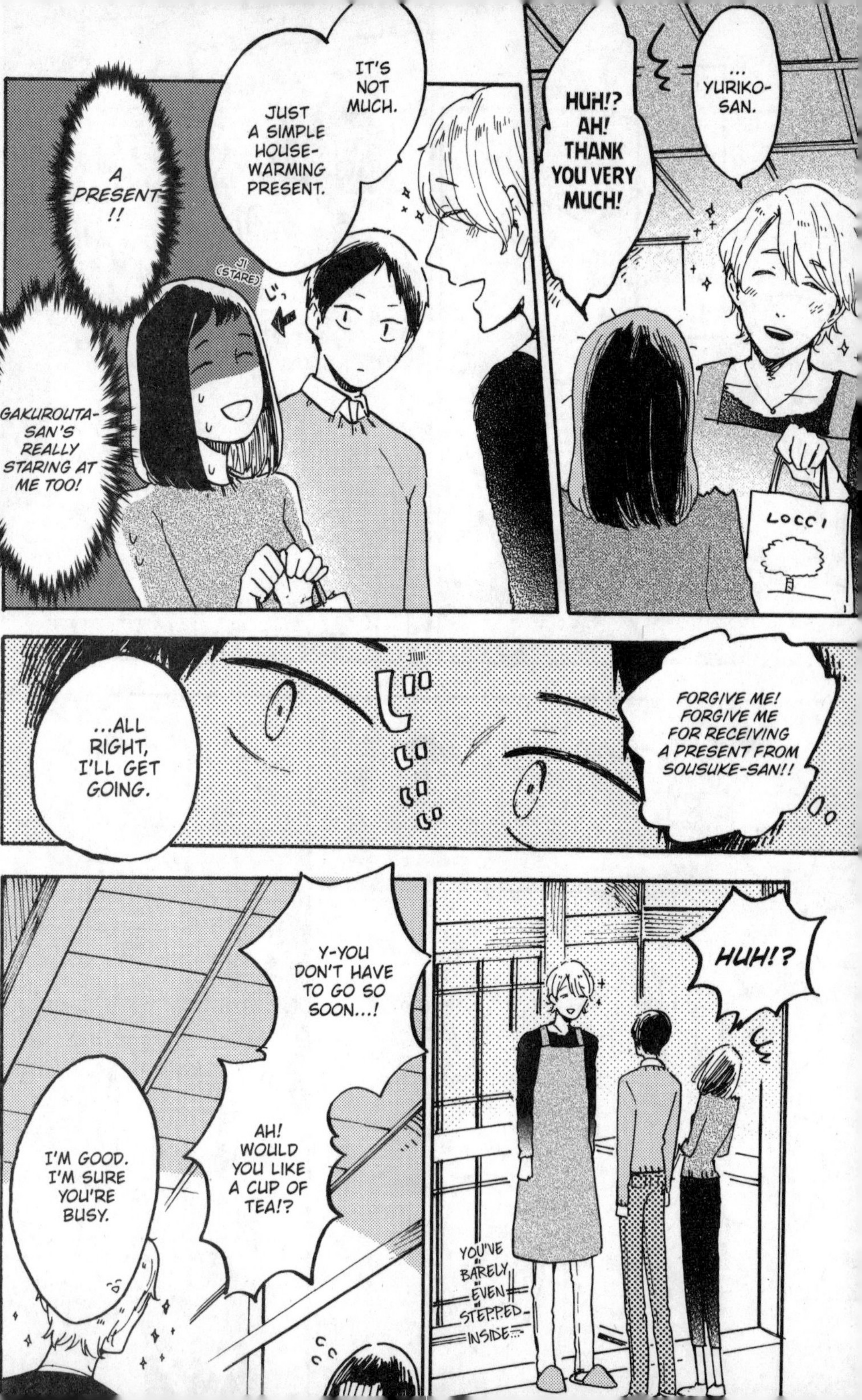
...YURIKO-SAN.
HUH!? AH! THANK YOU VERY MUCH!
LOCCI
IT'S NOT MUCH.
JUST A SIMPLE HOUSE-WARMING PRESENT.
A PRESENT!!
JI (STARE)
GAKUROUTA-SAN'S REALLY STARING AT ME TOO!
FORGIVE ME! FORGIVE ME FOR RECEIVING A PRESENT FROM SOUSUKE-SAN!!
JIIII
...ALL RIGHT, I'LL GET GOING.
HUH!?
YOU'VE BARELY EVEN STEPPED INSIDE...
Y-YOU DON'T HAVE TO GO SO SOON...!
AH! WOULD YOU LIKE A CUP OF TEA!?
I'M GOOD. I'M SURE YOU'RE BUSY.

Want to win a Free Gift Card!?

Enter the Reading Raffle Today…

All you need to do to enter:

- Read a library book from the shortlist (pictured below)
- Complete the short review form inside and return it to the library with the book…

GRAPHIC NOVELS

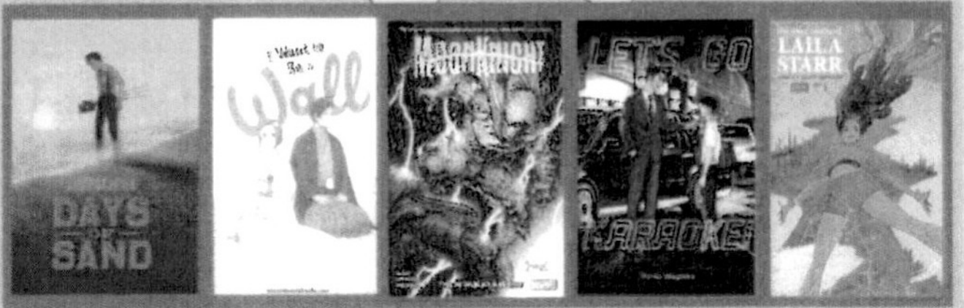
DAYS
SAND
Wall
LET'S GO
KARAOKE!
LAILA STARR

RAFFLE WINNINER PRIZE = GIFT CARD OF YOUR CHOICE!!!

Steam, X-Box, PlayStation, Switch…

Amazon, Waterstones, Love 2 Shop, Dining out…

Jorvik, York Dungeons, Yorkshire Wildlife Park…

(**Maximum 5 entries per person 1 for each book**).

Every Book on the shortlist can be found in the library and loaned for up to a week at a time.

Raffle will be drawn at the end of May…

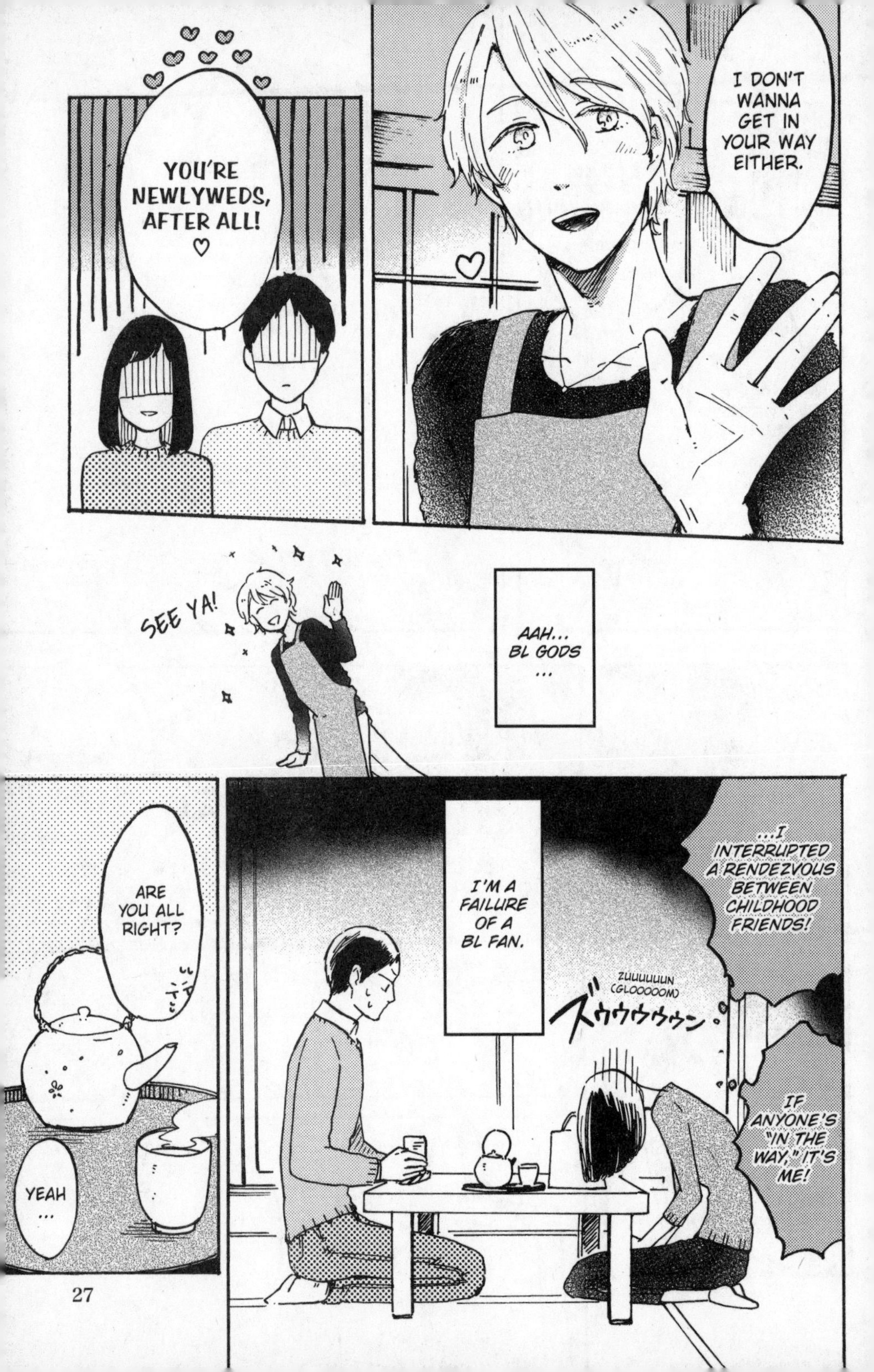

I DON'T WANNA GET IN YOUR WAY EITHER.
YOU'RE NEWLYWEDS, AFTER ALL! ♡
AAH... BL GODS ...
SEE YA!
...I INTERRUPTED A RENDEZVOUS BETWEEN CHILDHOOD FRIENDS!
I'M A FAILURE OF A BL FAN.
ズウウウウン
ZUUUUUUN (GLOOOOOM)
IF ANYONE'S "IN THE WAY," IT'S ME!
ARE YOU ALL RIGHT?
YEAH ...

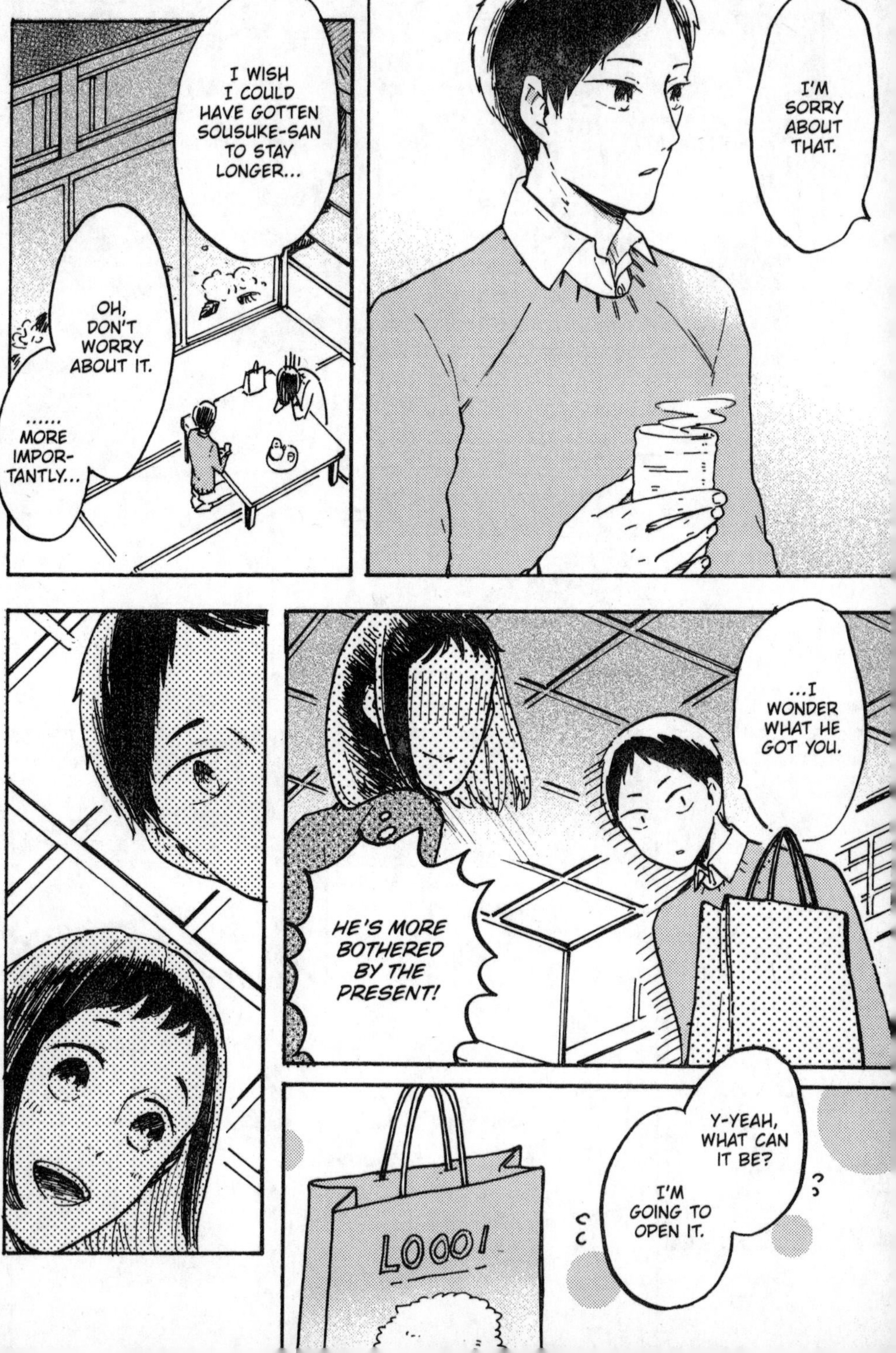
I'M SORRY ABOUT THAT.
I WISH I COULD HAVE GOTTEN SOUSUKE-SAN TO STAY LONGER...
OH, DON'T WORRY ABOUT IT.
...... MORE IMPORTANTLY...
...I WONDER WHAT HE GOT YOU.
HE'S MORE BOTHERED BY THE PRESENT!
Y-YEAH, WHAT CAN IT BE?
I'M GOING TO OPEN IT.
LOOO!

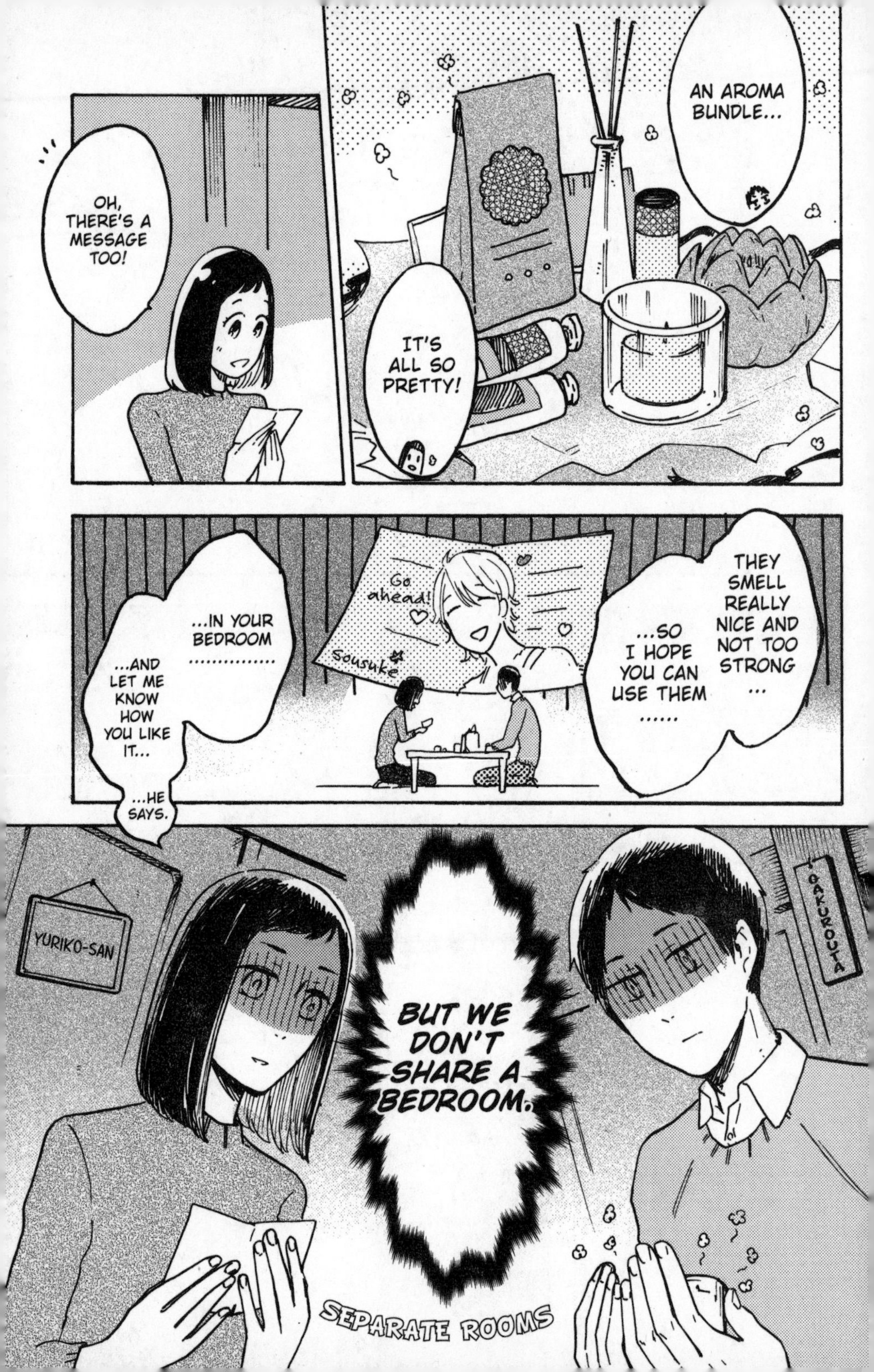
AN AROMA BUNDLE...
IT'S ALL SO PRETTY!
OH, THERE'S A MESSAGE TOO!
THEY SMELL REALLY NICE AND NOT TOO STRONG...
...SO I HOPE YOU CAN USE THEM......
Go ahead!
Sousuke
...IN YOUR BEDROOM..............
...AND LET ME KNOW HOW YOU LIKE IT...
...HE SAYS.
GAKUROUTA
YURIKO-SAN
BUT WE DON'T SHARE A BEDROOM.
SEPARATE ROOMS

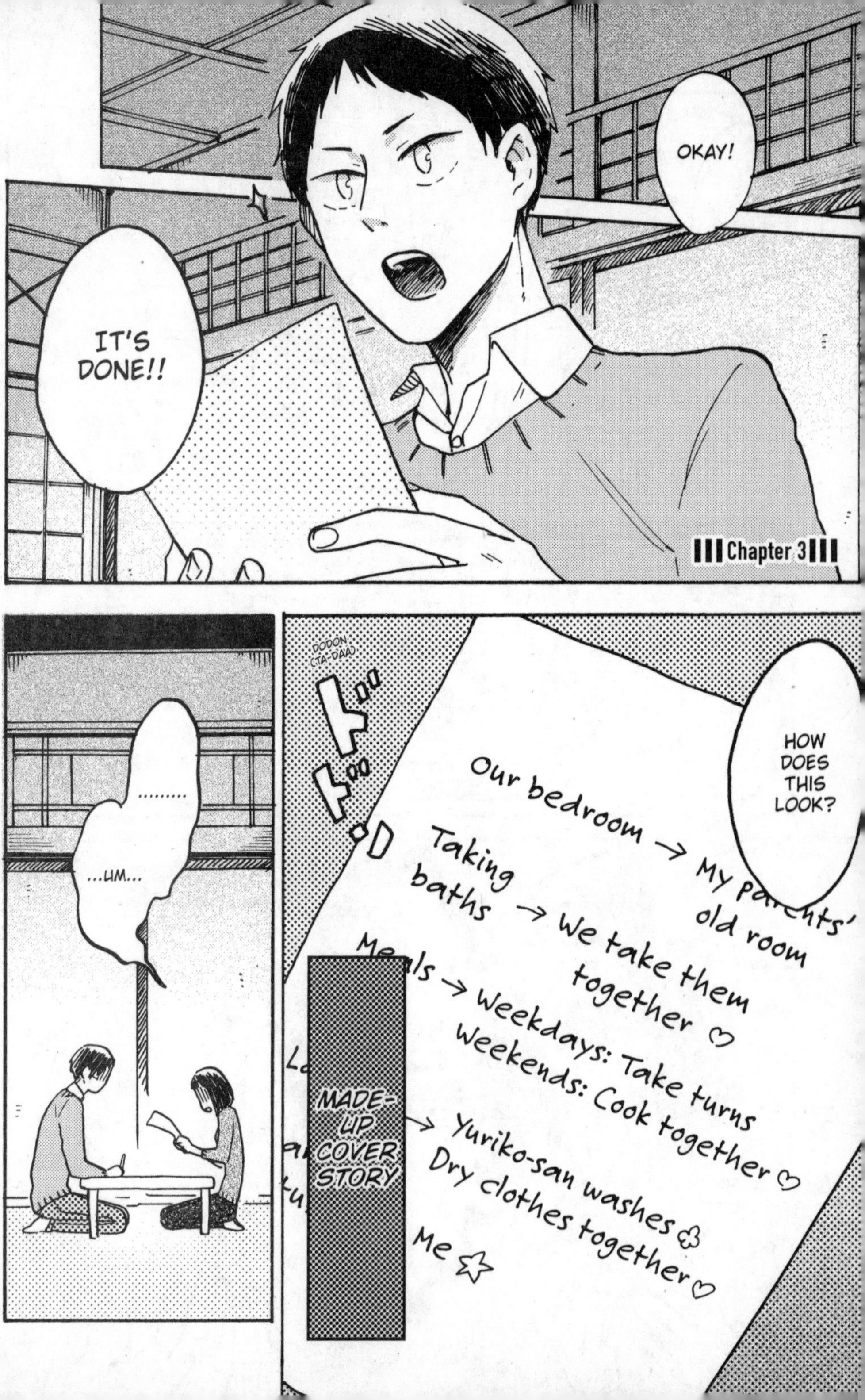
OKAY!
IT'S DONE!!
Chapter 3
DODON (TA-DAA)
HOW DOES THIS LOOK?
Our bedroom → My parents' old room
Taking baths → We take them together ♡
Meals → Weekdays: Take turns
Weekends: Cook together ♡
MADE-UP COVER STORY
→ Yuriko-san washes ✿
Dry clothes together ♡
Me ☆
....
...UM...

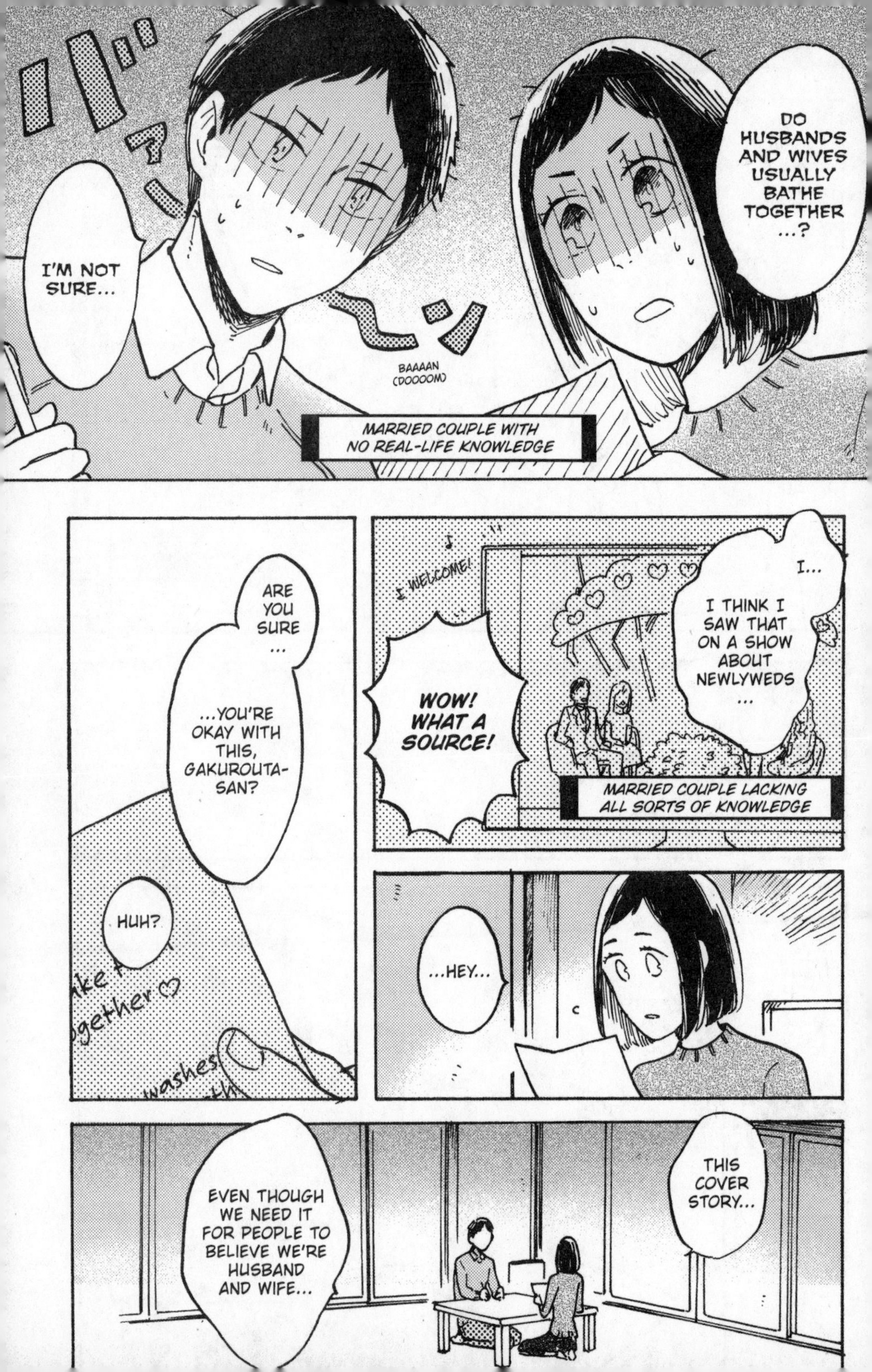
DO HUSBANDS AND WIVES USUALLY BATHE TOGETHER ...?
I'M NOT SURE...
BAAAAN (DOOOOM)
MARRIED COUPLE WITH NO REAL-LIFE KNOWLEDGE
I... I THINK I SAW THAT ON A SHOW ABOUT NEWLYWEDS ...
I WELCOME!
WOW! WHAT A SOURCE!
MARRIED COUPLE LACKING ALL SORTS OF KNOWLEDGE
...HEY...
ARE YOU SURE ...
...YOU'RE OKAY WITH THIS, GAKUROUTA-SAN?
HUH?
THIS COVER STORY...
EVEN THOUGH WE NEED IT FOR PEOPLE TO BELIEVE WE'RE HUSBAND AND WIFE...

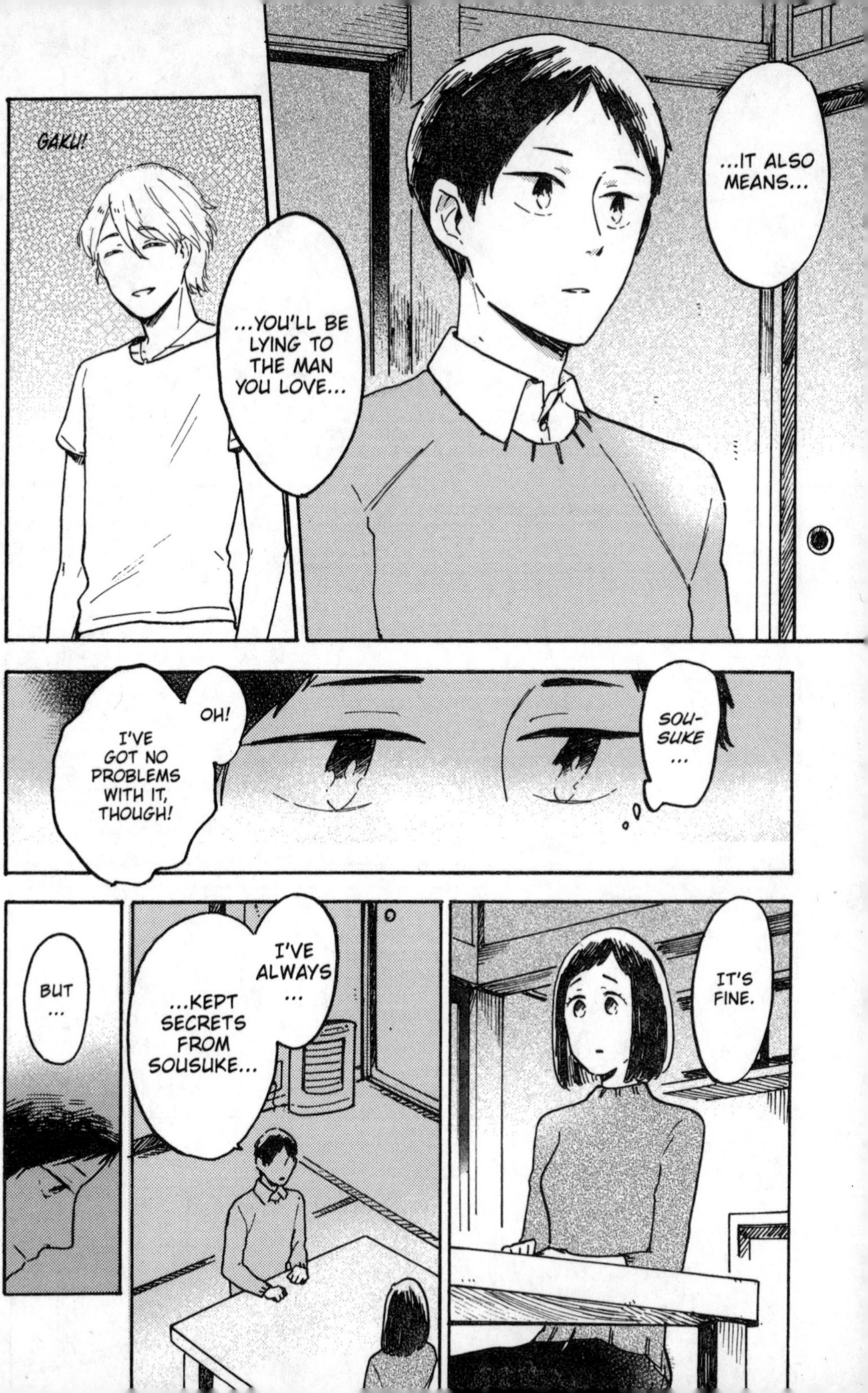
...IT ALSO MEANS...
...YOU'LL BE LYING TO THE MAN YOU LOVE...
GAKU!
SOU-SUKE ...
OH! I'VE GOT NO PROBLEMS WITH IT, THOUGH!
IT'S FINE.
...
I'VE ALWAYS ...
...KEPT SECRETS FROM SOUSUKE...
BUT ...

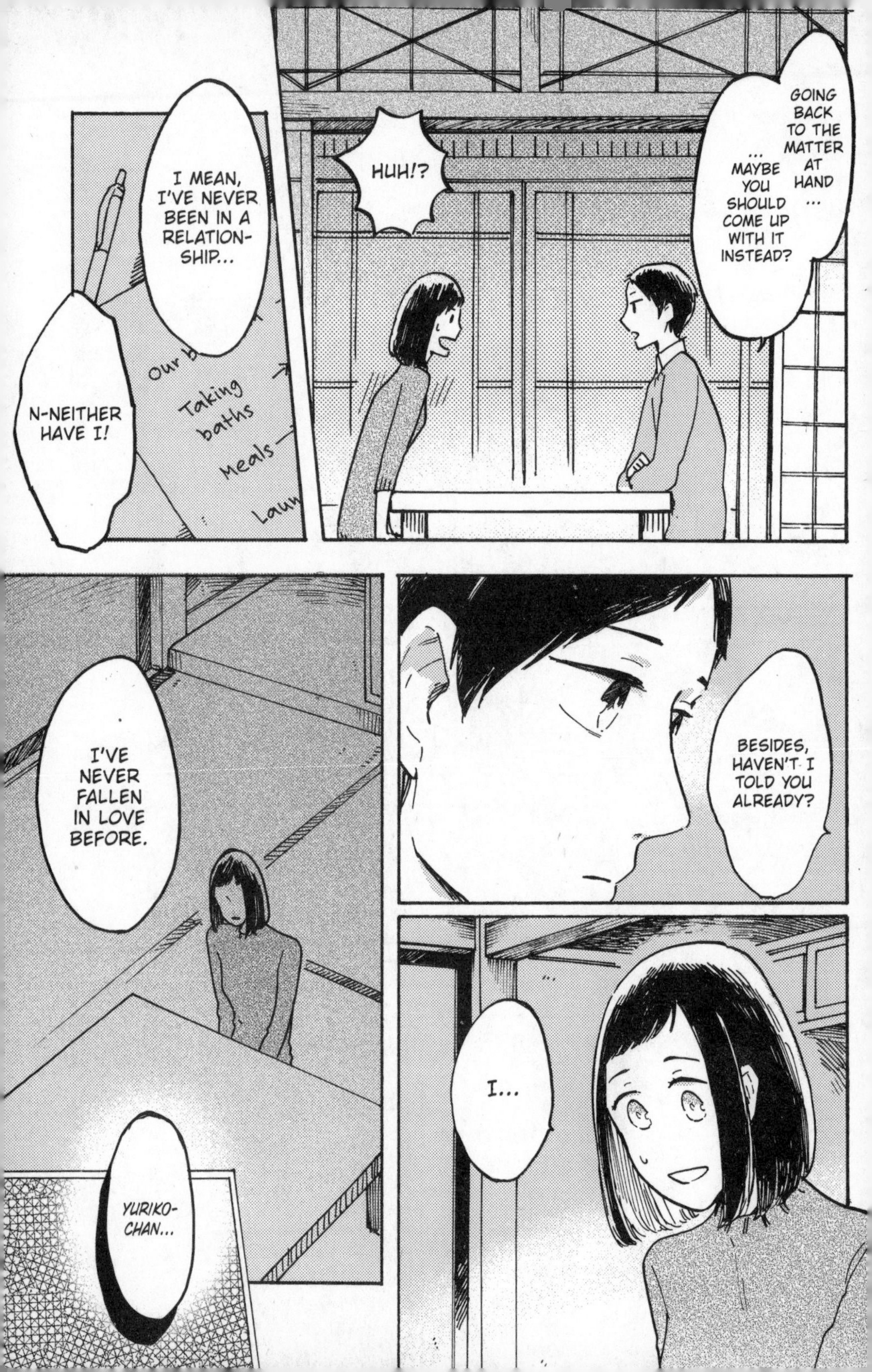
GOING BACK TO THE MATTER AT HAND...
...MAYBE YOU SHOULD COME UP WITH IT INSTEAD?
HUH!?
I MEAN, I'VE NEVER BEEN IN A RELATIONSHIP...
Taking baths
Meals
N-NEITHER HAVE I!
BESIDES, HAVEN'T I TOLD YOU ALREADY?
I...
I'VE NEVER FALLEN IN LOVE BEFORE.
YURIKO-CHAN...

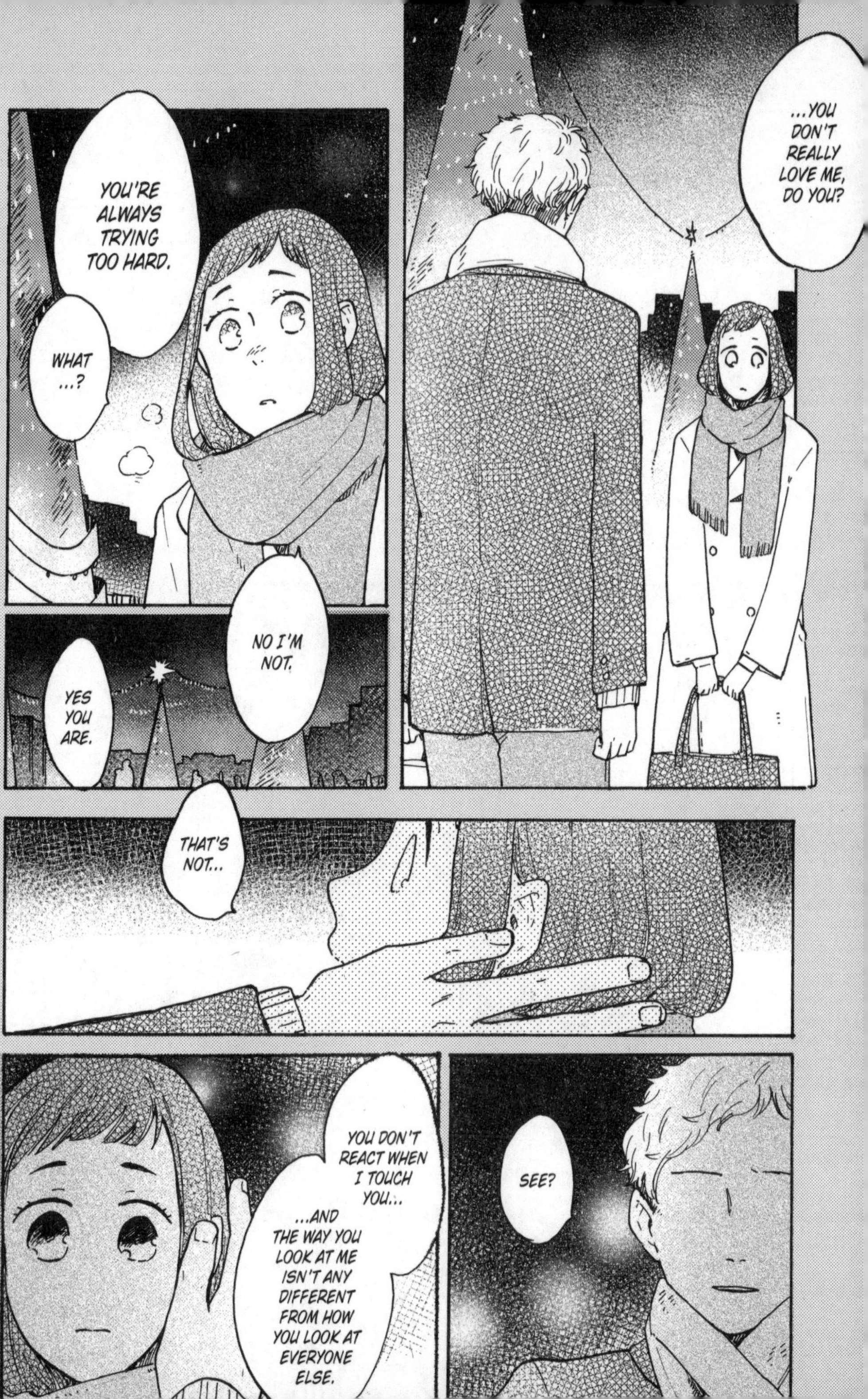
...YOU DON'T REALLY LOVE ME, DO YOU?
YOU'RE ALWAYS TRYING TOO HARD.
WHAT ...?
NO I'M NOT.
YES YOU ARE.
THAT'S NOT...
SEE?
YOU DON'T REACT WHEN I TOUCH YOU...
...AND THE WAY YOU LOOK AT ME ISN'T ANY DIFFERENT FROM HOW YOU LOOK AT EVERYONE ELSE.

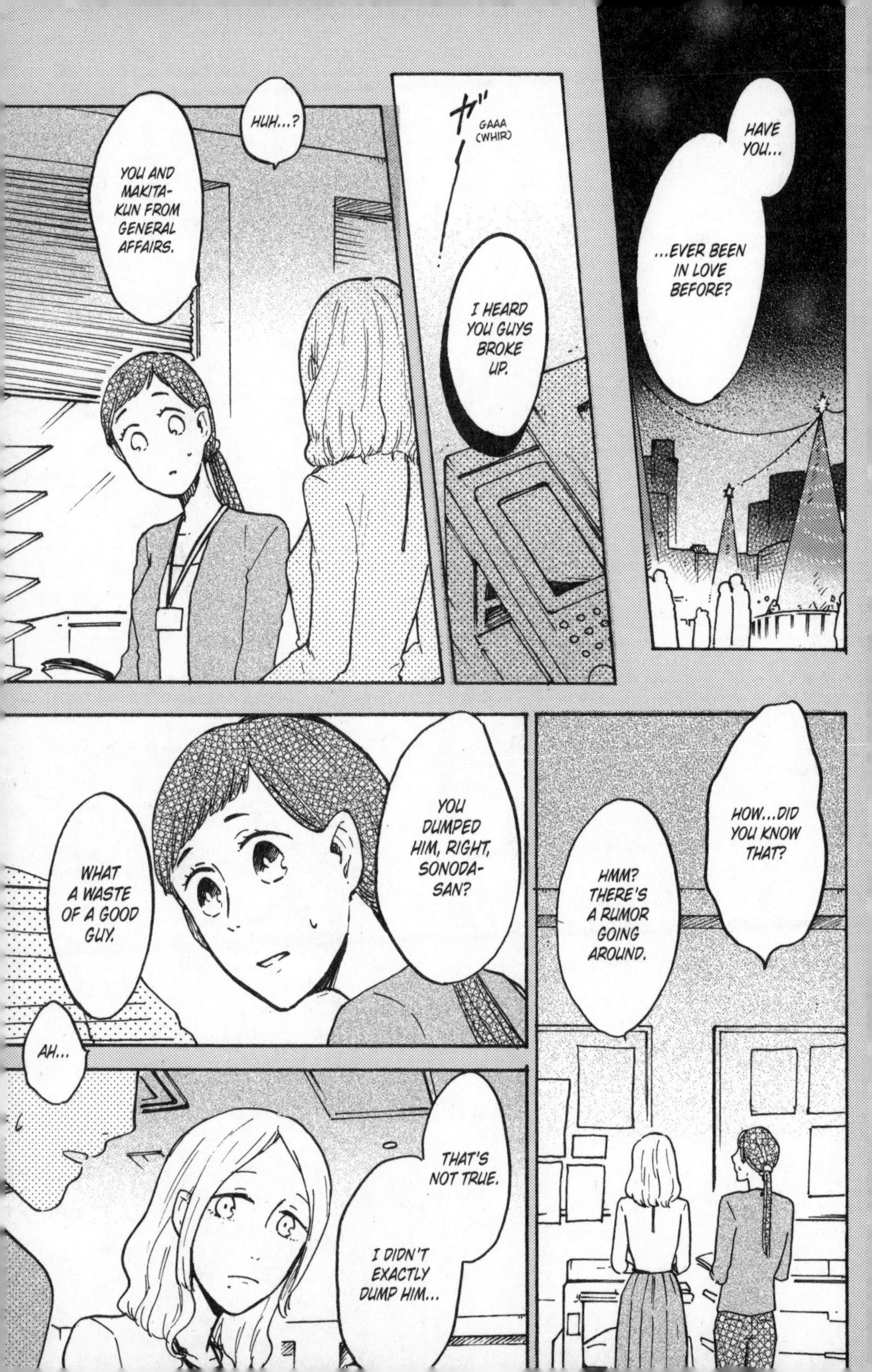
HAVE YOU...
...EVER BEEN IN LOVE BEFORE?
ガ
GAAA (WHIR)
I HEARD YOU GUYS BROKE UP.
HUH...?
YOU AND MAKITA-KUN FROM GENERAL AFFAIRS.
HOW...DID YOU KNOW THAT?
HMM? THERE'S A RUMOR GOING AROUND.
YOU DUMPED HIM, RIGHT, SONODA-SAN?
WHAT A WASTE OF A GOOD GUY.
AH...
THAT'S NOT TRUE.
I DIDN'T EXACTLY DUMP HIM...

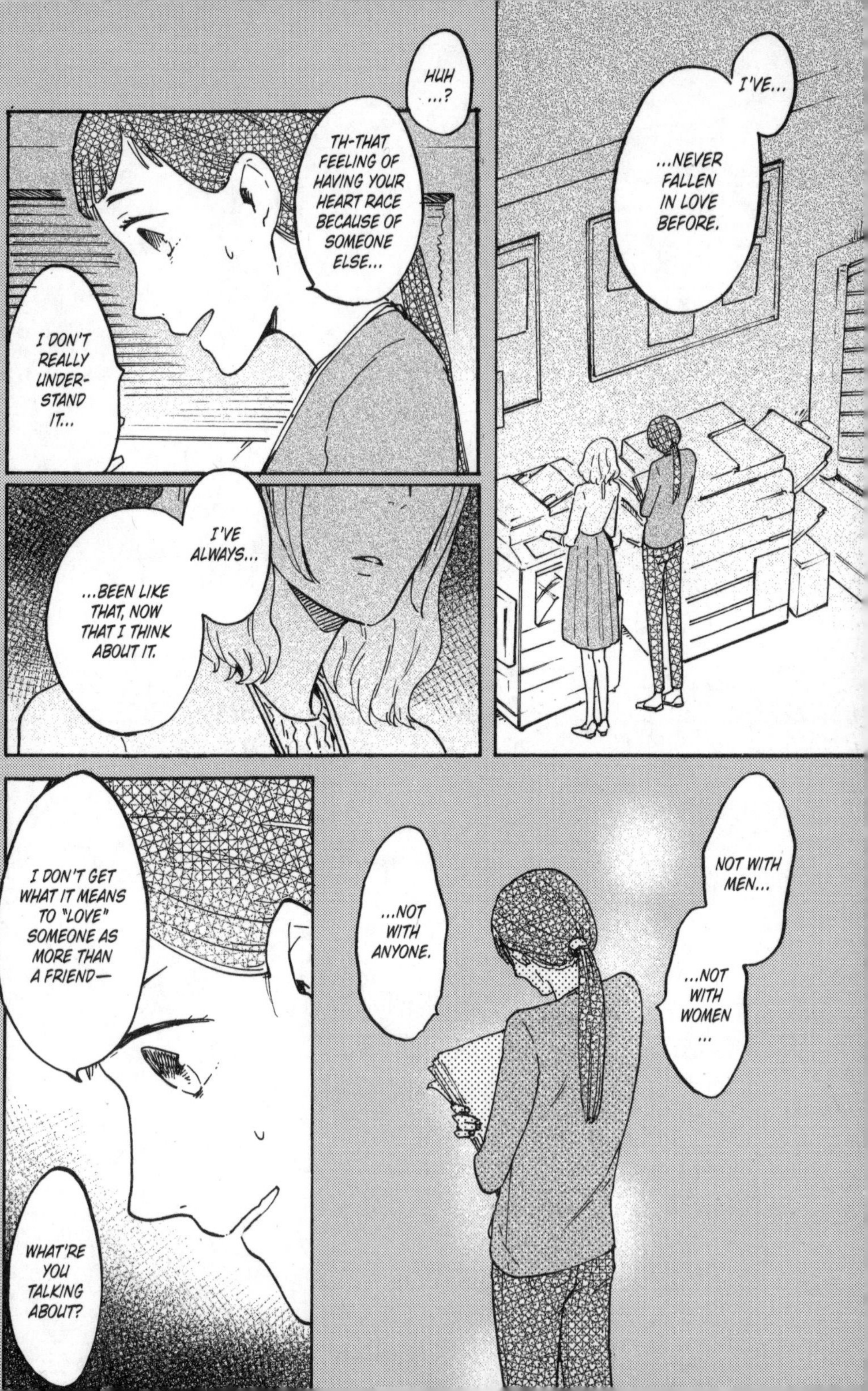
I'VE...
...NEVER FALLEN IN LOVE BEFORE.
HUH ...?
TH-THAT FEELING OF HAVING YOUR HEART RACE BECAUSE OF SOMEONE ELSE...
I DON'T REALLY UNDER-STAND IT...
I'VE ALWAYS...
...BEEN LIKE THAT, NOW THAT I THINK ABOUT IT.
NOT WITH MEN...
...NOT WITH WOMEN ...
...NOT WITH ANYONE.
I DON'T GET WHAT IT MEANS TO "LOVE" SOMEONE AS MORE THAN A FRIEND—
WHAT'RE YOU TALKING ABOUT?

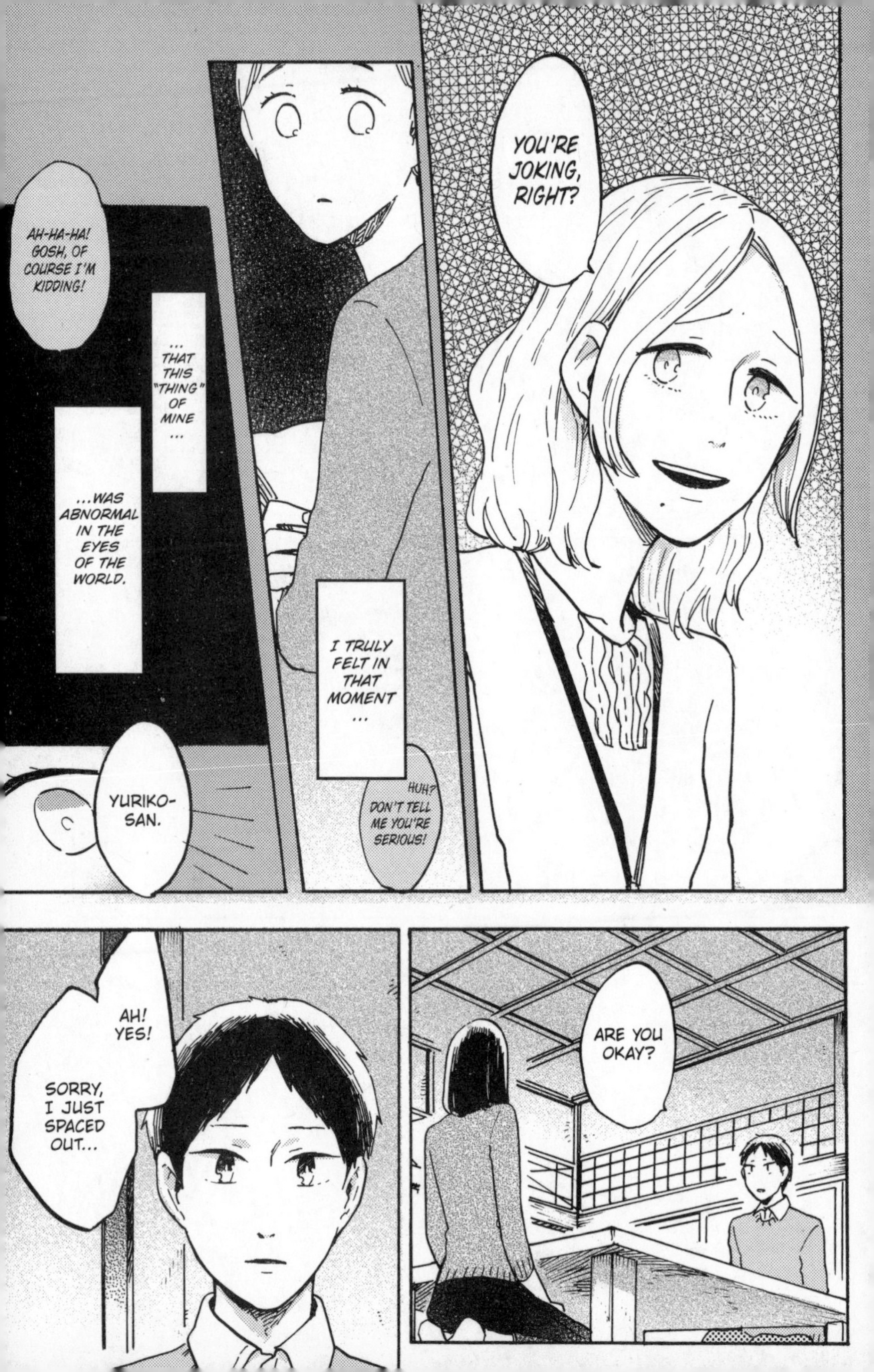
YOU'RE JOKING, RIGHT?
HUH? DON'T TELL ME YOU'RE SERIOUS!
AH-HA-HA! GOSH, OF COURSE I'M KIDDING!
I TRULY FELT IN THAT MOMENT...
...THAT THIS "THING" OF MINE...
...WAS ABNORMAL IN THE EYES OF THE WORLD.
YURIKO-SAN.
ARE YOU OKAY?
AH! YES!
SORRY, I JUST SPACED OUT...

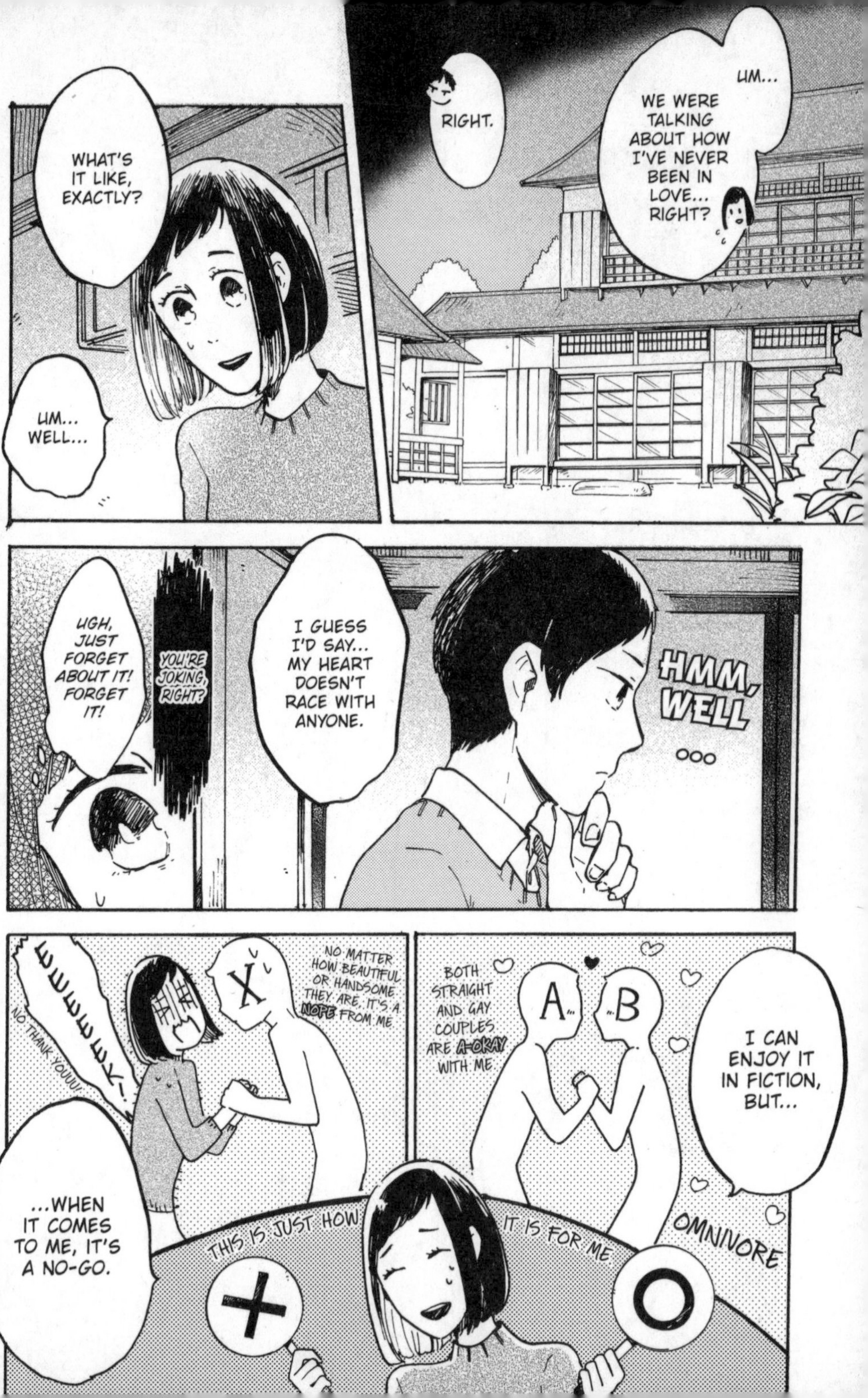
UM... WE WERE TALKING ABOUT HOW I'VE NEVER BEEN IN LOVE... RIGHT?
RIGHT.
WHAT'S IT LIKE, EXACTLY?
UM... WELL...
HMM, WELL
I GUESS I'D SAY... MY HEART DOESN'T RACE WITH ANYONE.
YOU'RE JOKING, RIGHT?
UGH, JUST FORGET ABOUT IT! FORGET IT!
I CAN ENJOY IT IN FICTION, BUT...
BOTH STRAIGHT AND GAY COUPLES ARE A-OKAY WITH ME
A
B
OMNIVORE
NO MATTER HOW BEAUTIFUL OR HANDSOME THEY ARE, IT'S A NOPE FROM ME
X
EEEEEK!
NO THANK YOUUU!
...WHEN IT COMES TO ME, IT'S A NO-GO.
THIS IS JUST HOW IT IS FOR ME

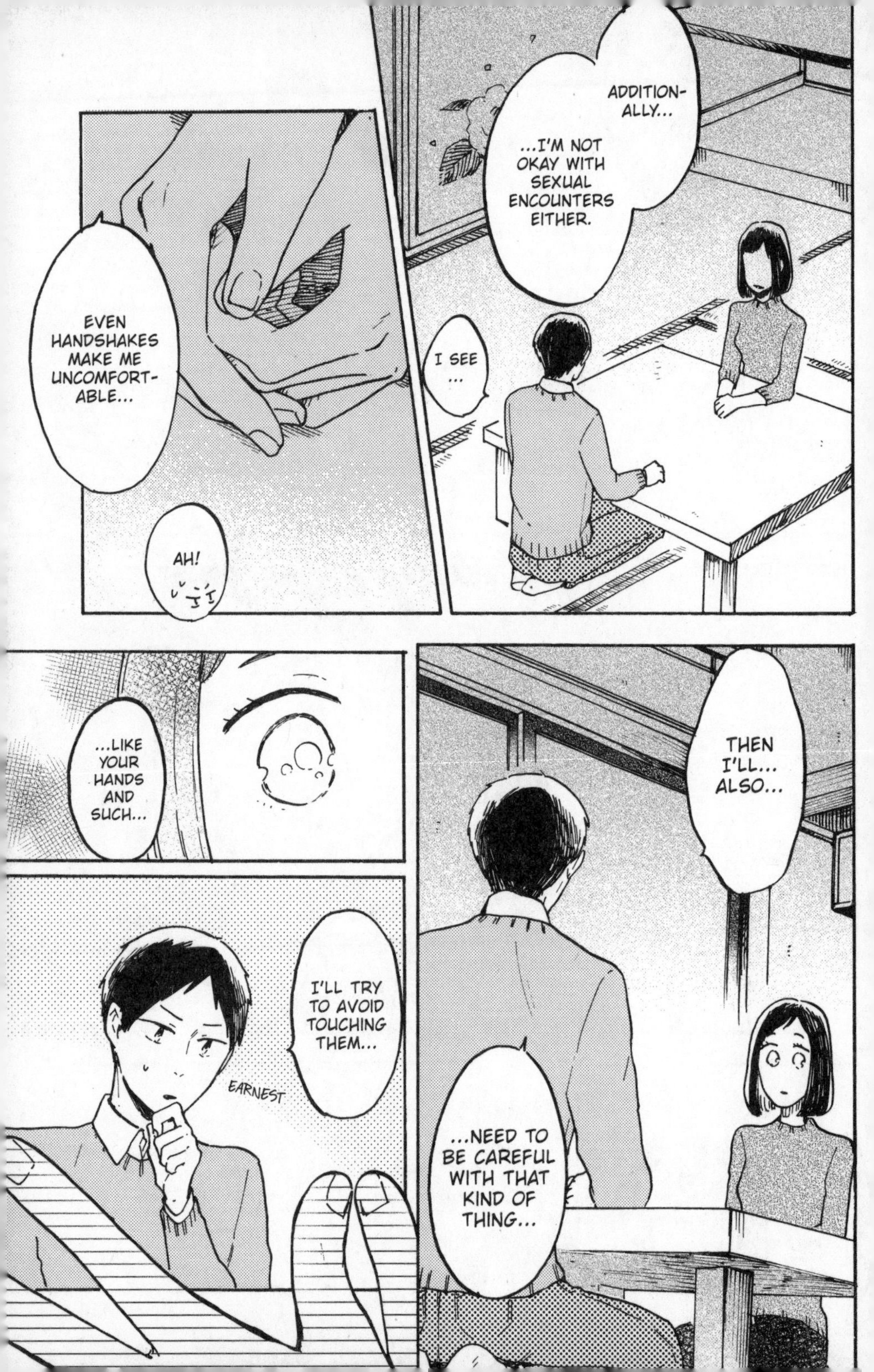
ADDITION-ALLY...
...I'M NOT OKAY WITH SEXUAL ENCOUNTERS EITHER.
I SEE ...
EVEN HANDSHAKES MAKE ME UNCOMFORTABLE...
AH!
THEN I'LL... ALSO...
...NEED TO BE CAREFUL WITH THAT KIND OF THING...
...LIKE YOUR HANDS AND SUCH...
I'LL TRY TO AVOID TOUCHING THEM...
EARNEST

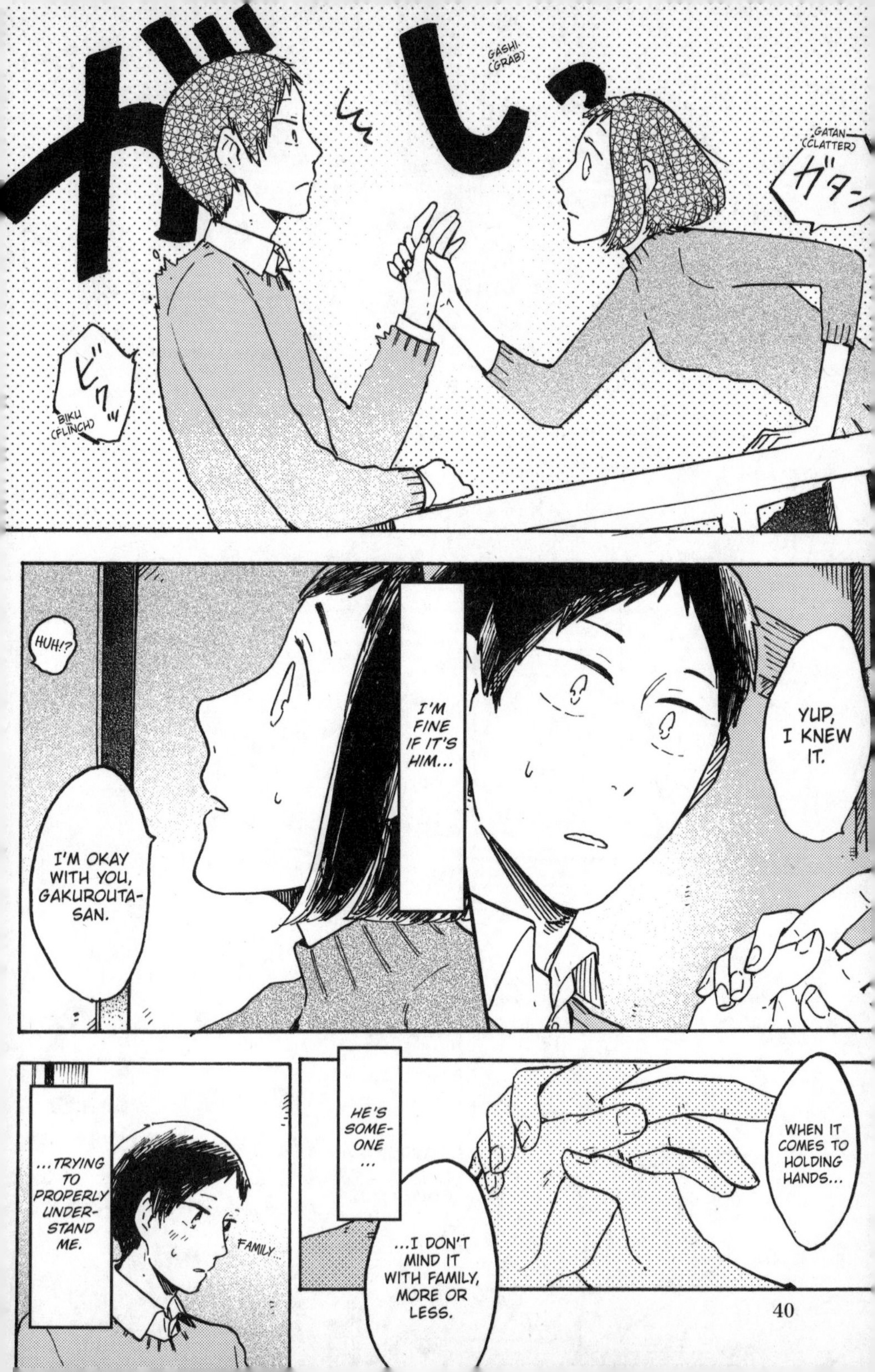
GASHI (GRAB)
GATAN (CLATTER)
BIKU (FLINCH)
YUP, I KNEW IT.
I'M FINE IF IT'S HIM...
HUH!?
I'M OKAY WITH YOU, GAKUROUTA-SAN.
WHEN IT COMES TO HOLDING HANDS...
HE'S SOMEONE...
...I DON'T MIND IT WITH FAMILY, MORE OR LESS.
...TRYING TO PROPERLY UNDERSTAND ME.
FAMILY...

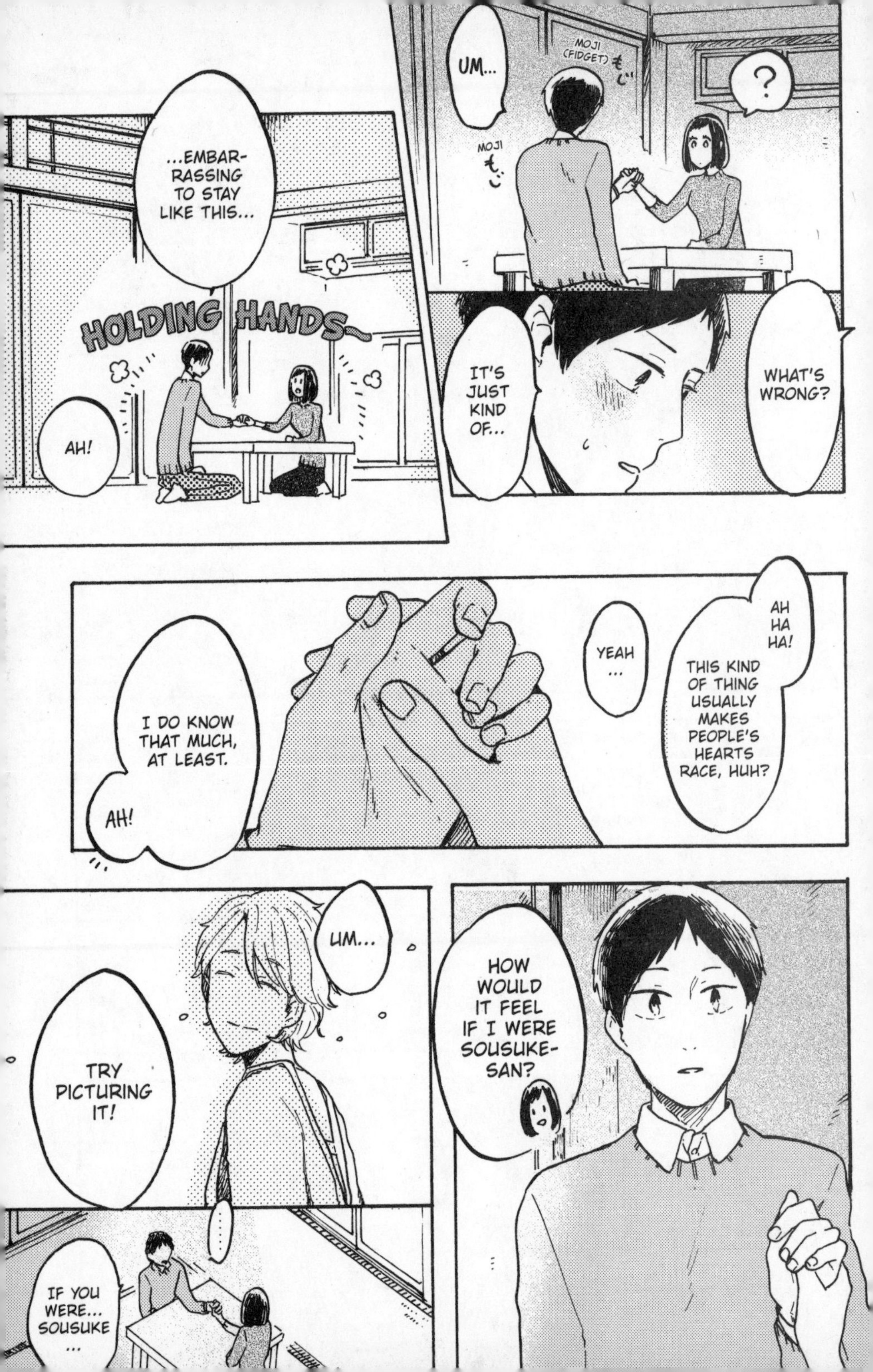
UM...
MOJI (FIDGET) もじ
?
MOJI もじ
WHAT'S WRONG?
IT'S JUST KIND OF...
...EMBAR-RASSING TO STAY LIKE THIS...
HOLDING HANDS~
AH!
AH HA HA!
THIS KIND OF THING USUALLY MAKES PEOPLE'S HEARTS RACE, HUH?
YEAH...
I DO KNOW THAT MUCH, AT LEAST.
AH!
HOW WOULD IT FEEL IF I WERE SOUSUKE-SAN?
UM...
TRY PICTURING IT!
...
IF YOU WERE... SOUSUKE ...

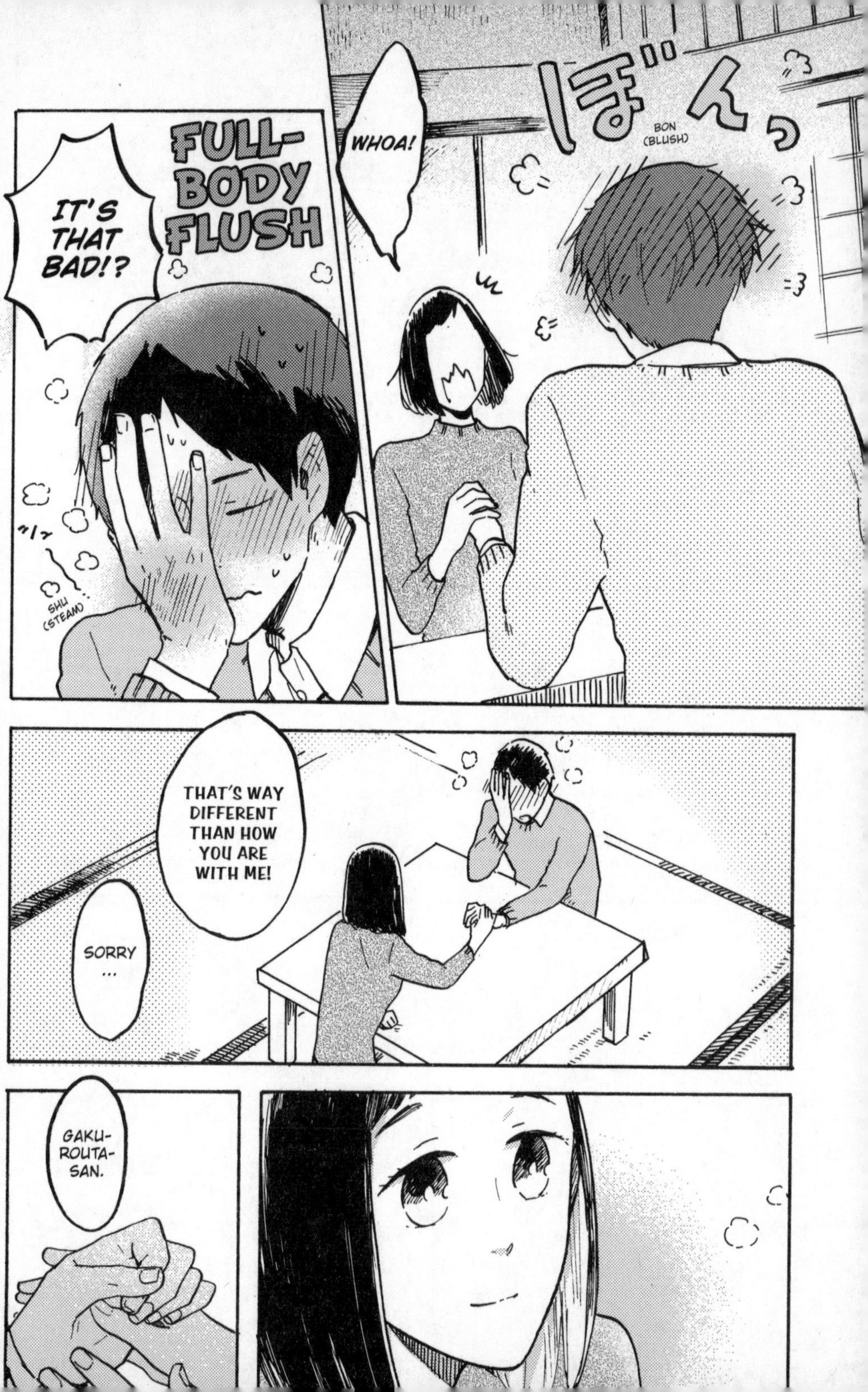
ぼんっ
BON (BLUSH)
WHOA!
FULL-BODY FLUSH
IT'S THAT BAD!?
SHU (STEAM)
THAT'S WAY DIFFERENT THAN HOW YOU ARE WITH ME!
SORRY ...
GAKU-ROUTA-SAN.

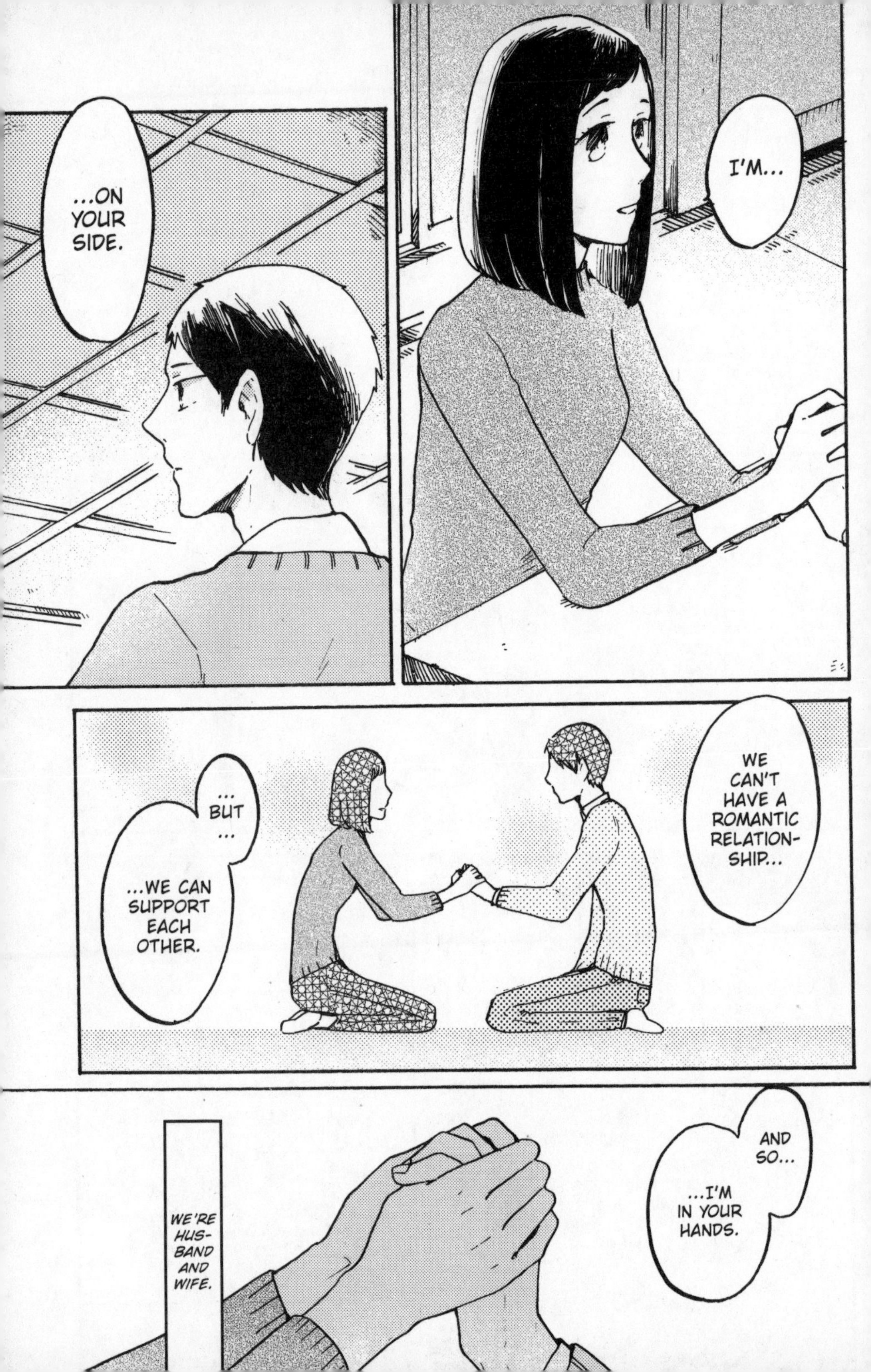
I'M...
...ON YOUR SIDE.
WE CAN'T HAVE A ROMANTIC RELATION-SHIP...
... BUT ...
...WE CAN SUPPORT EACH OTHER.
AND SO...
...I'M IN YOUR HANDS.
WE'RE HUS-BAND AND WIFE.

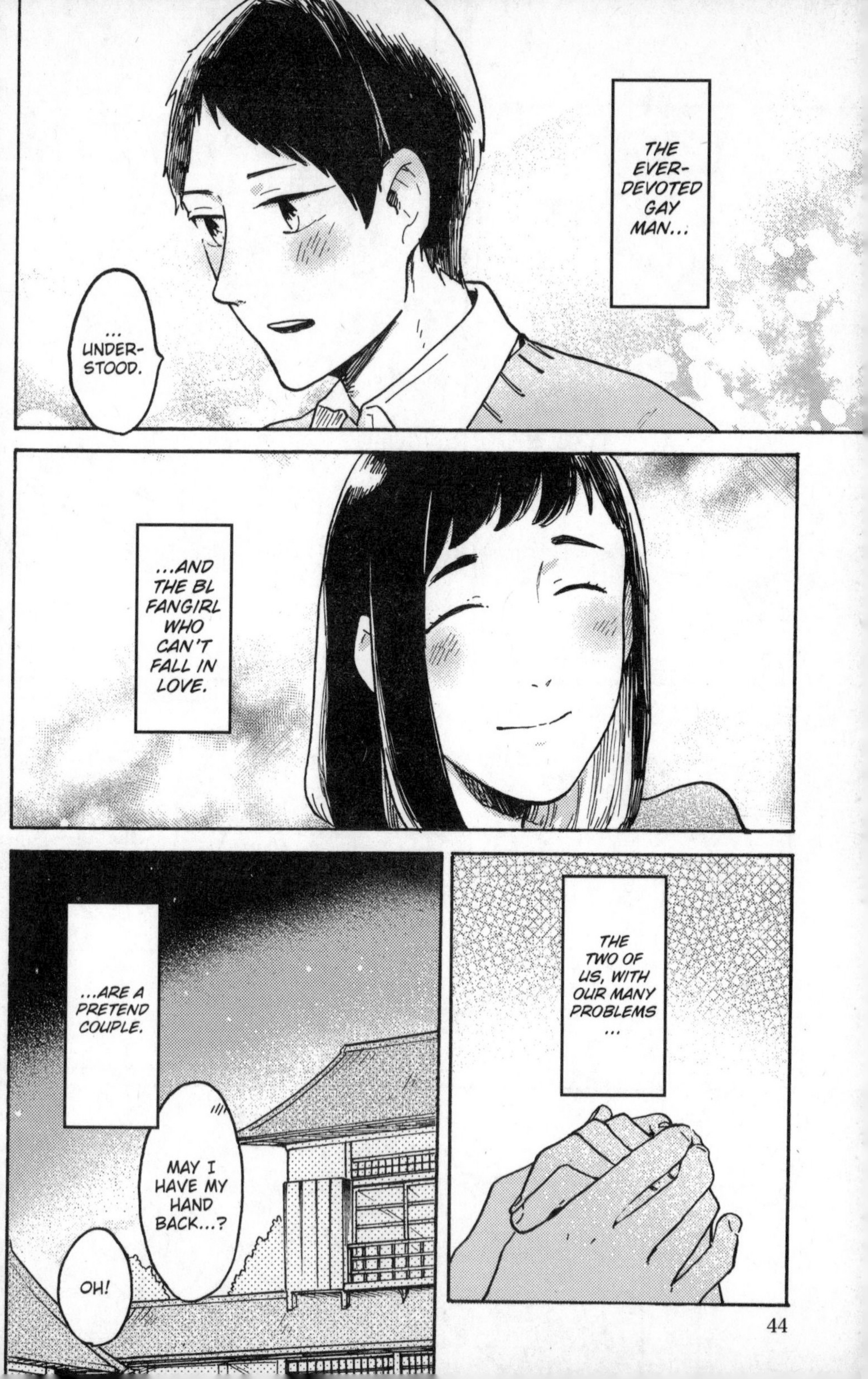
THE EVER-DEVOTED GAY MAN...
...UNDERSTOOD.
...AND THE BL FANGIRL WHO CAN'T FALL IN LOVE.
THE TWO OF US, WITH OUR MANY PROBLEMS...
...ARE A PRETEND COUPLE.
MAY I HAVE MY HAND BACK...?
OH!

I Want
to Be a
Wall

I Want
to Be a
Wall

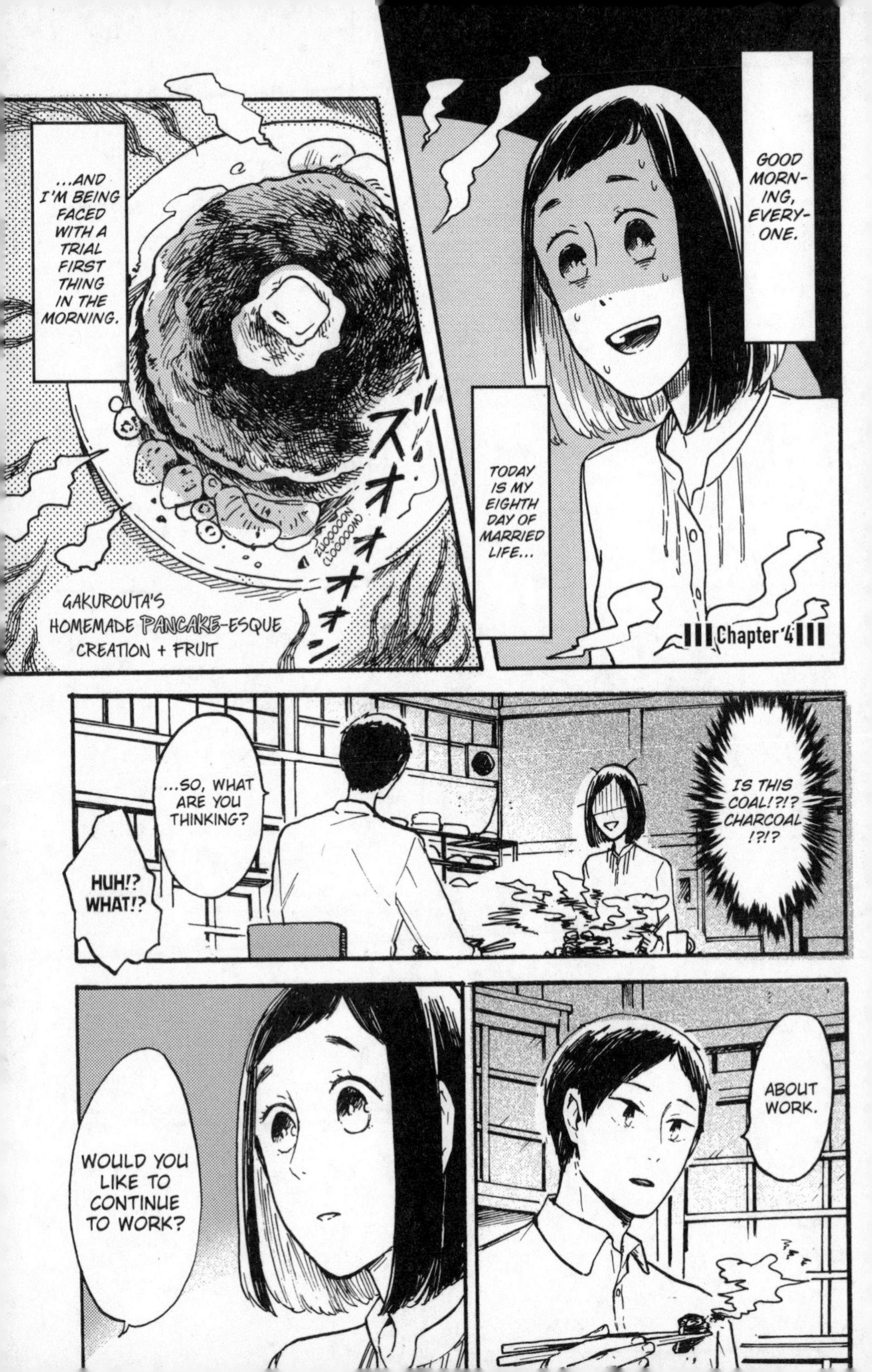
GOOD MORNING, EVERYONE.
TODAY IS MY EIGHTH DAY OF MARRIED LIFE...
Chapter 4
...AND I'M BEING FACED WITH A TRIAL FIRST THING IN THE MORNING.
ズオオオオオン
ZUOOOOOON (CLOOOOOOM)
GAKUROUTA'S HOMEMADE PANCAKE-ESQUE CREATION + FRUIT
IS THIS COAL!?!? CHARCOAL!?!?
...SO, WHAT ARE YOU THINKING?
HUH!? WHAT!?
ABOUT WORK.
WOULD YOU LIKE TO CONTINUE TO WORK?

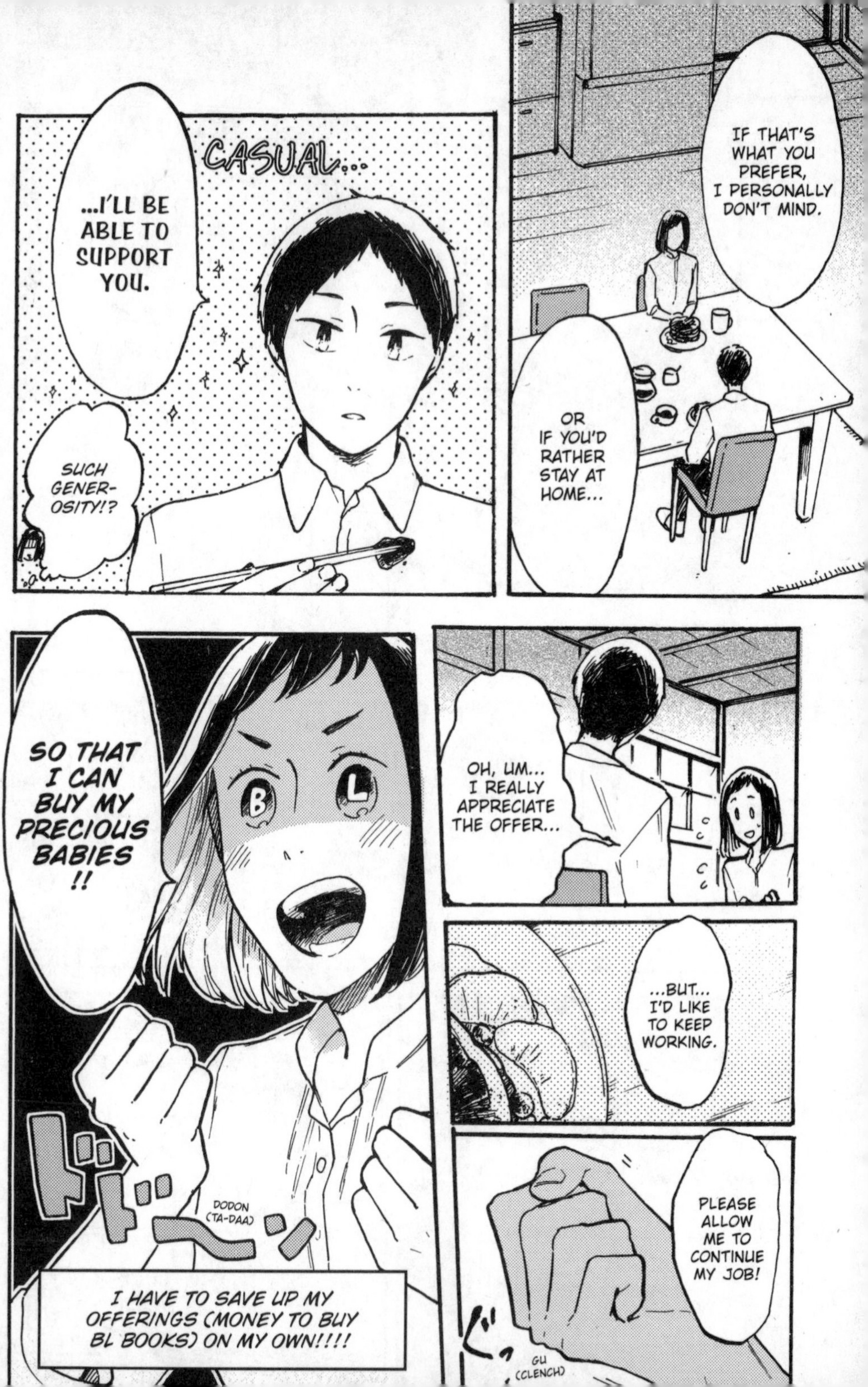
IF THAT'S WHAT YOU PREFER, I PERSONALLY DON'T MIND.
OR IF YOU'D RATHER STAY AT HOME...
...I'LL BE ABLE TO SUPPORT YOU.
CASUAL...
SUCH GENER-OSITY!?
OH, UM... I REALLY APPRECIATE THE OFFER...
...BUT... I'D LIKE TO KEEP WORKING.
PLEASE ALLOW ME TO CONTINUE MY JOB!
GU (CLENCH)
SO THAT I CAN BUY MY PRECIOUS BABIES !!
DODON (TA-DAA)
I HAVE TO SAVE UP MY OFFERINGS (MONEY TO BUY BL BOOKS) ON MY OWN!!!!

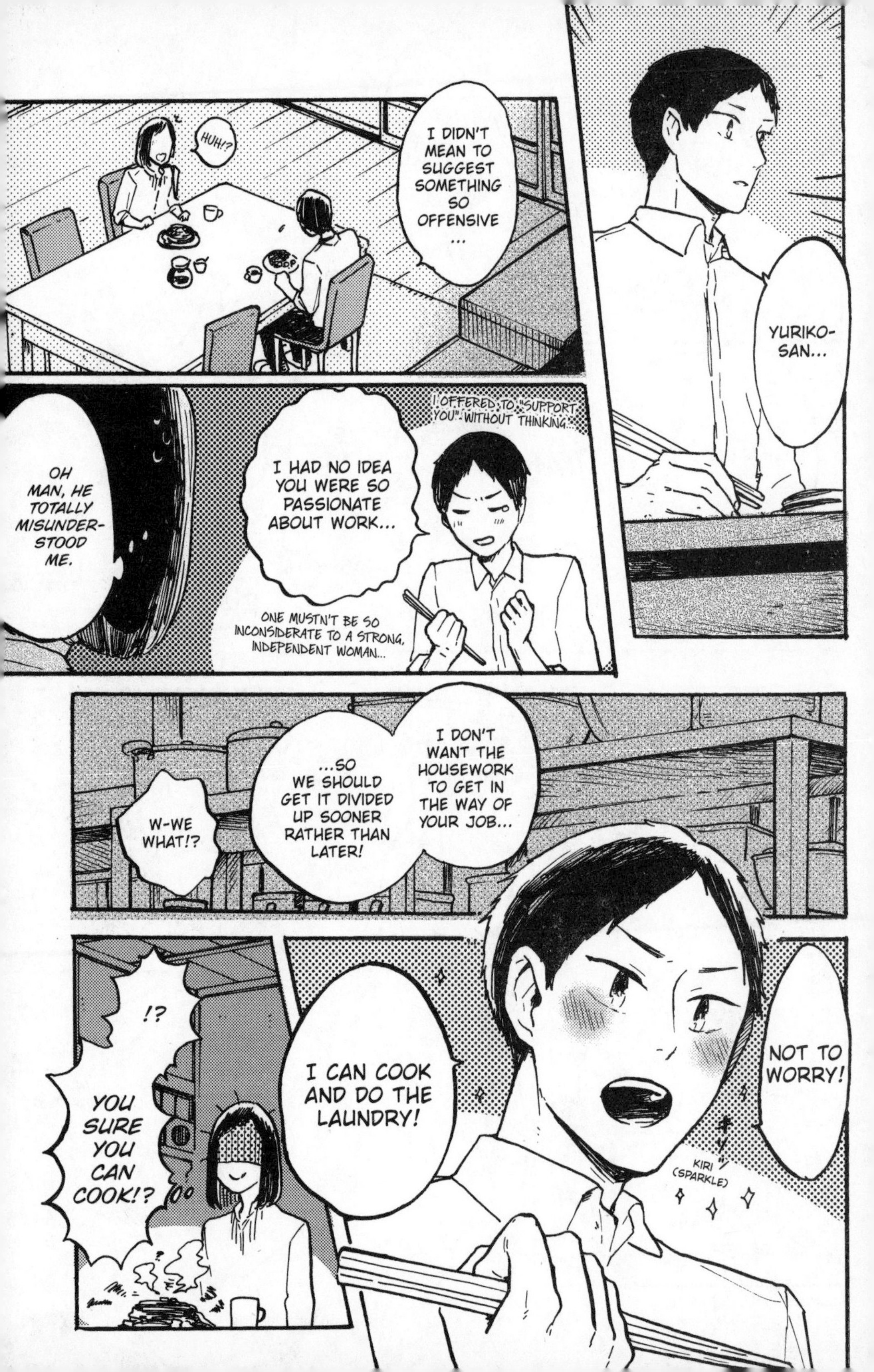
YURIKO-SAN...
I DIDN'T MEAN TO SUGGEST SOMETHING SO OFFENSIVE...
HUH!?
I OFFERED TO "SUPPORT YOU" WITHOUT THINKING...
I HAD NO IDEA YOU WERE SO PASSIONATE ABOUT WORK...
ONE MUSTN'T BE SO INCONSIDERATE TO A STRONG, INDEPENDENT WOMAN...
OH MAN, HE TOTALLY MISUNDERSTOOD ME.
I DON'T WANT THE HOUSEWORK TO GET IN THE WAY OF YOUR JOB...
...SO WE SHOULD GET IT DIVIDED UP SOONER RATHER THAN LATER!
W-WE WHAT!?
NOT TO WORRY!
KIRI (SPARKLE)
I CAN COOK AND DO THE LAUNDRY!
!?
YOU SURE YOU CAN COOK!?

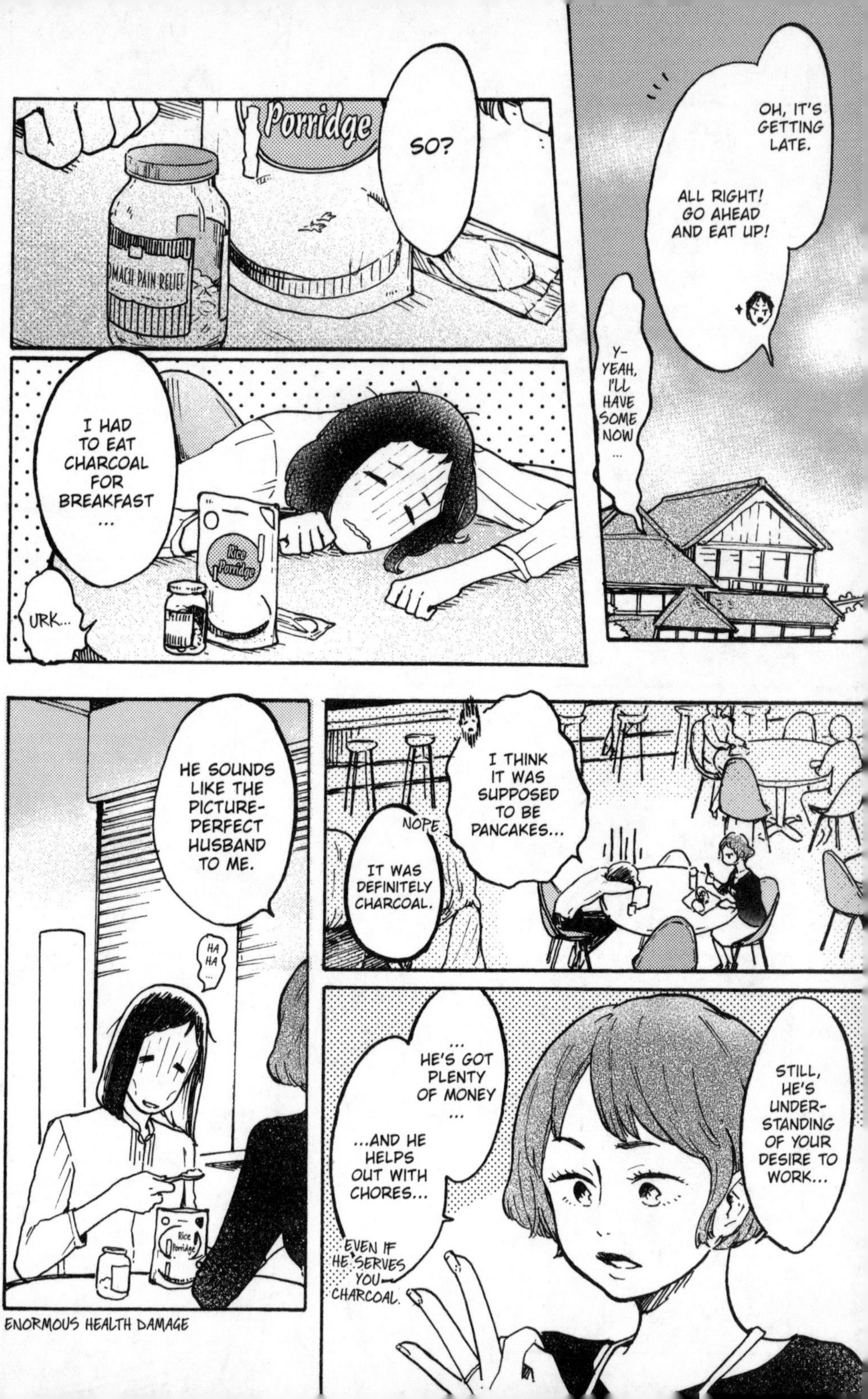
OH, IT'S GETTING LATE.
ALL RIGHT! GO AHEAD AND EAT UP!
Y-YEAH, I'LL HAVE SOME NOW...
Porridge
SO?
OMACH PAIN RELIEF
I HAD TO EAT CHARCOAL FOR BREAKFAST...
Rice Porridge
URK...
I THINK IT WAS SUPPOSED TO BE PANCAKES...
NOPE
IT WAS DEFINITELY CHARCOAL.
STILL, HE'S UNDER-STANDING OF YOUR DESIRE TO WORK...
...HE'S GOT PLENTY OF MONEY...
...AND HE HELPS OUT WITH CHORES...
EVEN IF HE SERVES YOU CHARCOAL.
HE SOUNDS LIKE THE PICTURE-PERFECT HUSBAND TO ME.
HA HA...
Rice Porridge
ENORMOUS HEALTH DAMAGE

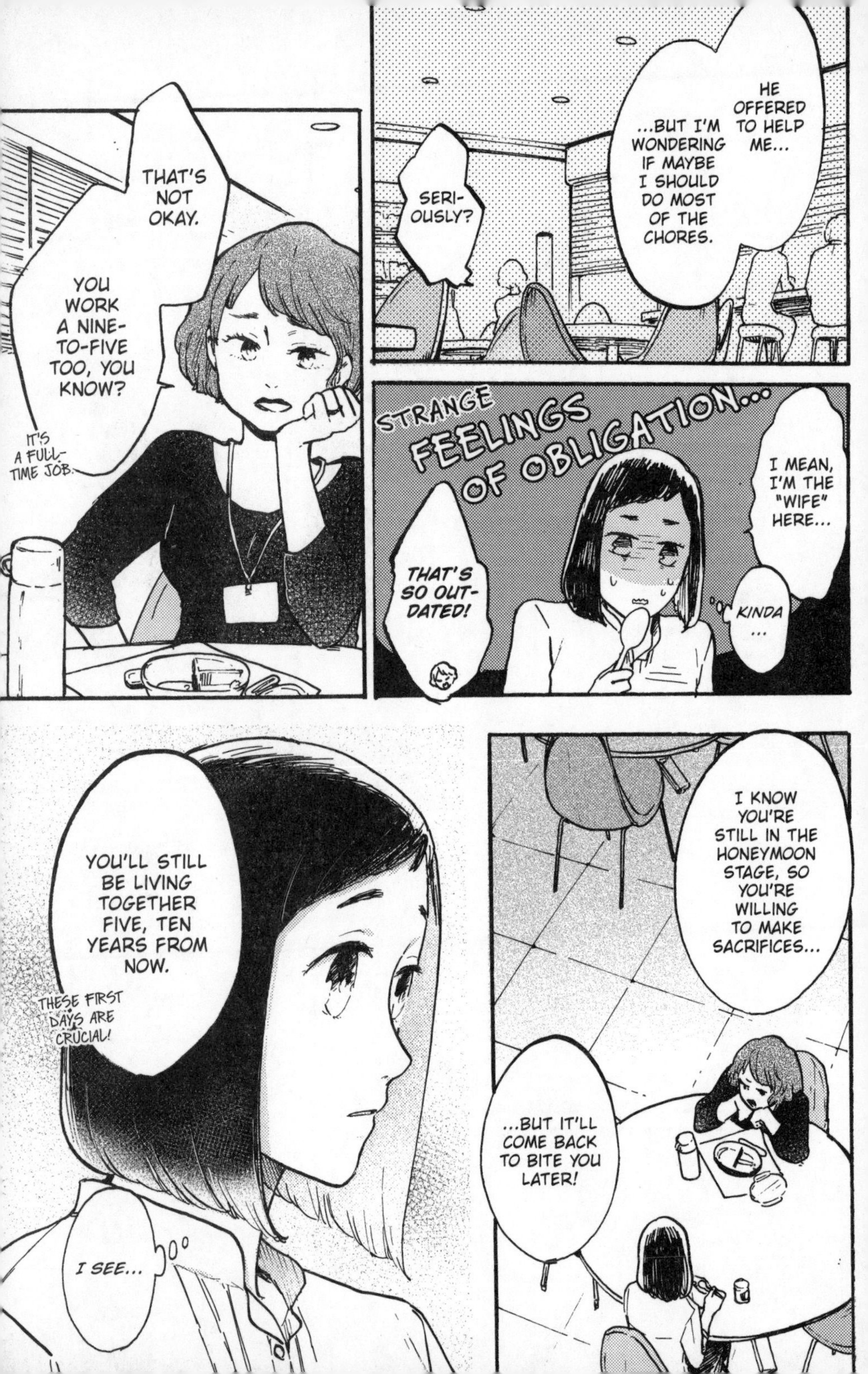
HE OFFERED TO HELP ME...
...BUT I'M WONDERING IF MAYBE I SHOULD DO MOST OF THE CHORES.
SERI-OUSLY?
STRANGE FEELINGS OF OBLIGATION...
I MEAN, I'M THE "WIFE" HERE...
KINDA...
THAT'S SO OUT-DATED!
THAT'S NOT OKAY.
YOU WORK A NINE-TO-FIVE TOO, YOU KNOW?
IT'S A FULL-TIME JOB.
I KNOW YOU'RE STILL IN THE HONEYMOON STAGE, SO YOU'RE WILLING TO MAKE SACRIFICES...
...BUT IT'LL COME BACK TO BITE YOU LATER!
YOU'LL STILL BE LIVING TOGETHER FIVE, TEN YEARS FROM NOW.
THESE FIRST DAYS ARE CRUCIAL!
I SEE...

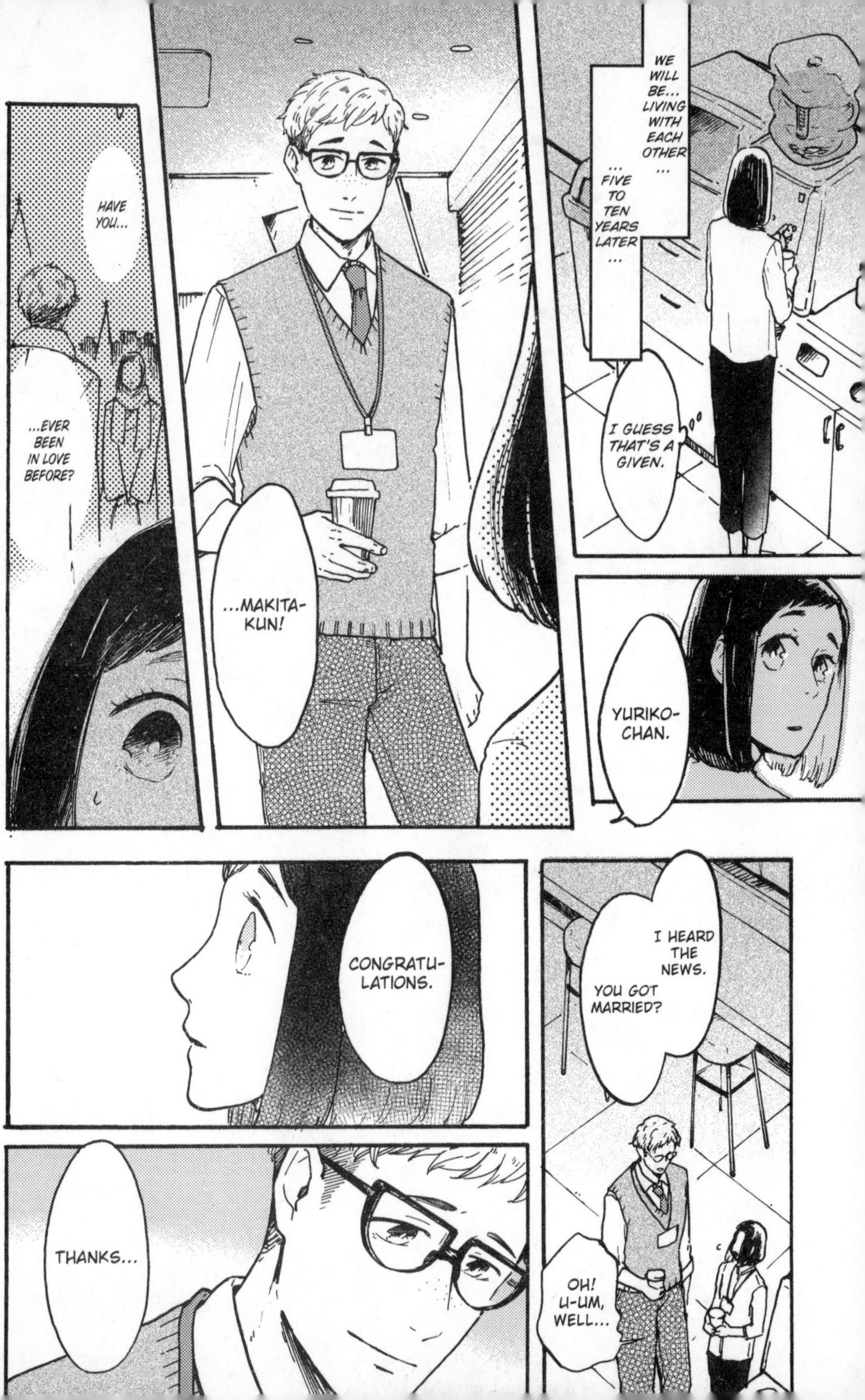
WE WILL BE... LIVING WITH EACH OTHER ... FIVE TO TEN YEARS LATER ...
I GUESS THAT'S A GIVEN.
YURIKO-CHAN.
...MAKITA-KUN!
HAVE YOU...
...EVER BEEN IN LOVE BEFORE?
I HEARD THE NEWS.
YOU GOT MARRIED?
OH! U-UM, WELL...
CONGRATU-LATIONS.
THANKS...

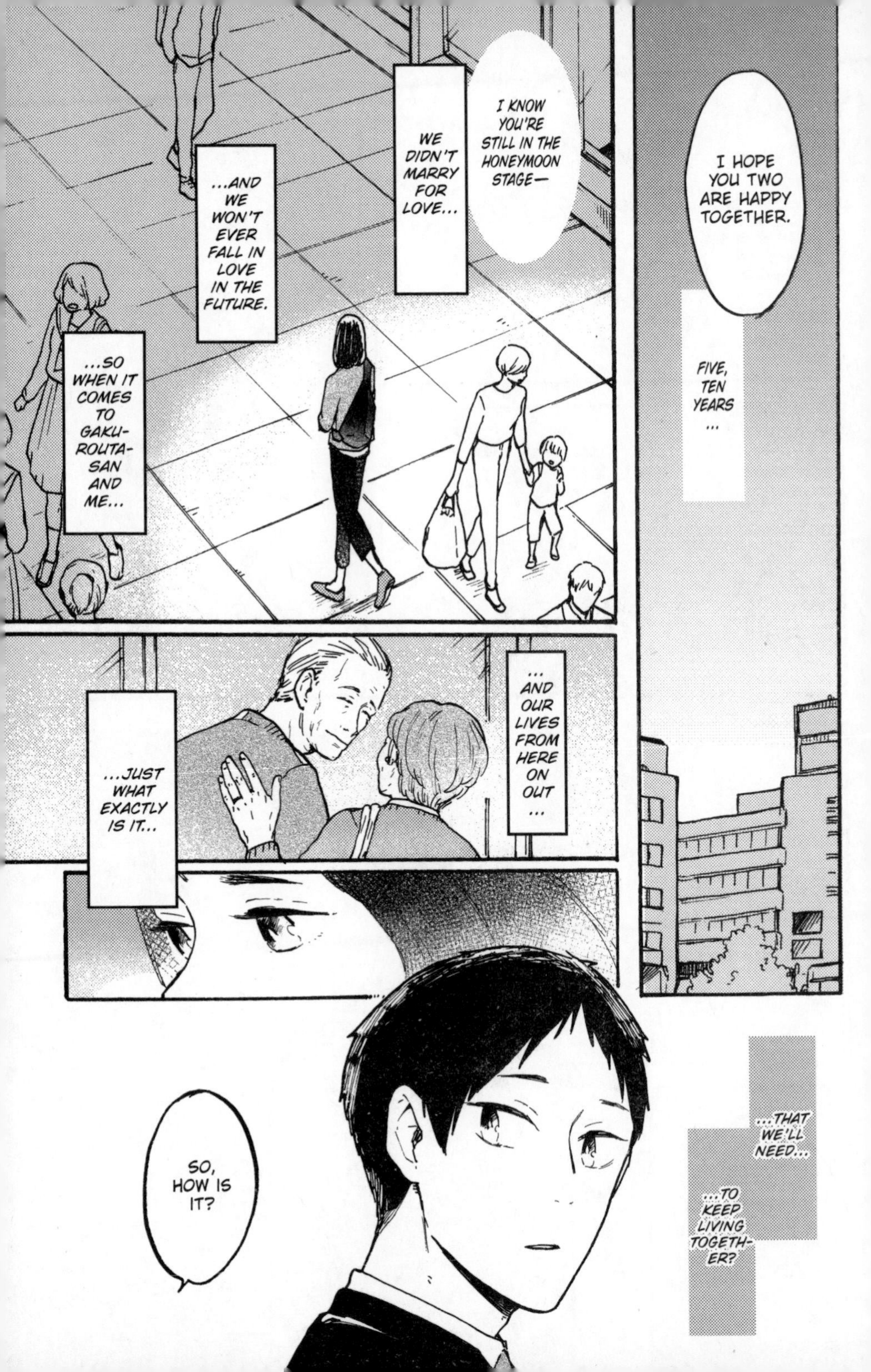
I HOPE YOU TWO ARE HAPPY TOGETHER.
FIVE, TEN YEARS ...
I KNOW YOU'RE STILL IN THE HONEYMOON STAGE—
WE DIDN'T MARRY FOR LOVE...
...AND WE WON'T EVER FALL IN LOVE IN THE FUTURE.
...SO WHEN IT COMES TO GAKU-ROUTA-SAN AND ME...
... AND OUR LIVES FROM HERE ON OUT ...
...JUST WHAT EXACTLY IS IT...
...THAT WE'LL NEED...
...TO KEEP LIVING TOGETH-ER?
SO, HOW IS IT?

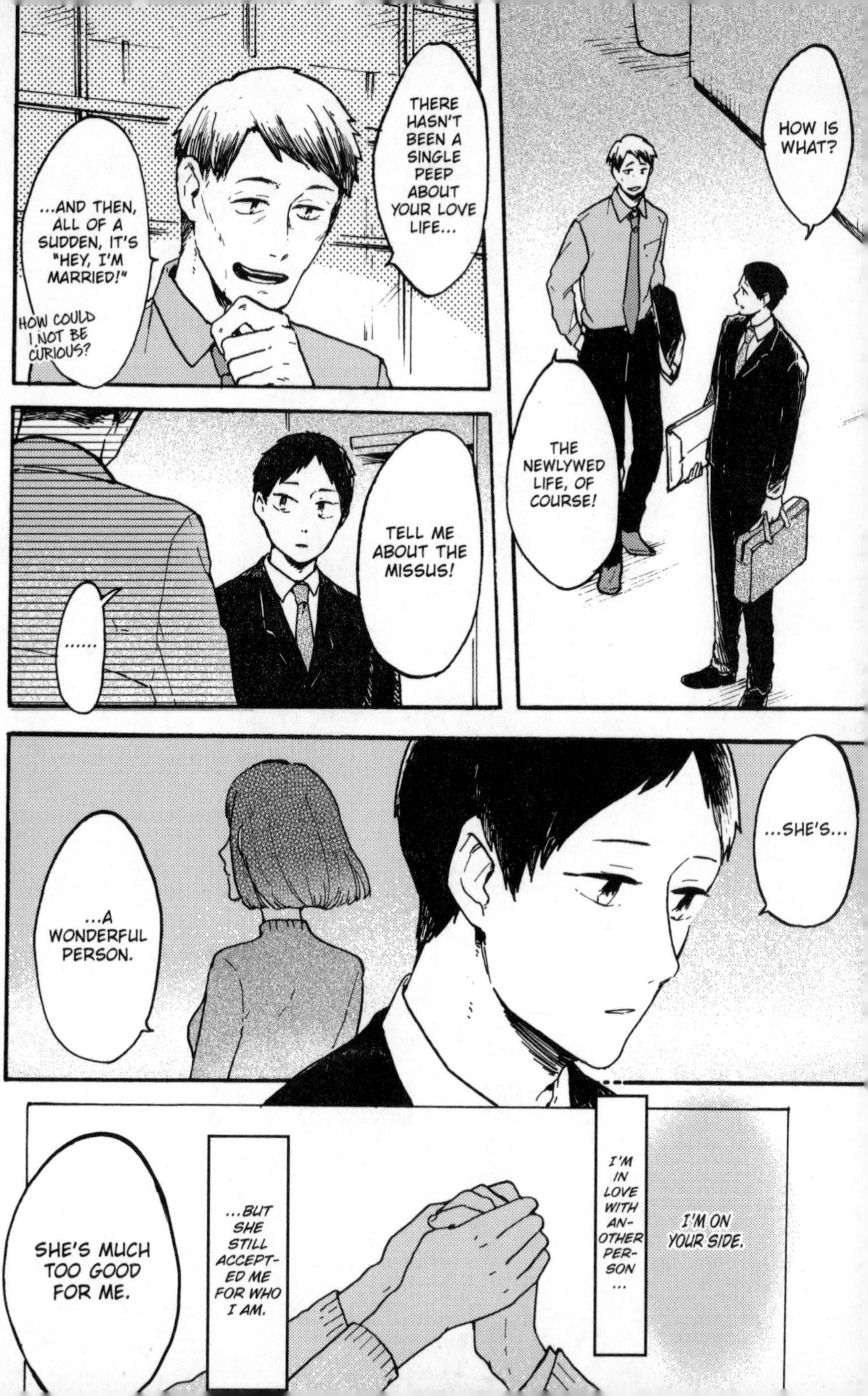
HOW IS WHAT?
THE NEWLYWED LIFE, OF COURSE!
THERE HASN'T BEEN A SINGLE PEEP ABOUT YOUR LOVE LIFE...
...AND THEN, ALL OF A SUDDEN, IT'S "HEY, I'M MARRIED!"
HOW COULD I NOT BE CURIOUS?
TELL ME ABOUT THE MISSUS!
......
...SHE'S...
...A WONDERFUL PERSON.
I'M ON YOUR SIDE.
I'M IN LOVE WITH AN-OTHER PER-SON...
...BUT SHE STILL ACCEPT-ED ME FOR WHO I AM.
SHE'S MUCH TOO GOOD FOR ME.

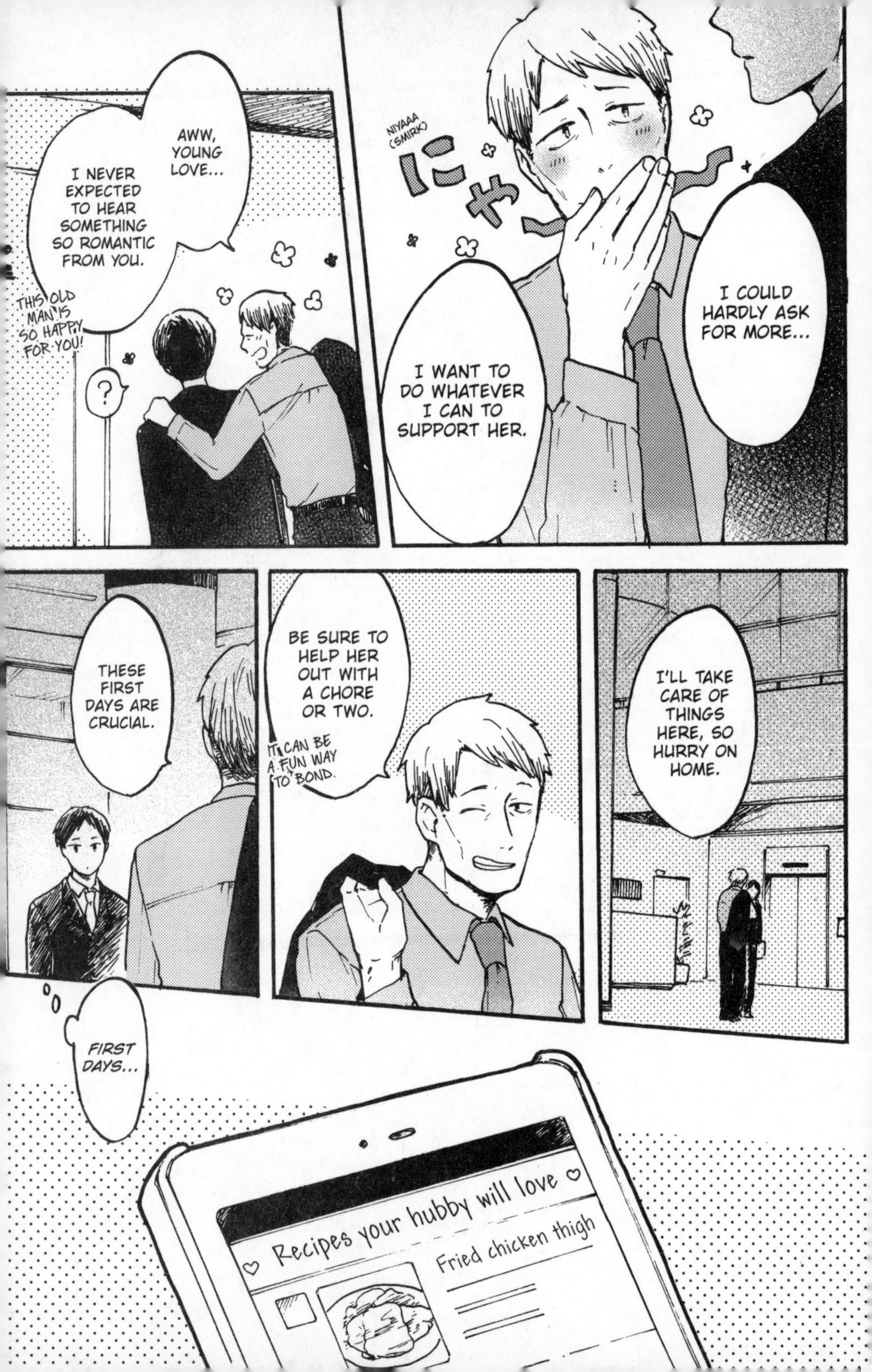
I COULD HARDLY ASK FOR MORE...
I WANT TO DO WHATEVER I CAN TO SUPPORT HER.
NIYAAA (SMIRK)
にやー
AWW, YOUNG LOVE...
I NEVER EXPECTED TO HEAR SOMETHING SO ROMANTIC FROM YOU.
THIS OLD MAN IS SO HAPPY FOR YOU!
?
I'LL TAKE CARE OF THINGS HERE, SO HURRY ON HOME.
BE SURE TO HELP HER OUT WITH A CHORE OR TWO.
IT CAN BE A FUN WAY TO BOND.
THESE FIRST DAYS ARE CRUCIAL.
FIRST DAYS...
Recipes your hubby will love
Fried chicken thigh

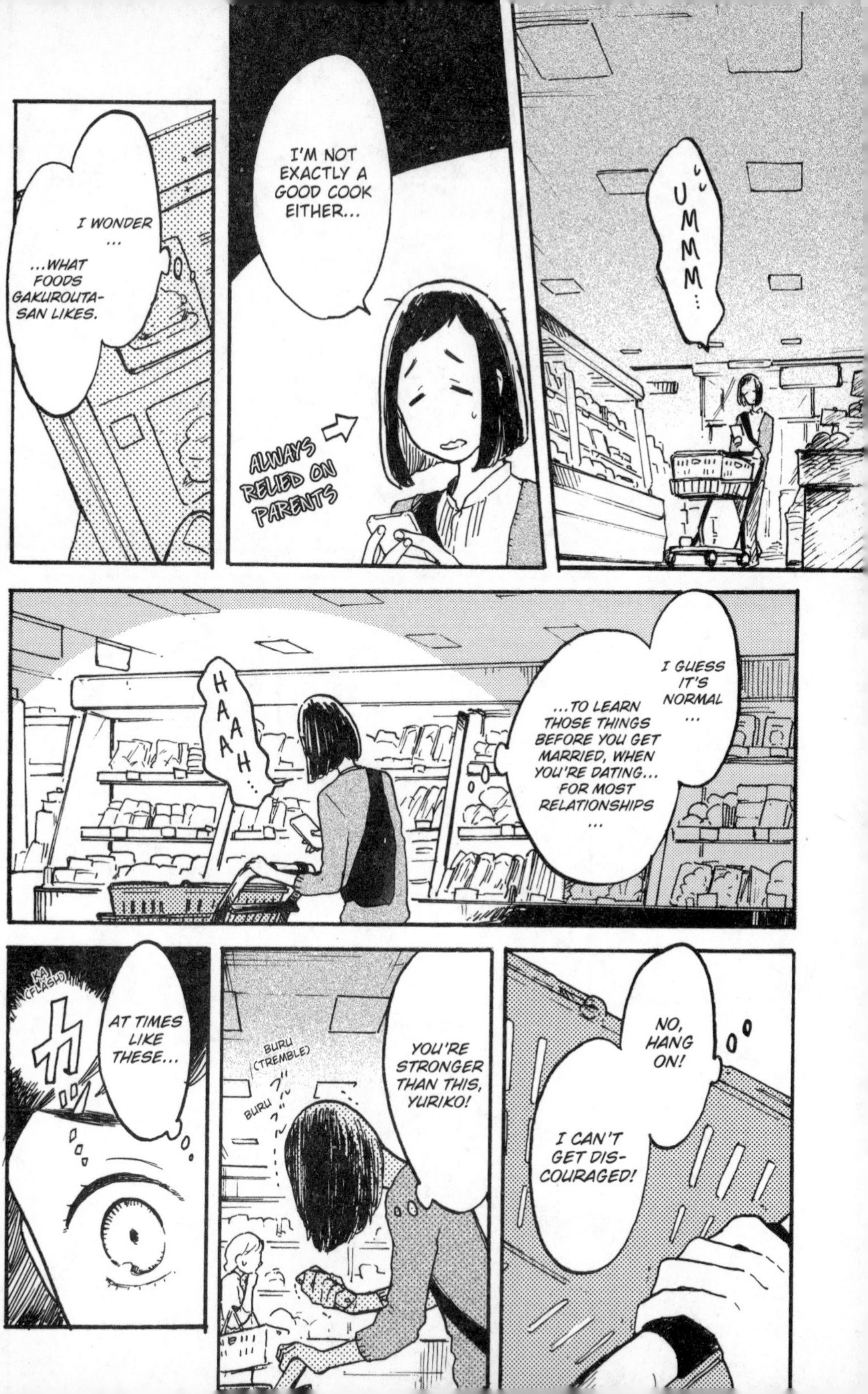
UMMM...
I'M NOT EXACTLY A GOOD COOK EITHER...
ALWAYS RELIED ON PARENTS
I WONDER...
...WHAT FOODS GAKUROUTA-SAN LIKES.
I GUESS IT'S NORMAL...
...TO LEARN THOSE THINGS BEFORE YOU GET MARRIED, WHEN YOU'RE DATING... FOR MOST RELATIONSHIPS...
HAAAH...
NO, HANG ON!
I CAN'T GET DIS-COURAGED!
YOU'RE STRONGER THAN THIS, YURIKO!
BURU (TREMBLE)
KA (FLASH)
AT TIMES LIKE THESE...

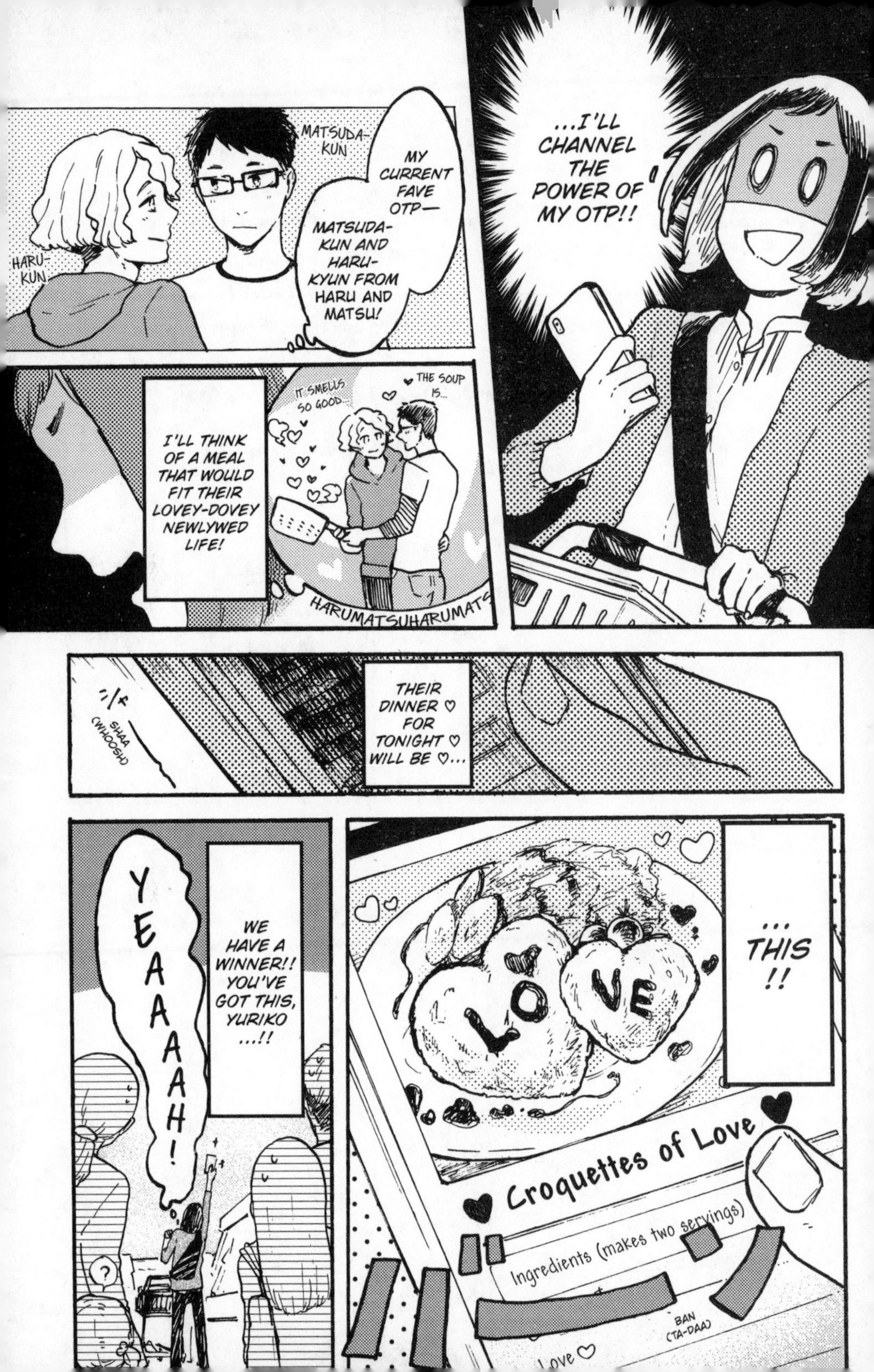
...I'LL CHANNEL THE POWER OF MY OTP!!
MY CURRENT FAVE OTP— MATSUDA-KUN AND HARU-KYUN FROM HARU AND MATSU!
MATSUDA-KUN
HARU-KUN
THE SOUP IS...
IT SMELLS SO GOOD
HARUMATSUHARUMATS
I'LL THINK OF A MEAL THAT WOULD FIT THEIR LOVEY-DOVEY NEWLYWED LIFE!
THEIR DINNER ♡ FOR TONIGHT ♡ WILL BE ♡...
SHAA (WHOOSH)
...THIS!!
LOVE
Croquettes of Love
Ingredients (makes two servings)
BAN (TA-DAA)
Love ♡
YEAAAAAH!
WE HAVE A WINNER!! YOU'VE GOT THIS, YURIKO ...!!
?

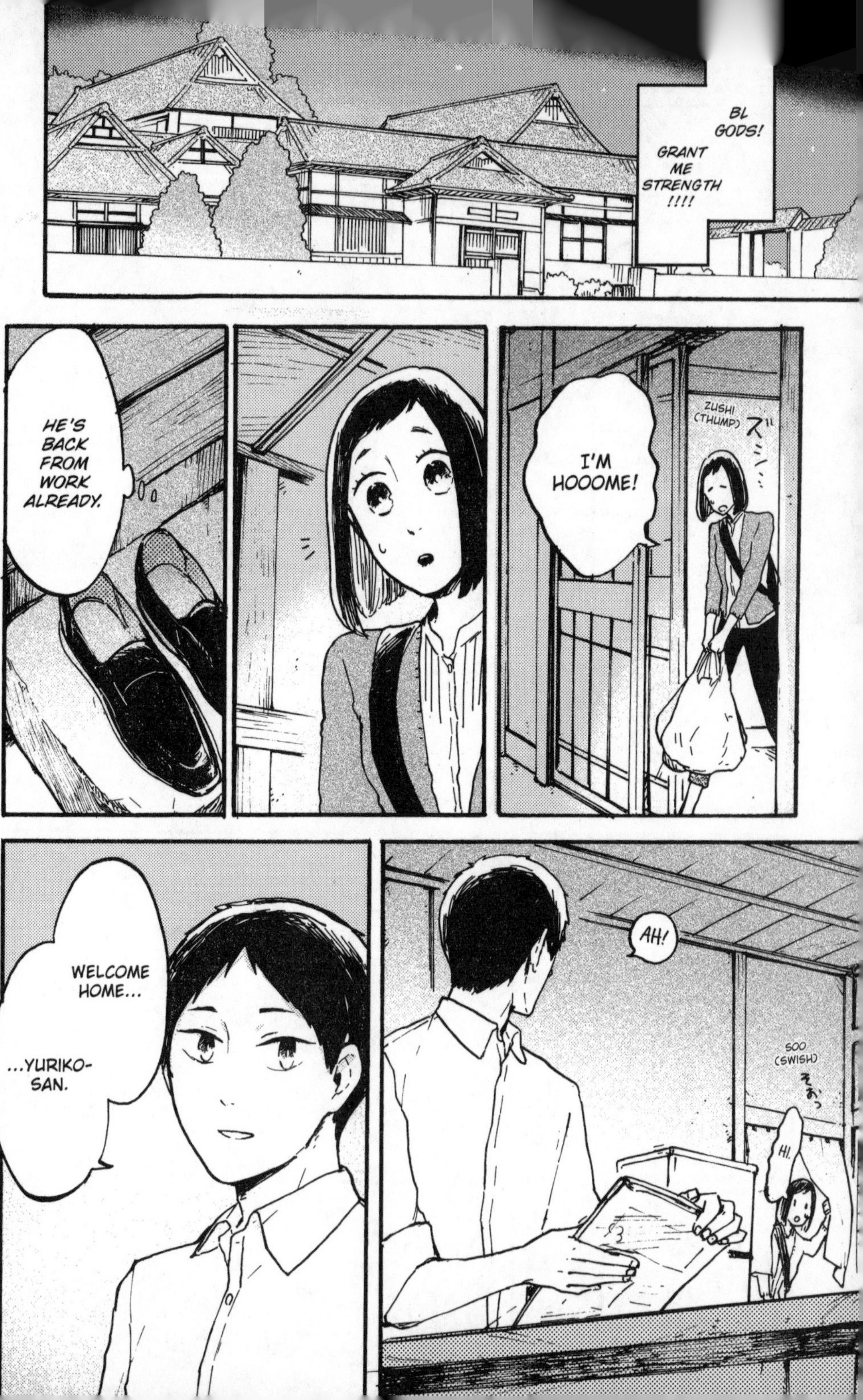
BL GODS!
GRANT ME STRENGTH !!!!
ZUSHI (THUMP)
I'M HOOOME!
HE'S BACK FROM WORK ALREADY.
AH!
SOO (SWISH)
HI.
WELCOME HOME...
...YURIKO-SAN.

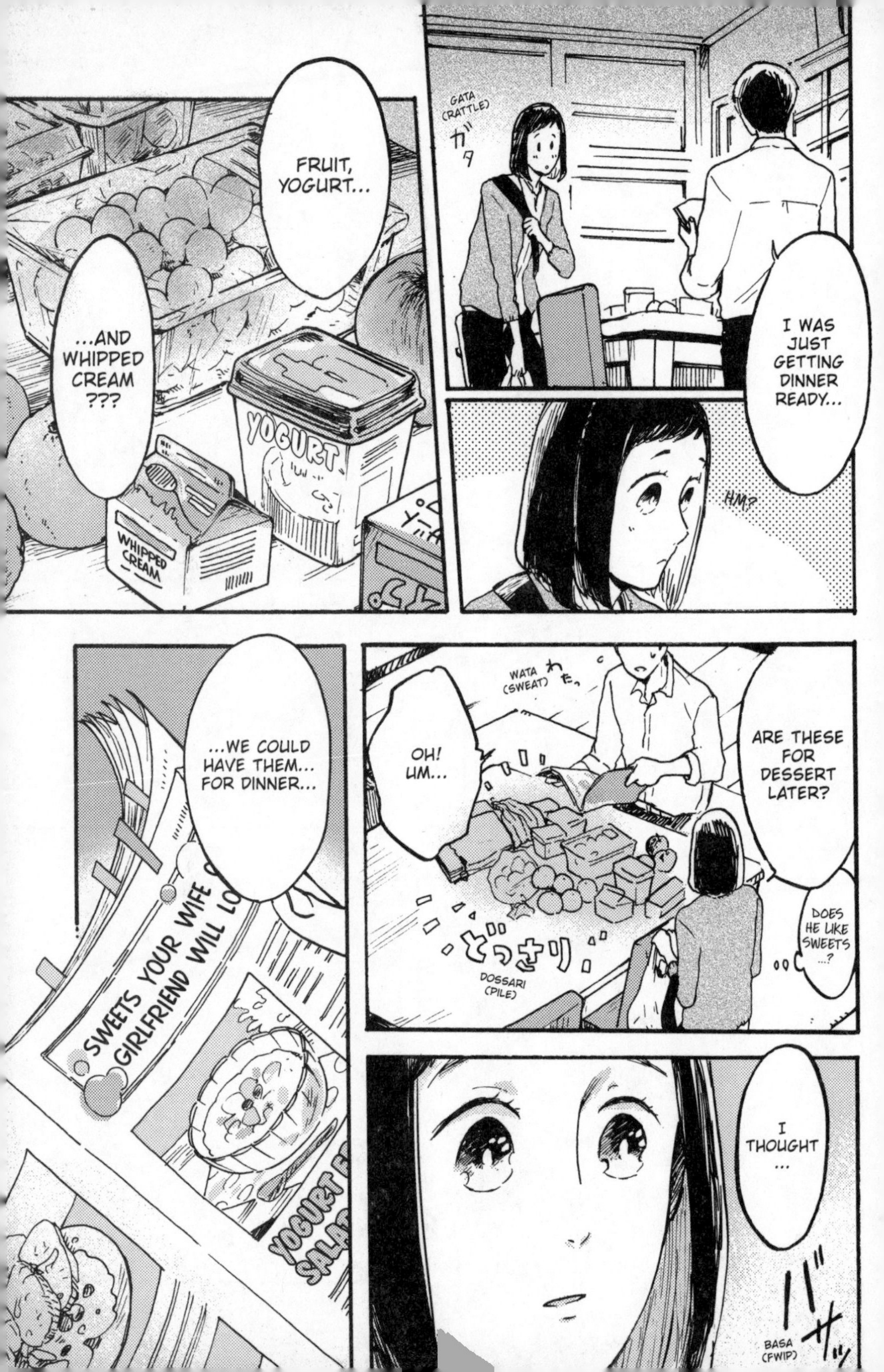
GATA (RATTLE)
I WAS JUST GETTING DINNER READY...
HM?
FRUIT, YOGURT...
...AND WHIPPED CREAM ???
YOGURT
WHIPPED CREAM
ARE THESE FOR DESSERT LATER?
DOES HE LIKE SWEETS ...?
WATA (SWEAT)
OH! UM...
DOSSARI (PILE)
I THOUGHT ...
BASA (FWIP)
...WE COULD HAVE THEM... FOR DINNER...
SWEETS YOUR WIFE
GIRLFRIEND WILL
YOGURT

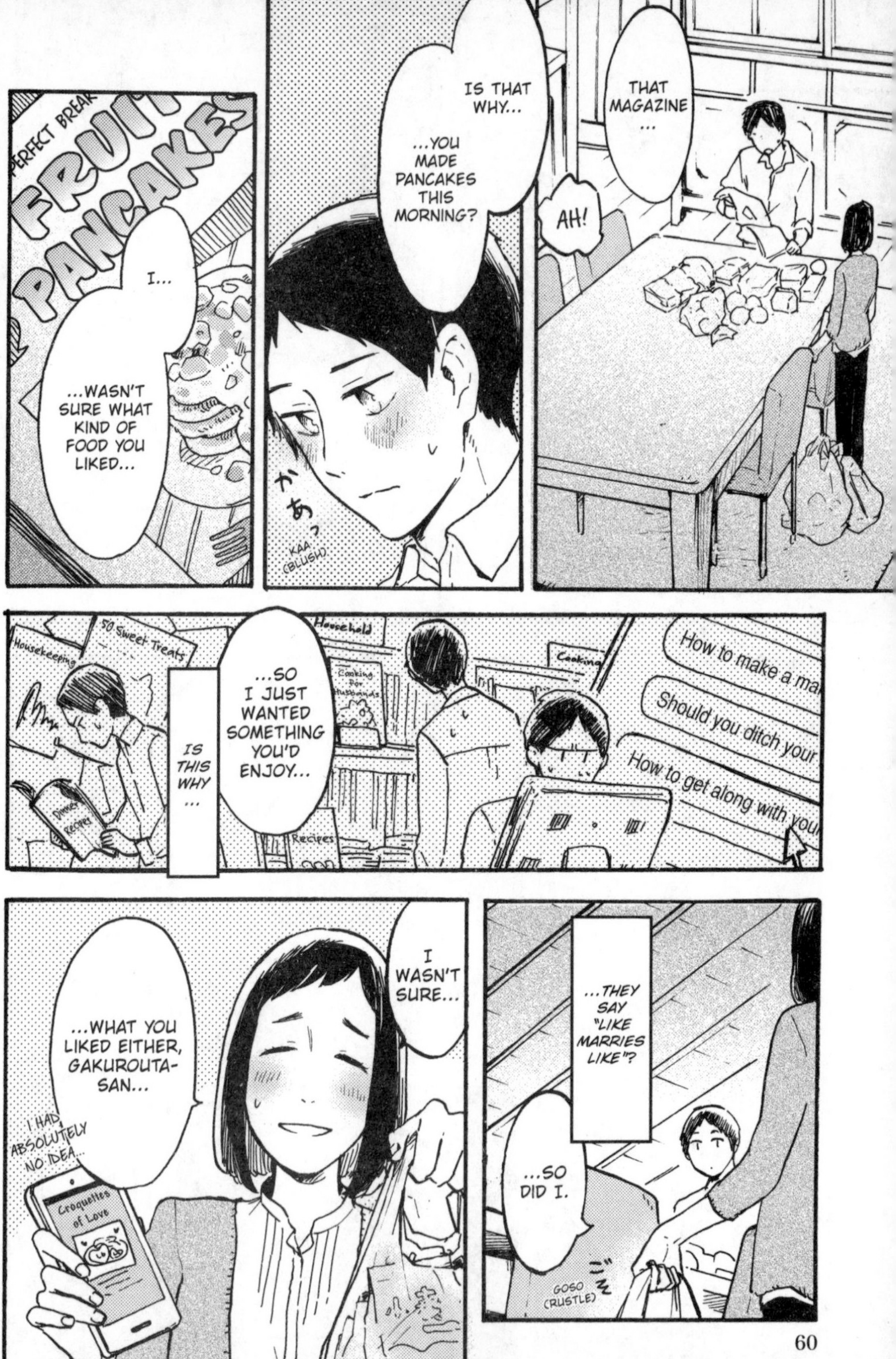
THAT MAGAZINE…
AH!
IS THAT WHY…
…YOU MADE PANCAKES THIS MORNING?
かあっ
KAA (BLUSH)
PERFECT BREAK
FRUIT PANCAKES
I…
…WASN'T SURE WHAT KIND OF FOOD YOU LIKED…
How to make a ma
Should you ditch your
How to get along with you
Household
Cooking
…SO I JUST WANTED SOMETHING YOU'D ENJOY…
Cooking for Husbands
50 Sweet Treats
Housekeeping
IS THIS WHY…
Dinner Recipes
Recipes
…THEY SAY "LIKE MARRIES LIKE"?
…SO DID I.
GOSO (RUSTLE)
I WASN'T SURE…
…WHAT YOU LIKED EITHER, GAKUROUTA-SAN…
I HAD ABSOLUTELY NO IDEA…
Croquettes of Love

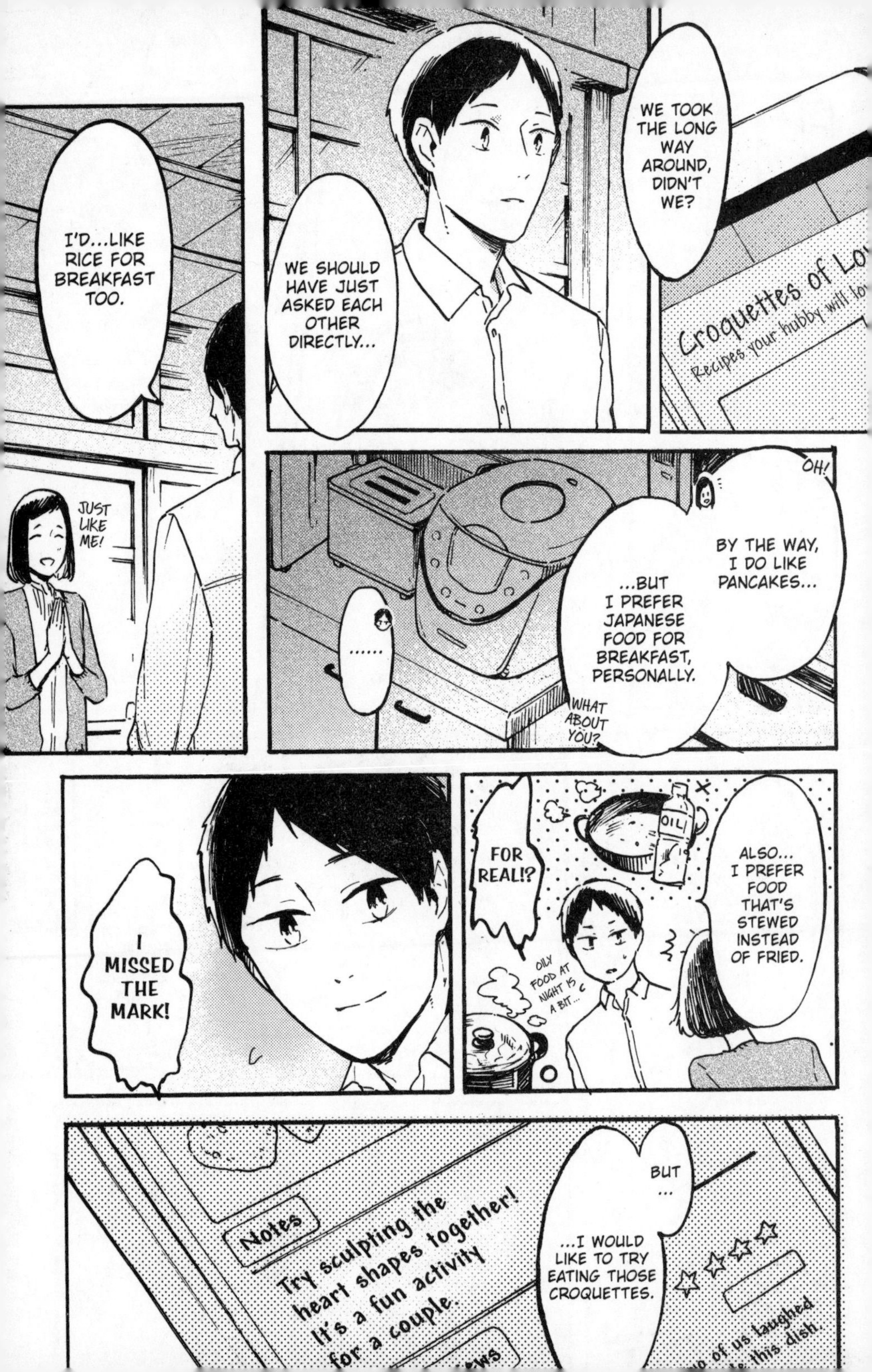
WE TOOK THE LONG WAY AROUND, DIDN'T WE?
WE SHOULD HAVE JUST ASKED EACH OTHER DIRECTLY...
OH!
BY THE WAY, I DO LIKE PANCAKES...
...BUT I PREFER JAPANESE FOOD FOR BREAKFAST, PERSONALLY.
WHAT ABOUT YOU?
....
I'D...LIKE RICE FOR BREAKFAST TOO.
JUST LIKE ME!
ALSO... I PREFER FOOD THAT'S STEWED INSTEAD OF FRIED.
OILY FOOD AT NIGHT IS A BIT...
OIL
FOR REAL!?
I MISSED THE MARK!
BUT ...
...I WOULD LIKE TO TRY EATING THOSE CROQUETTES.
Notes
Try sculpting the heart shapes together! It's a fun activity for a couple.

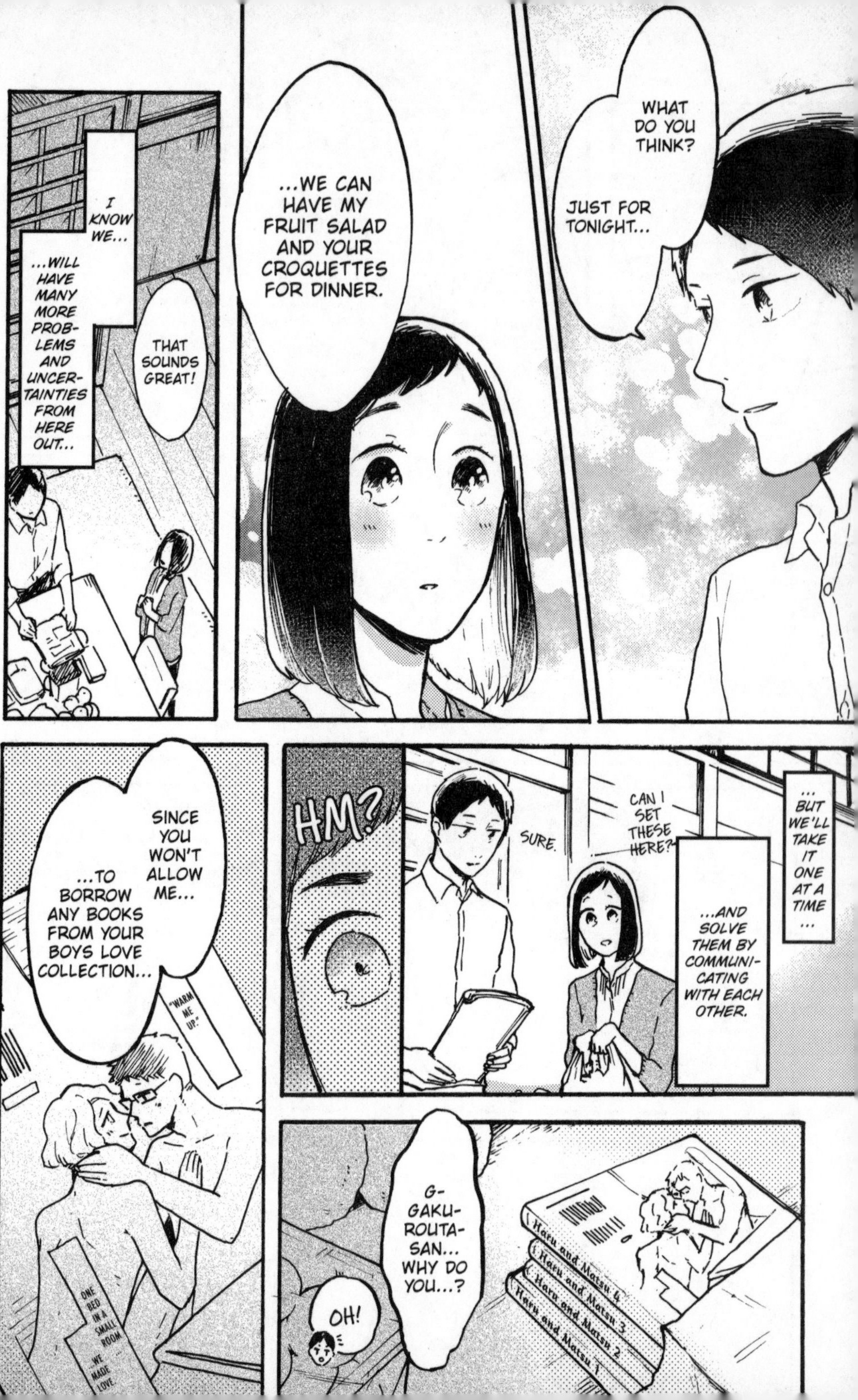
WHAT DO YOU THINK?
JUST FOR TONIGHT...
...WE CAN HAVE MY FRUIT SALAD AND YOUR CROQUETTES FOR DINNER.
I KNOW WE...
...WILL HAVE MANY MORE PROB-LEMS AND UNCER-TAINTIES FROM HERE OUT...
THAT SOUNDS GREAT!
...BUT WE'LL TAKE IT ONE AT A TIME...
CAN I SET THESE HERE?
SURE.
...AND SOLVE THEM BY COMMUNI-CATING WITH EACH OTHER.
HM?
G-GAKU-ROUTA-SAN... WHY DO YOU...?
OH!
Haru and Matsu 4
Haru and Matsu 3
Haru and Matsu 2
Haru and Matsu 1
SINCE YOU WON'T ALLOW ME...
...TO BORROW ANY BOOKS FROM YOUR BOYS LOVE COLLECTION...
"WARM ME UP."
ONE BED IN A SMALL ROOM...
...WE MADE LOVE.

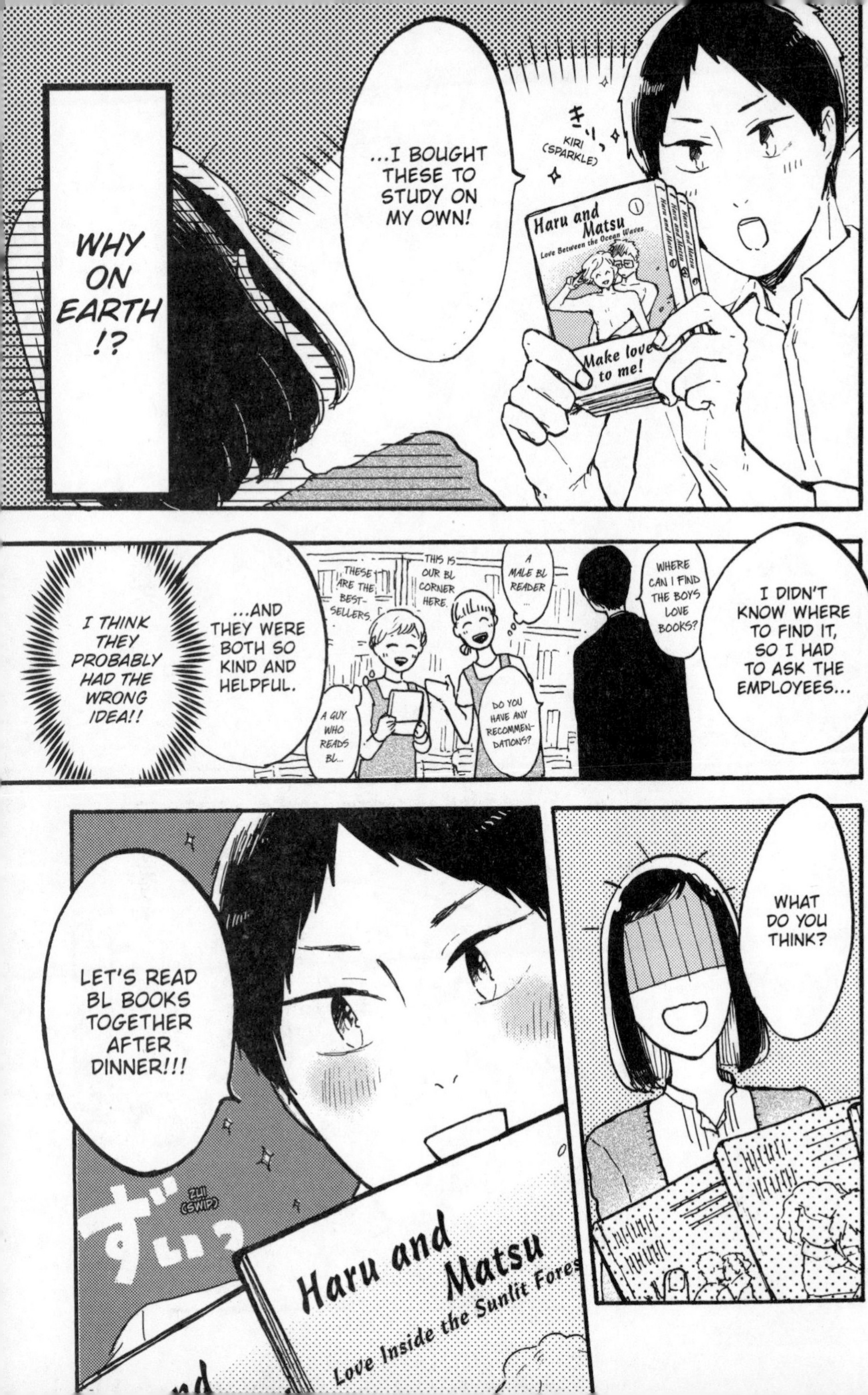
KIRI (SPARKLE)
...I BOUGHT THESE TO STUDY ON MY OWN!
Haru and Matsu
Love Between the Ocean Waves
Make love to me!
WHY ON EARTH!?
I DIDN'T KNOW WHERE TO FIND IT, SO I HAD TO ASK THE EMPLOYEES...
WHERE CAN I FIND THE BOYS LOVE BOOKS?
A MALE BL READER...
DO YOU HAVE ANY RECOMMEN-DATIONS?
THIS IS OUR BL CORNER HERE.
THESE ARE THE BEST-SELLERS.
A GUY WHO READS BL...
...AND THEY WERE BOTH SO KIND AND HELPFUL.
I THINK THEY PROBABLY HAD THE WRONG IDEA!!
WHAT DO YOU THINK?
LET'S READ BL BOOKS TOGETHER AFTER DINNER!!!
ZUI (SWIP)
Haru and Matsu
Love Inside the Sunlit Fores

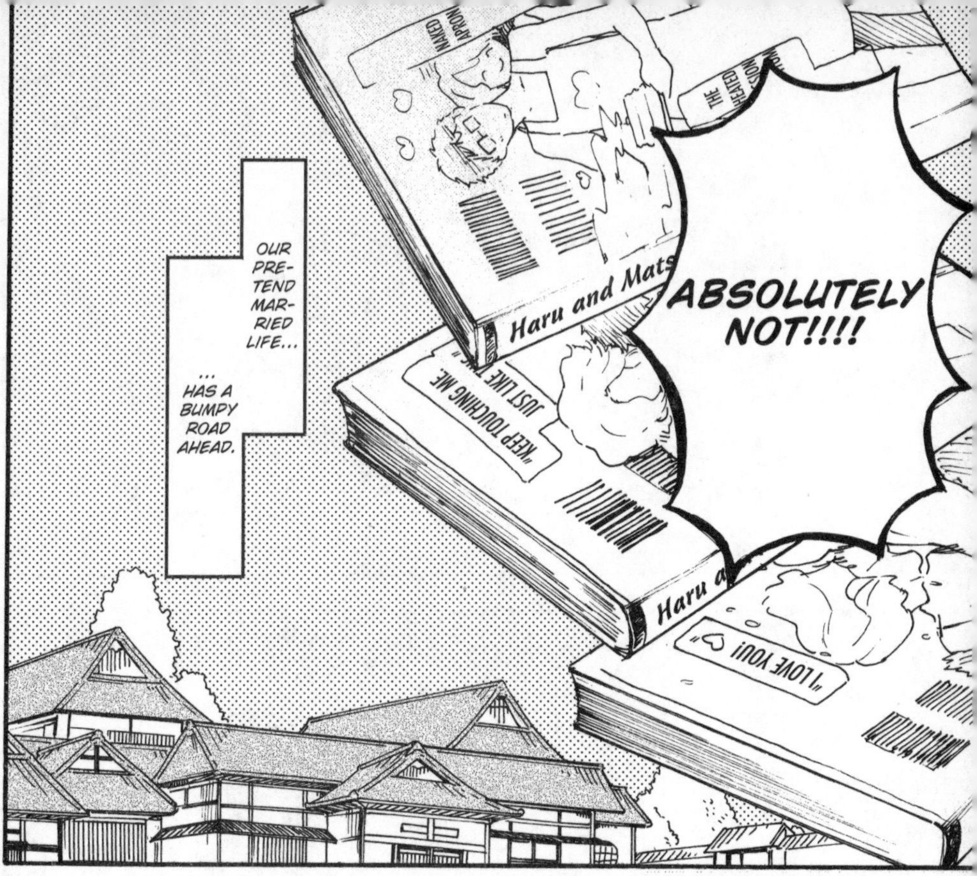
ABSOLUTELY NOT!!!!
NAKED APRON
"I LOVE YOU!"
OUR PRE-TEND MAR-RIED LIFE...
...HAS A BUMPY ROAD AHEAD.

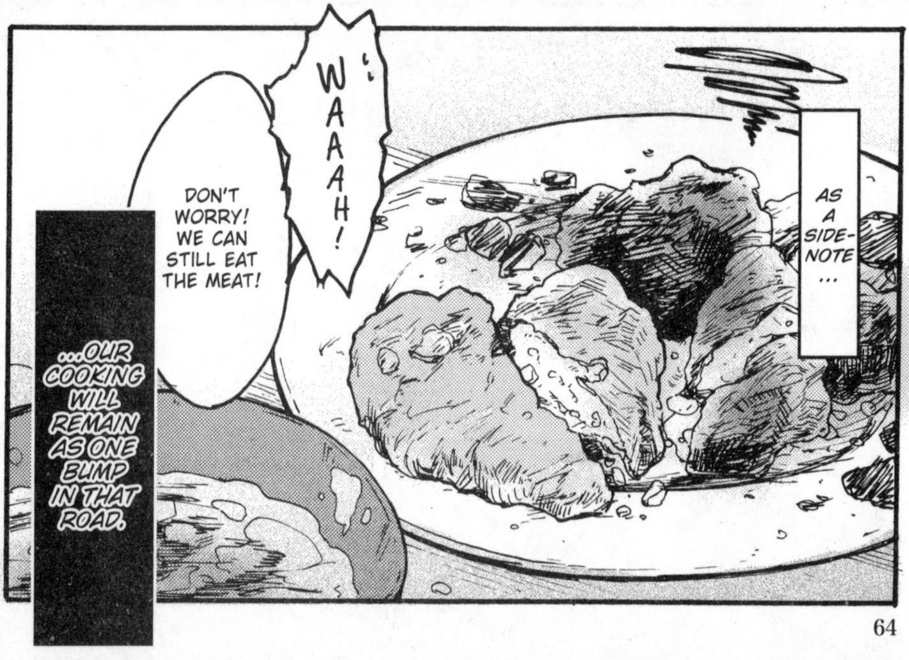
AS A SIDE-NOTE...
WAAAAH!
DON'T WORRY! WE CAN STILL EAT THE MEAT!
...OUR COOKING WILL REMAIN AS ONE BUMP IN THAT ROAD.

I Want
to Be a
Wall

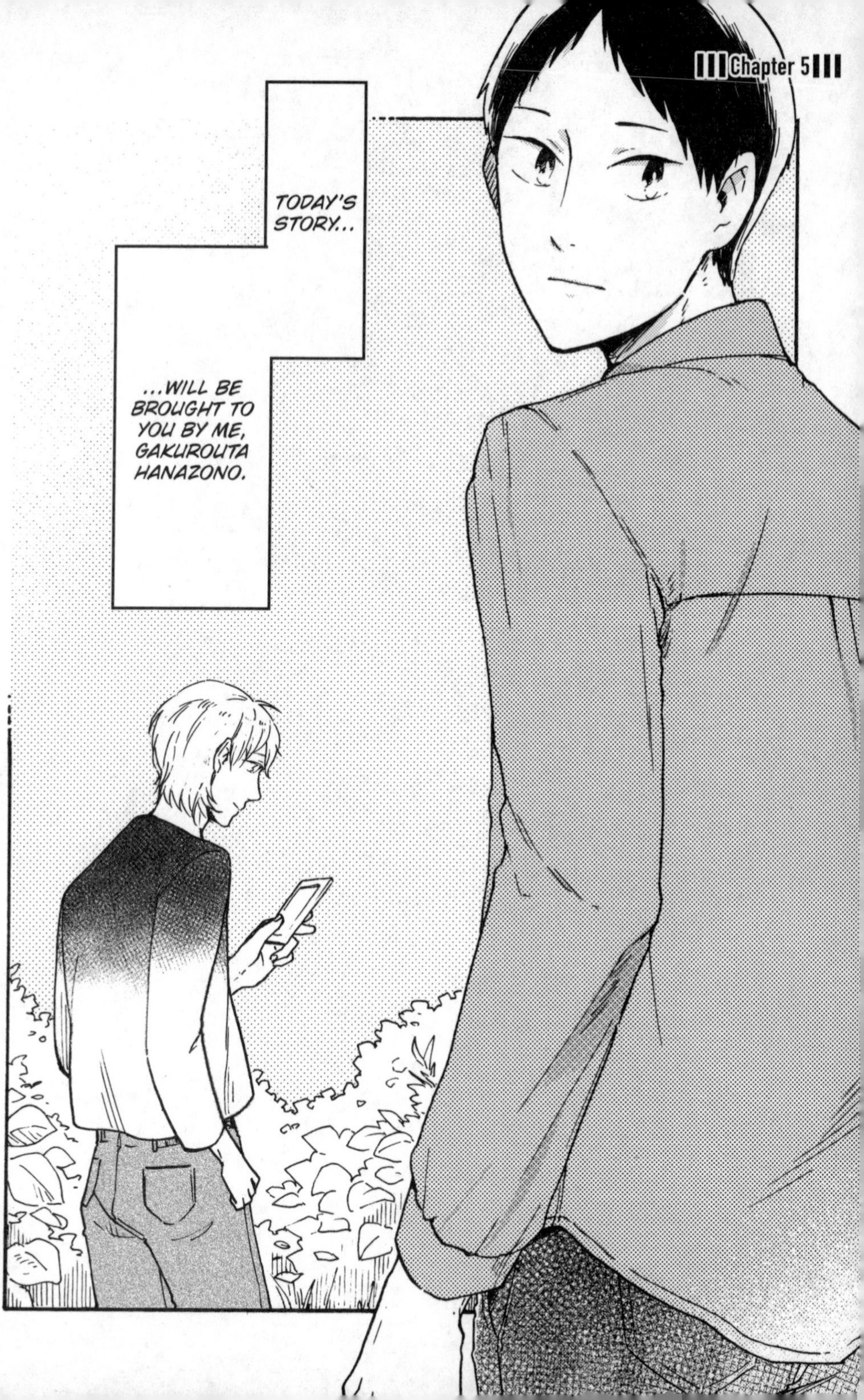
TODAY'S STORY...
...WILL BE BROUGHT TO YOU BY ME, GAKUROUTA HANAZONO.

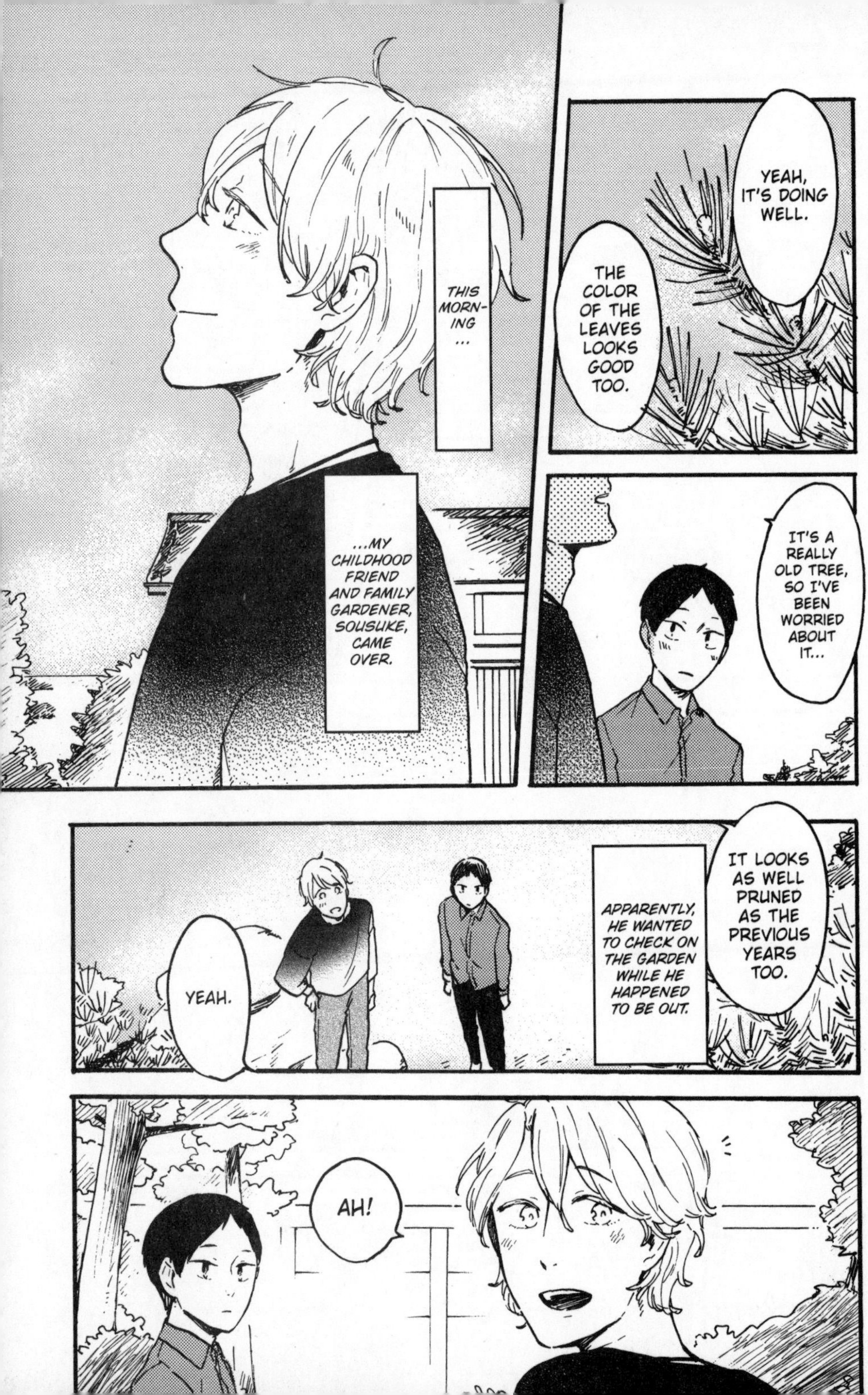
YEAH, IT'S DOING WELL.
THE COLOR OF THE LEAVES LOOKS GOOD TOO.
IT'S A REALLY OLD TREE, SO I'VE BEEN WORRIED ABOUT IT...
THIS MORN-ING...
...MY CHILDHOOD FRIEND AND FAMILY GARDENER, SOUSUKE, CAME OVER.
IT LOOKS AS WELL PRUNED AS THE PREVIOUS YEARS TOO.
APPARENTLY, HE WANTED TO CHECK ON THE GARDEN WHILE HE HAPPENED TO BE OUT.
YEAH.
AH!

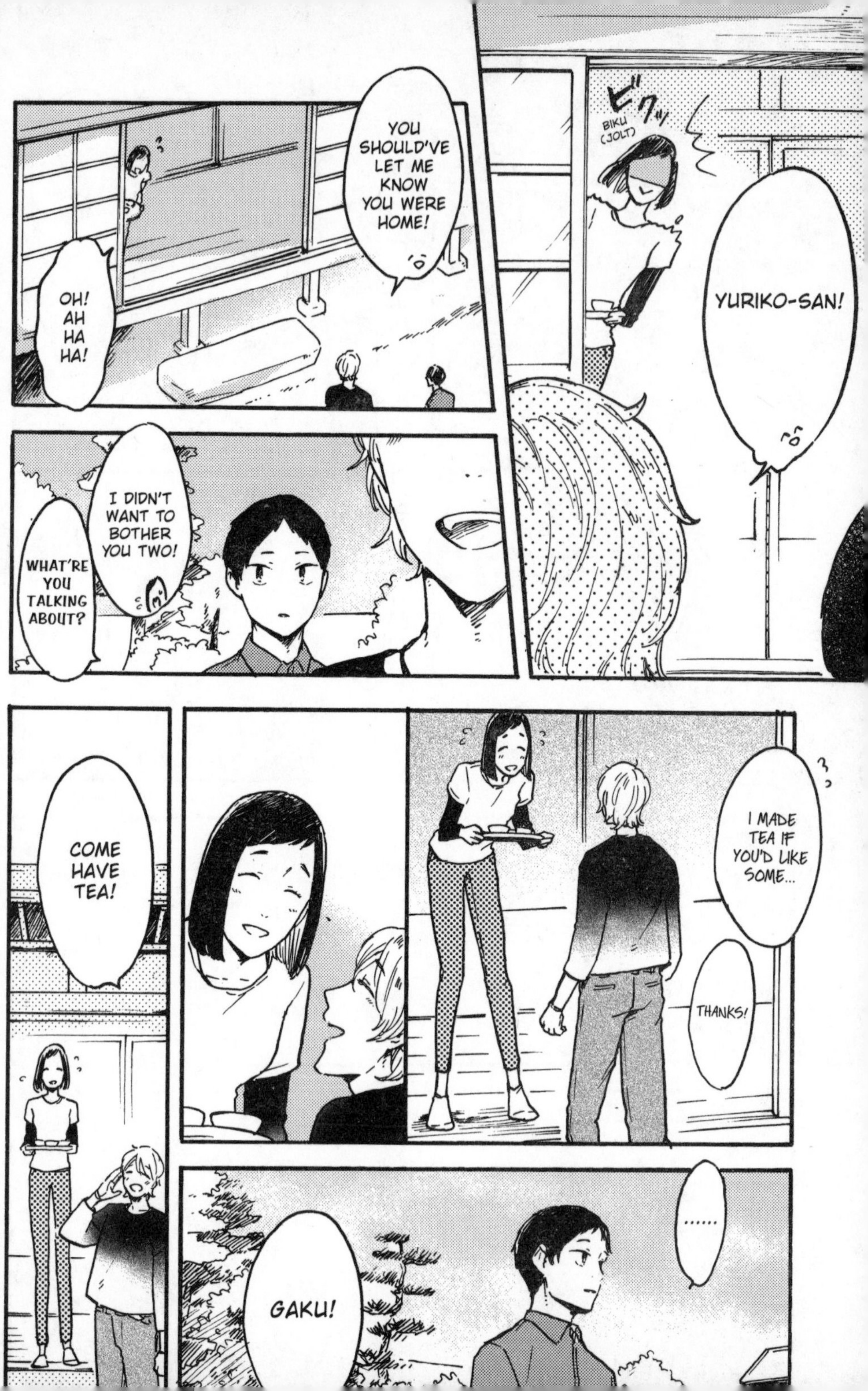
ビクッ
BIKU (JOLT)
YURIKO-SAN!
YOU SHOULD'VE LET ME KNOW YOU WERE HOME!
OH! AH HA HA!
I DIDN'T WANT TO BOTHER YOU TWO!
WHAT'RE YOU TALKING ABOUT?
I MADE TEA IF YOU'D LIKE SOME...
THANKS!
......
GAKU!
COME HAVE TEA!

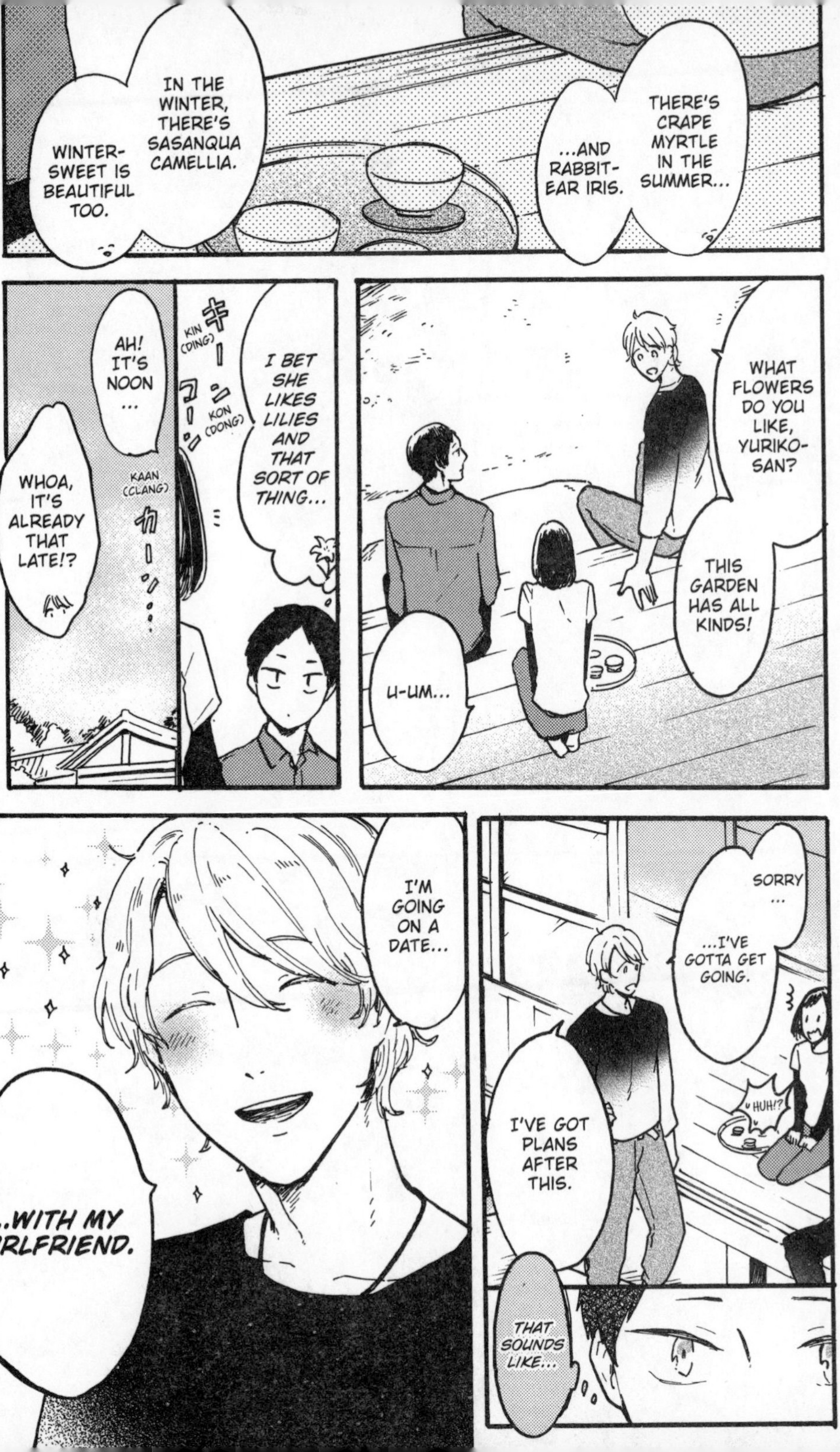
THERE'S CRAPE MYRTLE IN THE SUMMER...
...AND RABBIT-EAR IRIS.
IN THE WINTER, THERE'S SASANQUA CAMELLIA.
WINTER-SWEET IS BEAUTIFUL TOO.
WHAT FLOWERS DO YOU LIKE, YURIKO-SAN?
THIS GARDEN HAS ALL KINDS!
U-UM...
I BET SHE LIKES LILIES AND THAT SORT OF THING...
キーン KIN (DING)
コーン KON (DONG)
カーン KAAN (CLANG)
AH! IT'S NOON...
WHOA, IT'S ALREADY THAT LATE!?
SORRY...
...I'VE GOTTA GET GOING.
HUH!?
I'VE GOT PLANS AFTER THIS.
THAT SOUNDS LIKE...
I'M GOING ON A DATE...
...WITH MY GIRLFRIEND.

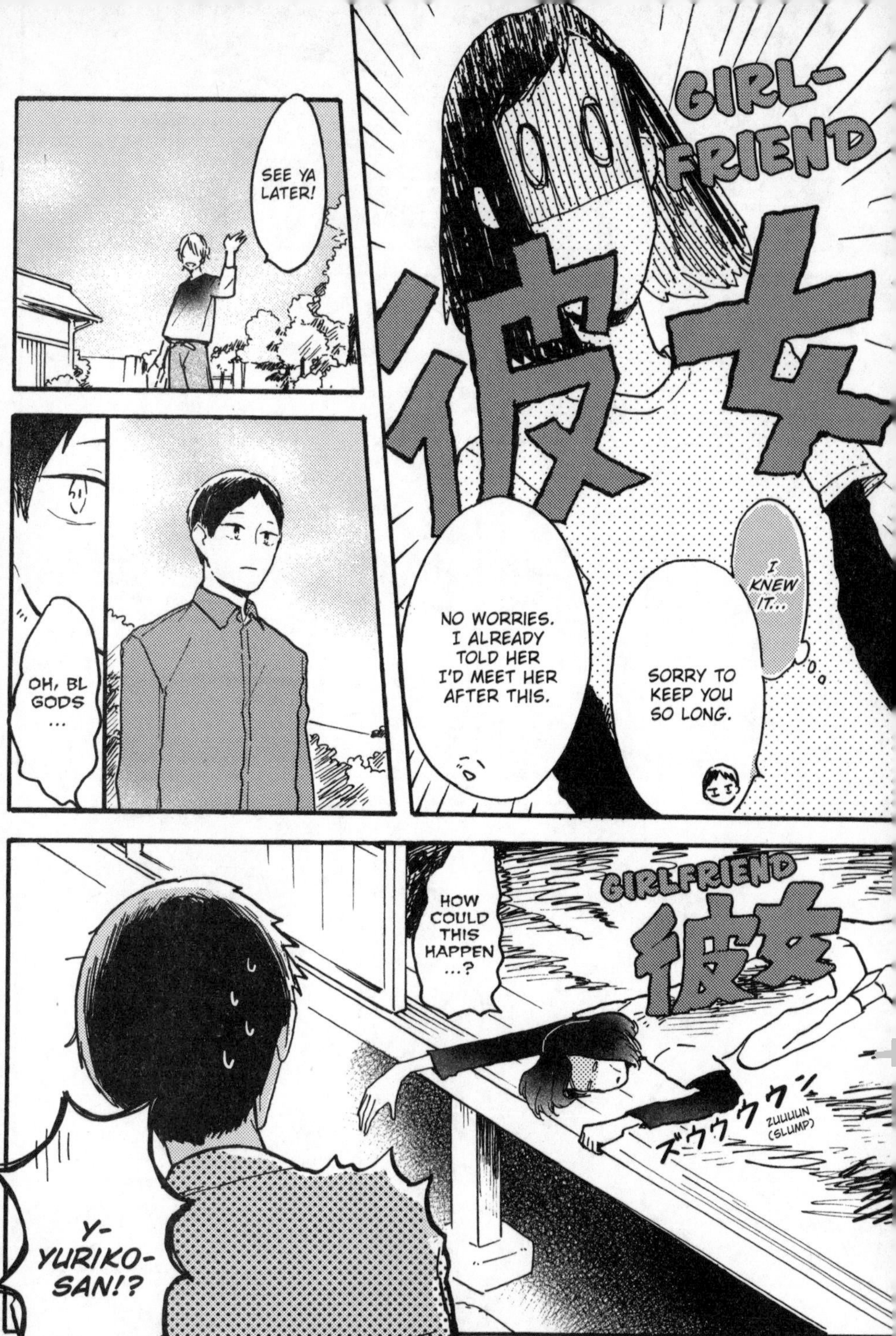
GIRL-FRIEND
彼女
I KNEW IT...
SORRY TO KEEP YOU SO LONG.
NO WORRIES. I ALREADY TOLD HER I'D MEET HER AFTER THIS.
SEE YA LATER!
OH, BL GODS ...
HOW COULD THIS HAPPEN ...?
GIRLFRIEND
彼女
ズウウウウ
ZUUUUN (SLUMP)
Y-YURIKO-SAN!?

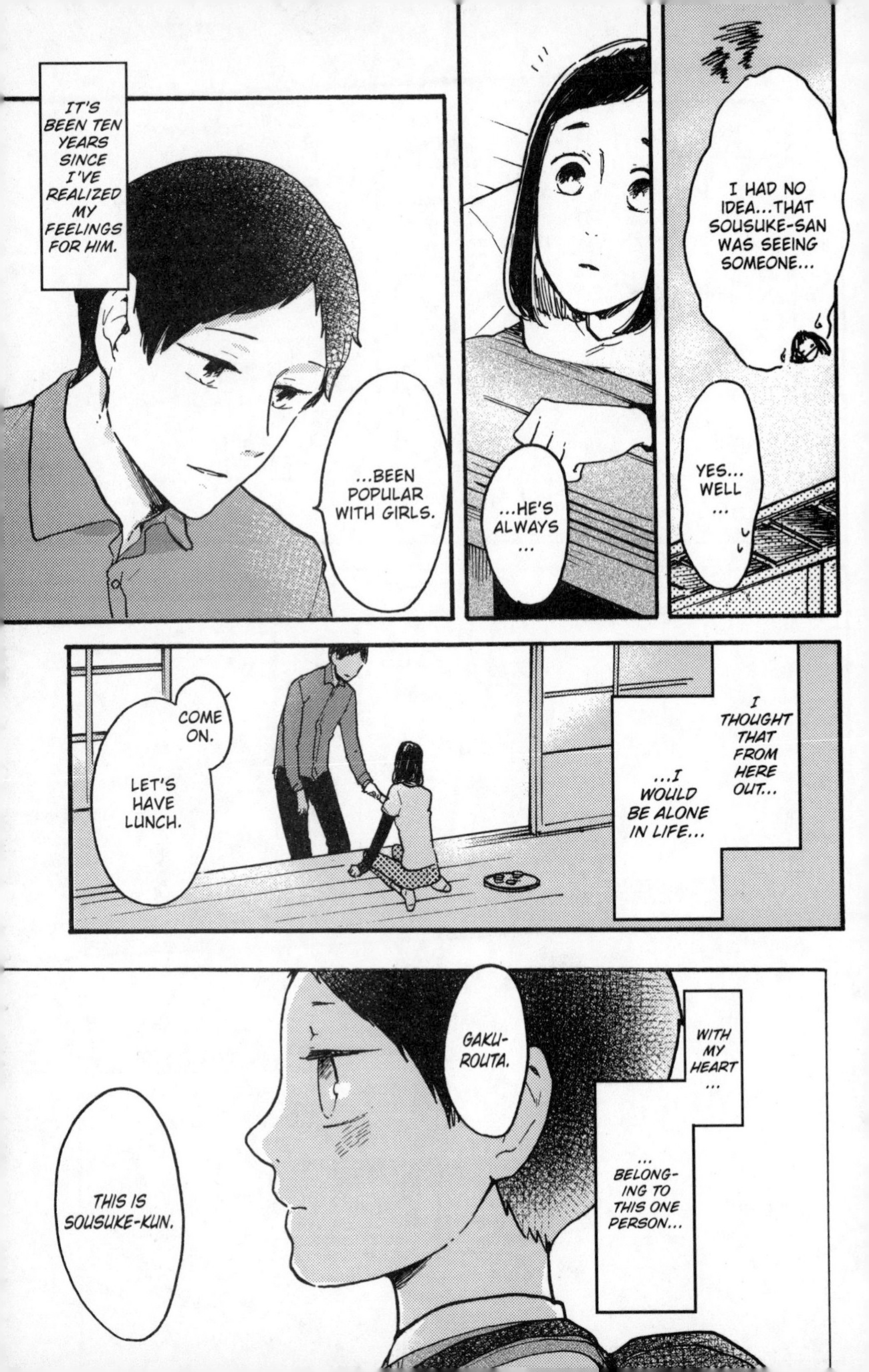
I HAD NO IDEA...THAT SOUSUKE-SAN WAS SEEING SOMEONE...
YES... WELL ...
...HE'S ALWAYS ...
...BEEN POPULAR WITH GIRLS.
IT'S BEEN TEN YEARS SINCE I'VE REALIZED MY FEELINGS FOR HIM.
I THOUGHT THAT FROM HERE OUT...
...I WOULD BE ALONE IN LIFE...
COME ON.
LET'S HAVE LUNCH.
WITH MY HEART ...
... BELONGING TO THIS ONE PERSON...
GAKU-ROUTA.
THIS IS SOUSUKE-KUN.

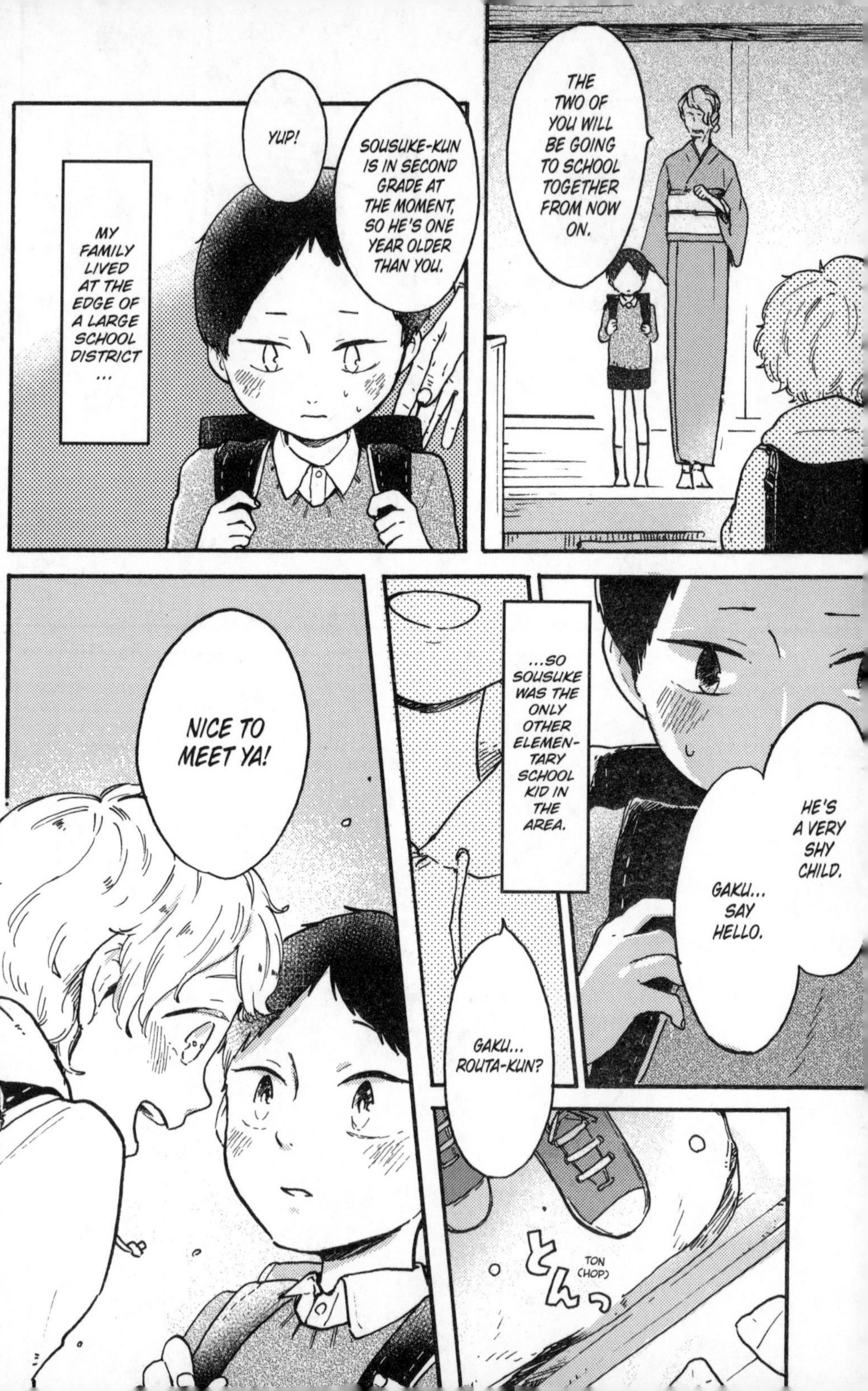
THE TWO OF YOU WILL BE GOING TO SCHOOL TOGETHER FROM NOW ON.
SOUSUKE-KUN IS IN SECOND GRADE AT THE MOMENT, SO HE'S ONE YEAR OLDER THAN YOU.
YUP!
MY FAMILY LIVED AT THE EDGE OF A LARGE SCHOOL DISTRICT...
HE'S A VERY SHY CHILD.
GAKU... SAY HELLO.
...SO SOUSUKE WAS THE ONLY OTHER ELEMENTARY SCHOOL KID IN THE AREA.
GAKU... ROUTA-KUN?
とんっ
TON (HOP)
NICE TO MEET YA!

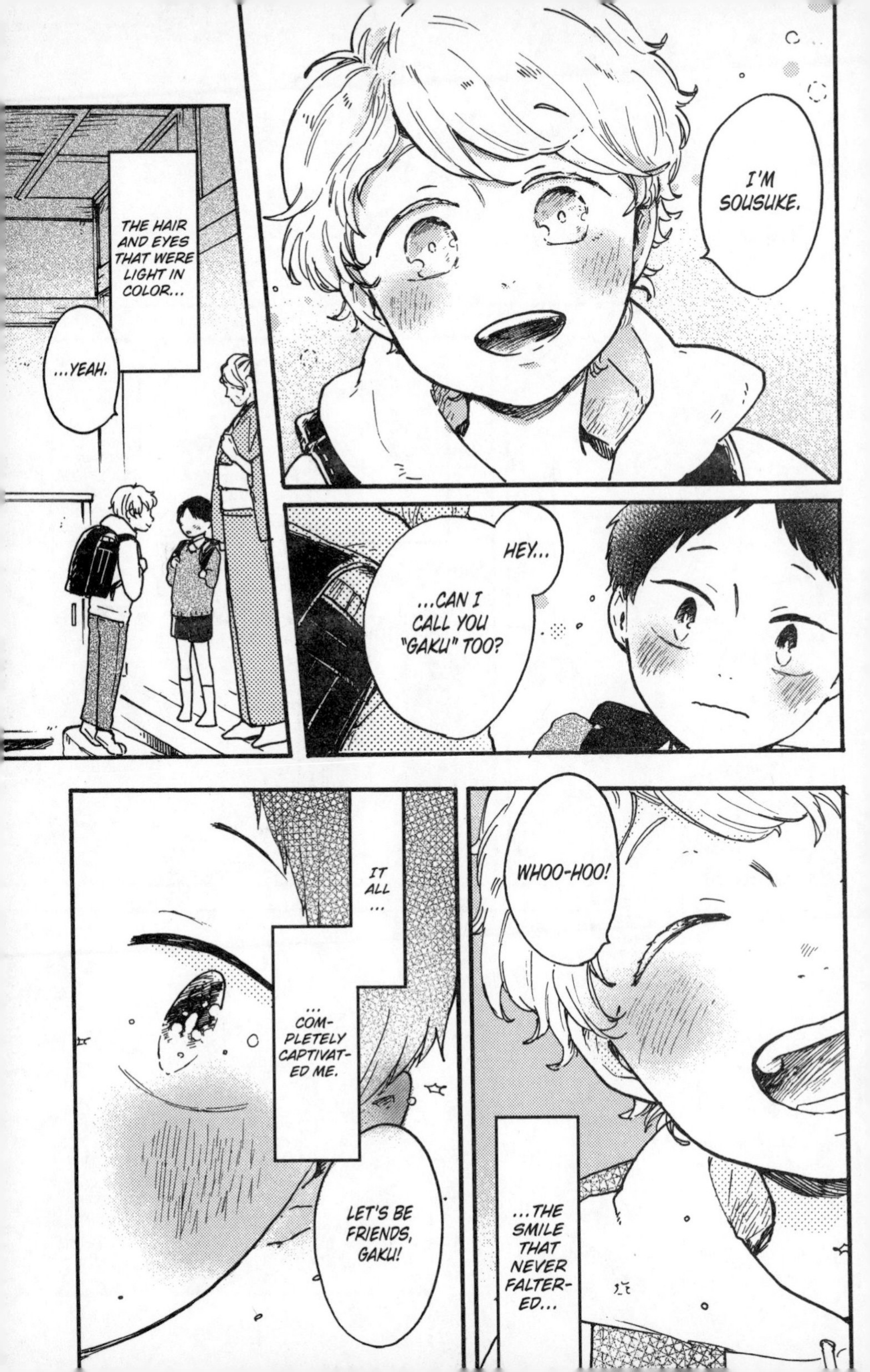
I'M SOUSUKE.
HEY... ...CAN I CALL YOU "GAKU" TOO?
THE HAIR AND EYES THAT WERE LIGHT IN COLOR...
...YEAH.
WHOO-HOO!
...THE SMILE THAT NEVER FALTERED...
IT ALL...
...COMPLETELY CAPTIVATED ME.
LET'S BE FRIENDS, GAKU!

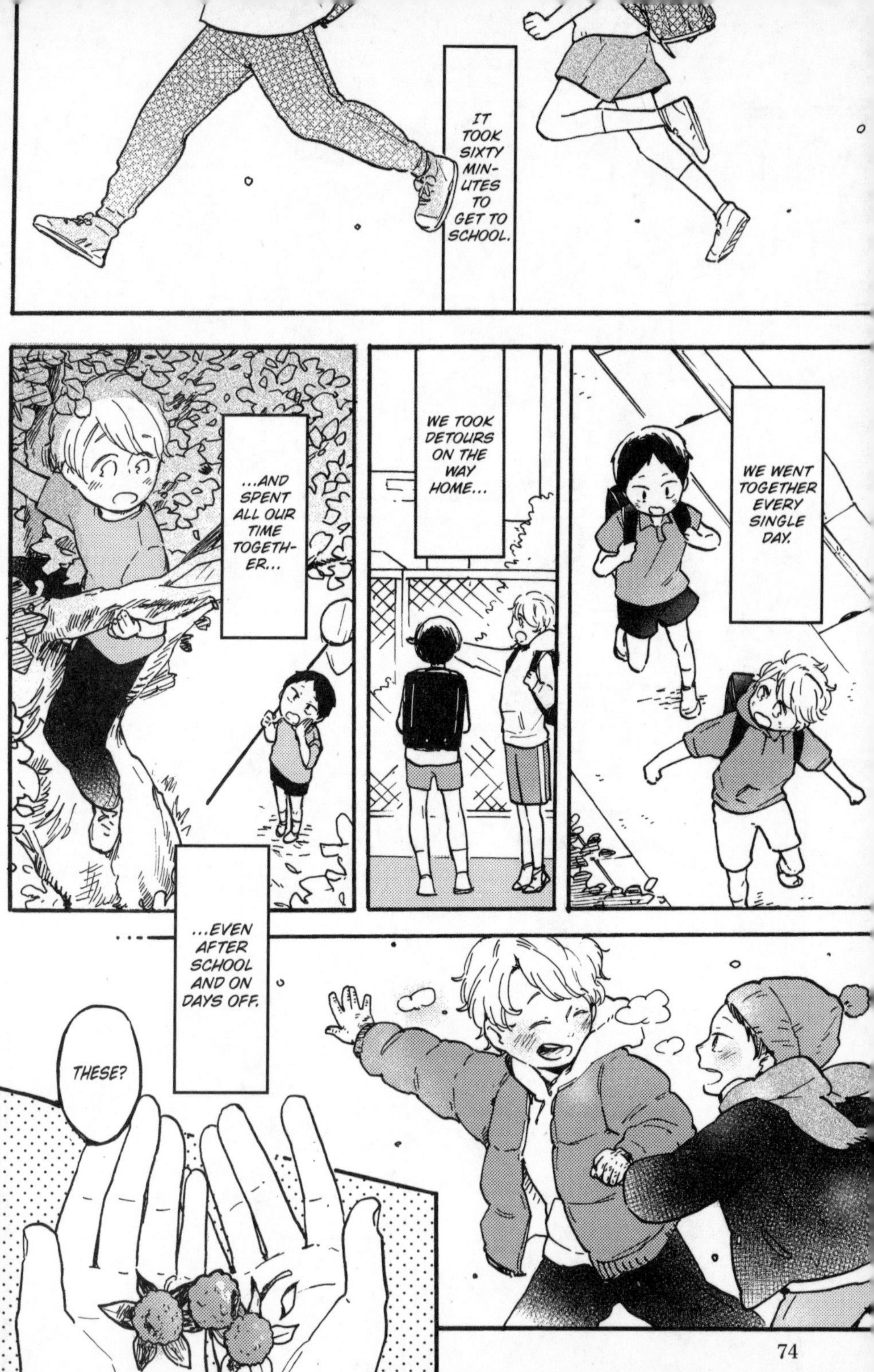
IT TOOK SIXTY MIN-UTES TO GET TO SCHOOL.
WE WENT TOGETHER EVERY SINGLE DAY.
WE TOOK DETOURS ON THE WAY HOME...
...AND SPENT ALL OUR TIME TOGETH-ER...
...EVEN AFTER SCHOOL AND ON DAYS OFF.
THESE?

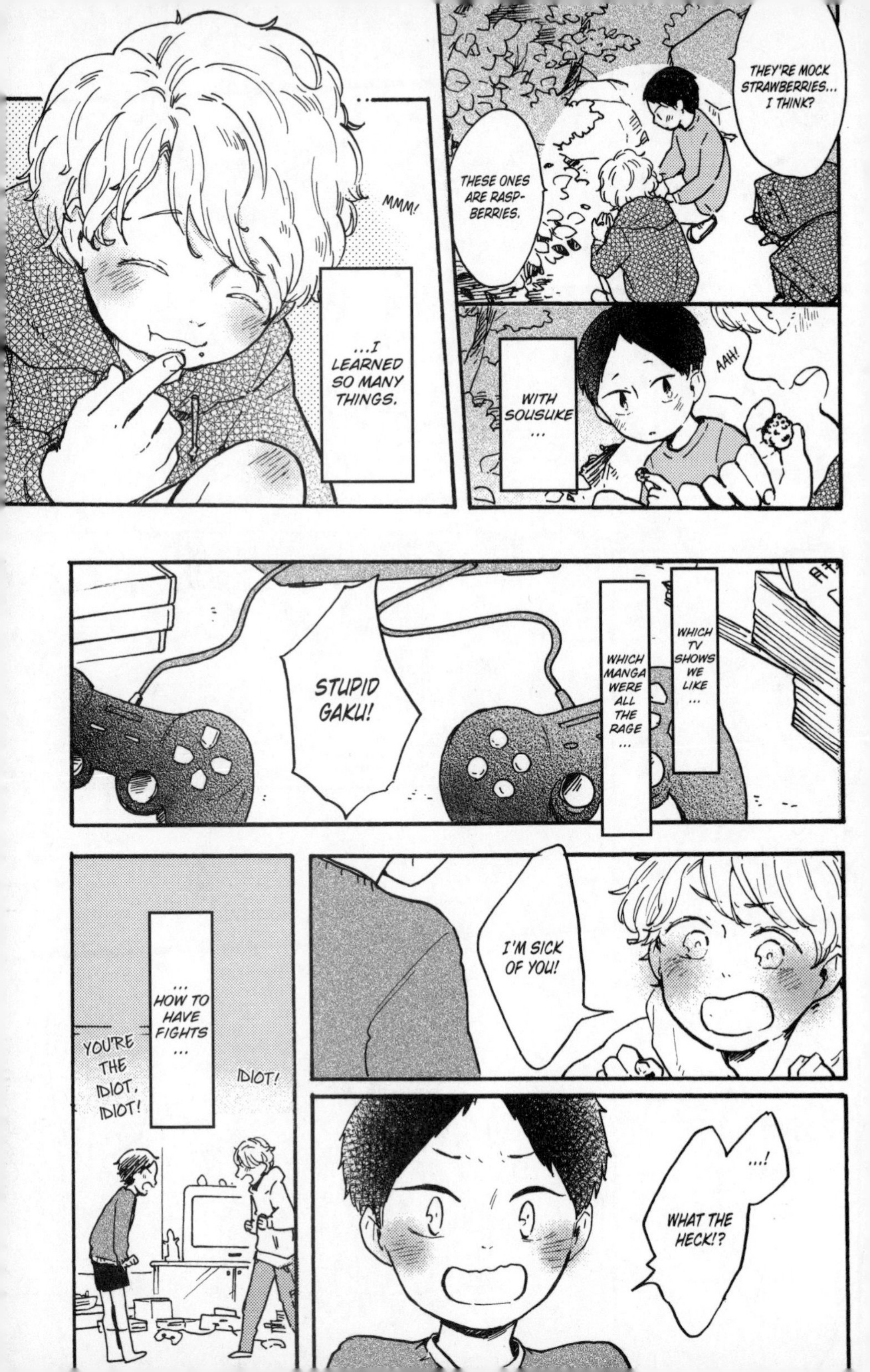

THEY'RE MOCK STRAWBERRIES... I THINK?
THESE ONES ARE RASP-BERRIES.
AAH!
WITH SOUSUKE ...
...
MMM!
...I LEARNED SO MANY THINGS.
WHICH TV SHOWS WE LIKE ...
WHICH MANGA WERE ALL THE RAGE ...
STUPID GAKU!
I'M SICK OF YOU!
...!
WHAT THE HECK!?
... HOW TO HAVE FIGHTS ...
IDIOT!
YOU'RE THE IDIOT, IDIOT!

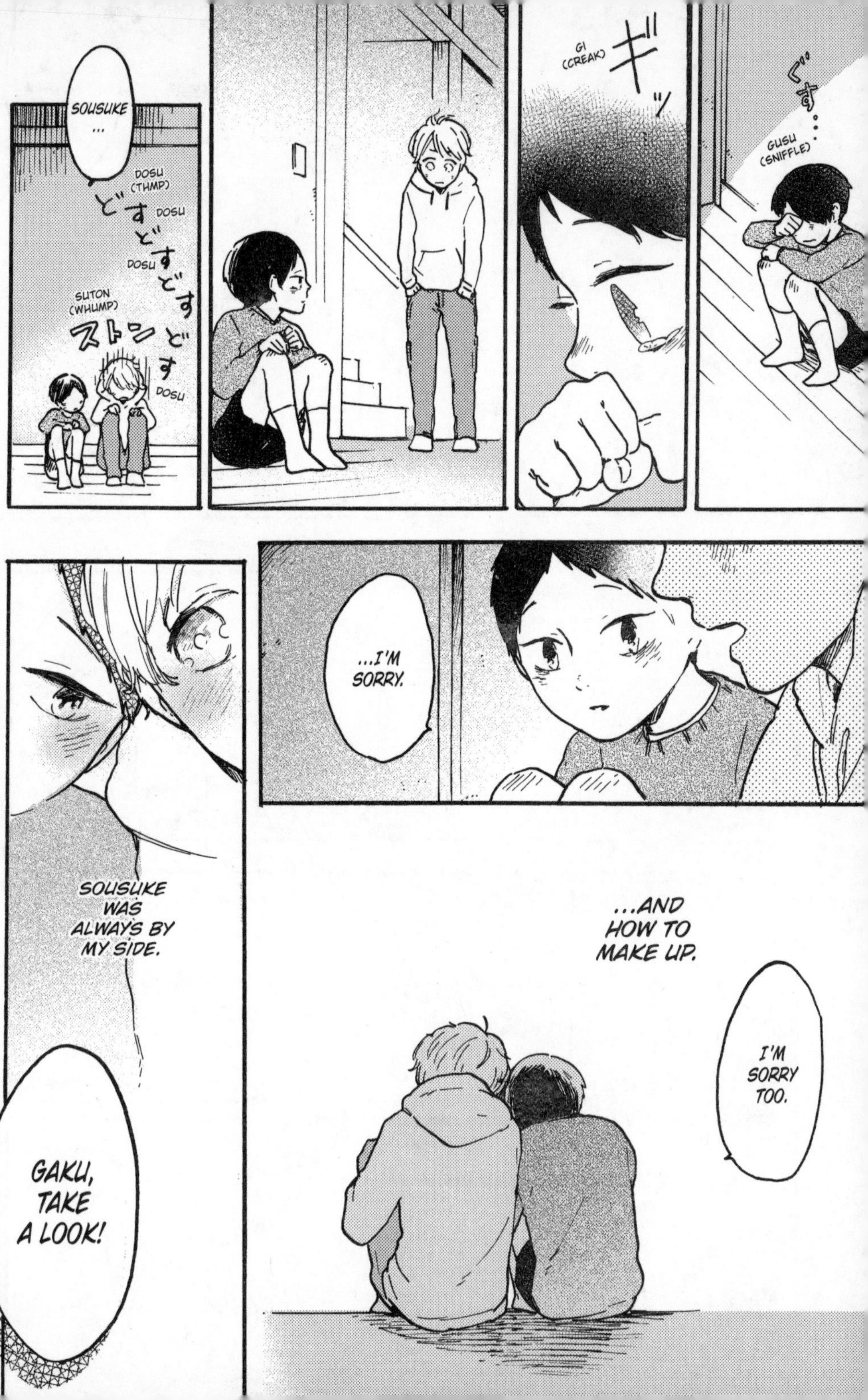
ぐす…
GUSU (SNIFFLE)
ギッ
GI (CREAK)
SOUSUKE ...
どす
DOSU (THMP)
どす
DOSU
どす
DOSU
ストン
SUTON (WHUMP)
どす
DOSU
...I'M SORRY.
...AND HOW TO MAKE UP.
I'M SORRY TOO.
SOUSUKE WAS ALWAYS BY MY SIDE.
GAKU, TAKE A LOOK!

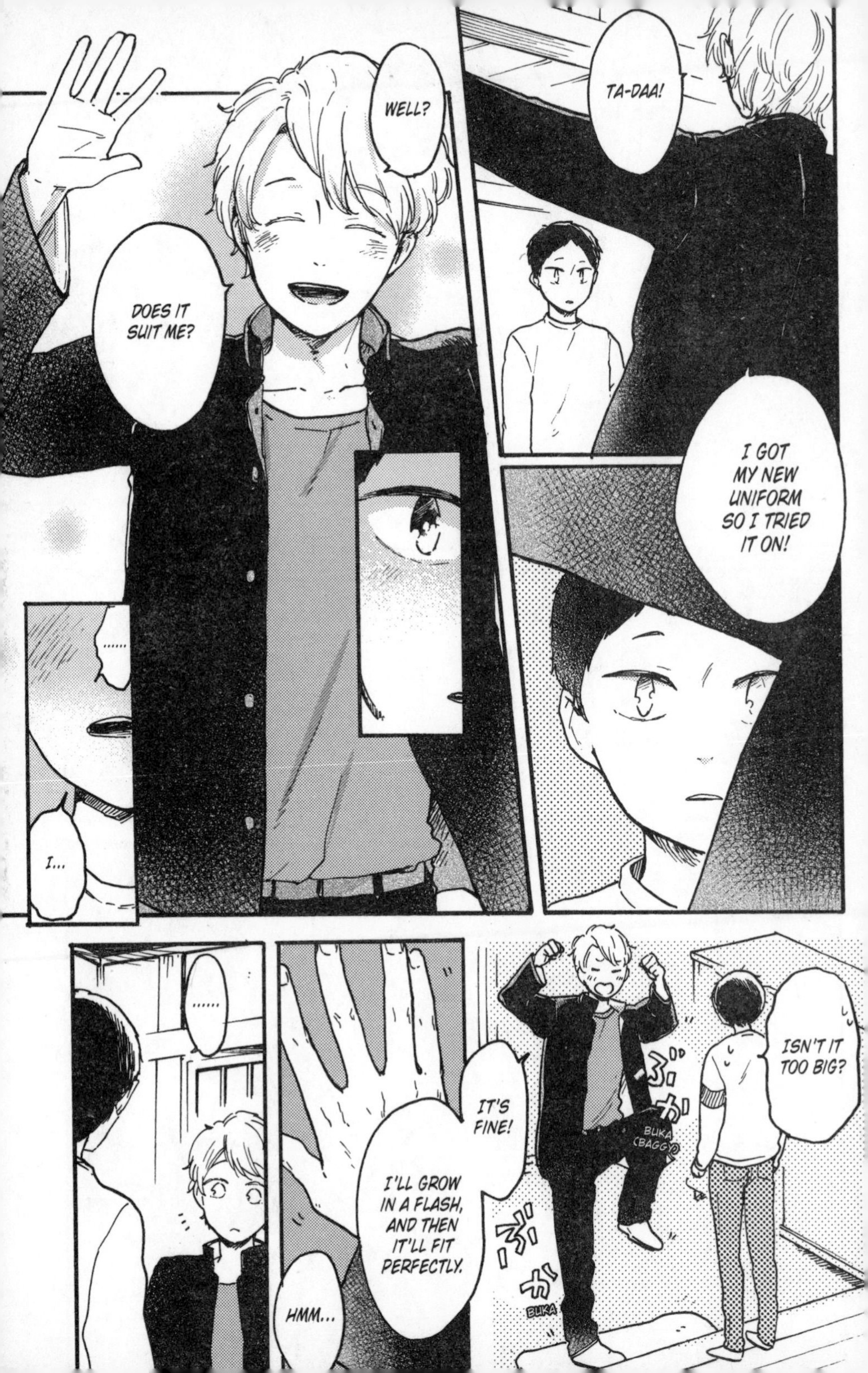

TA-DAA!
I GOT MY NEW UNIFORM SO I TRIED IT ON!
WELL?
DOES IT SUIT ME?
......
I...
ISN'T IT TOO BIG?
ぶか
BUKA (BAGGY)
ぶか
BUKA
IT'S FINE!
I'LL GROW IN A FLASH, AND THEN IT'LL FIT PERFECTLY.
HMM...
......

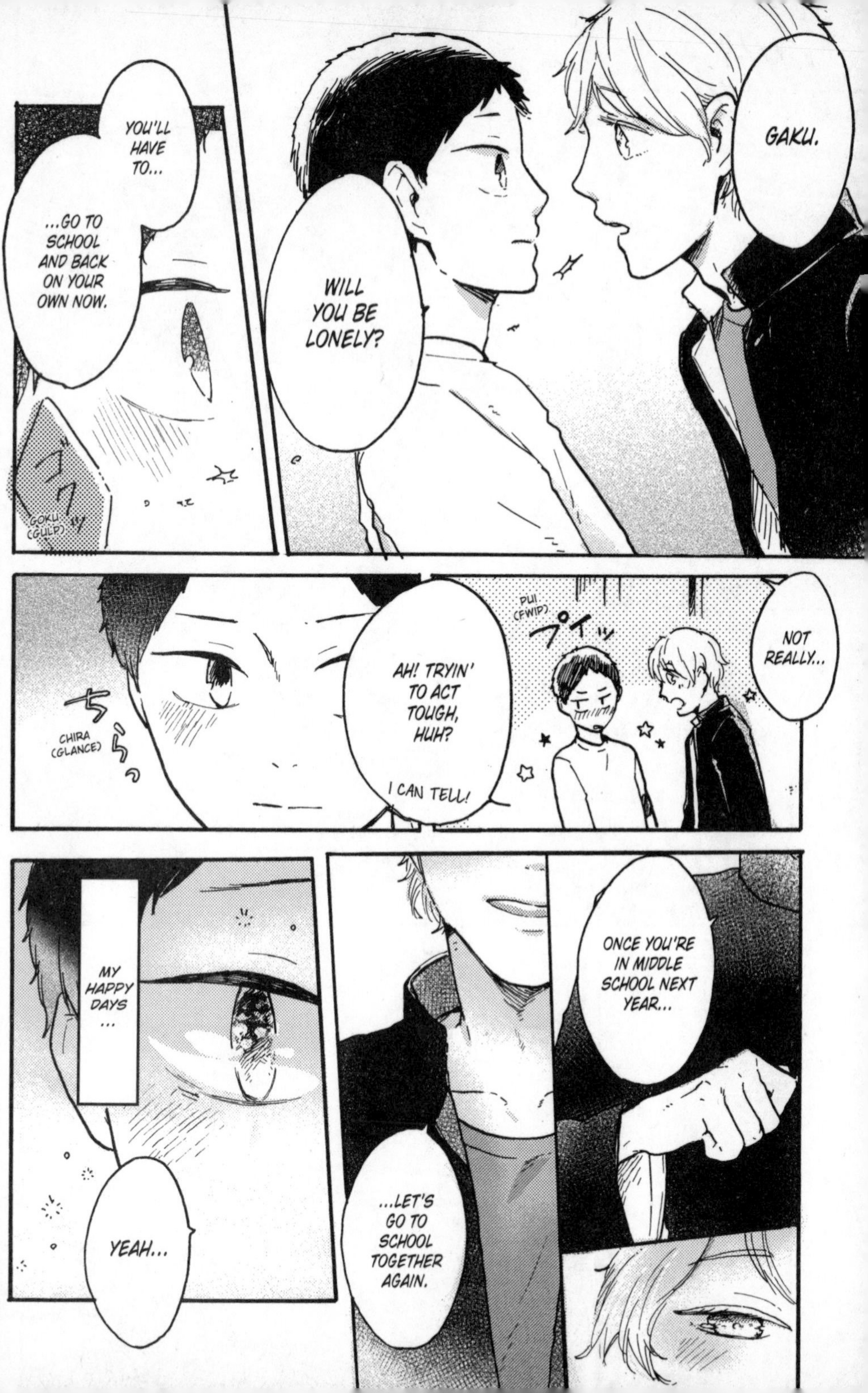
GAKU.
WILL YOU BE LONELY?
YOU'LL HAVE TO...
...GO TO SCHOOL AND BACK ON YOUR OWN NOW.
GOKU (GULP)
NOT REALLY...
PUI (FWIP)
AH! TRYIN' TO ACT TOUGH, HUH?
I CAN TELL!
CHIRA (GLANCE)
ONCE YOU'RE IN MIDDLE SCHOOL NEXT YEAR...
...LET'S GO TO SCHOOL TOGETHER AGAIN.
MY HAPPY DAYS...
YEAH...

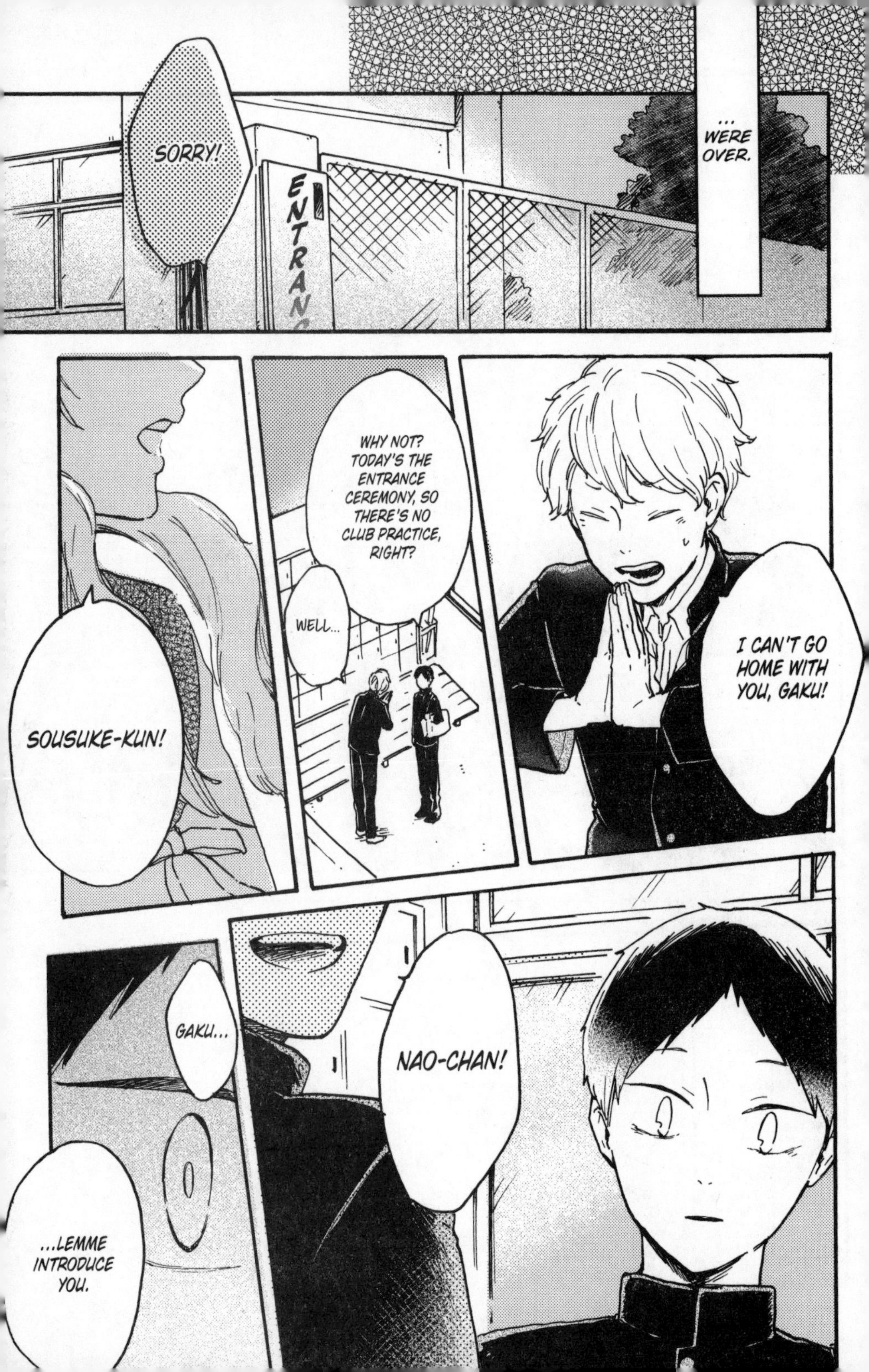

... WERE OVER.
SORRY!
ENTRANC
I CAN'T GO HOME WITH YOU, GAKU!
WHY NOT? TODAY'S THE ENTRANCE CEREMONY, SO THERE'S NO CLUB PRACTICE, RIGHT?
WELL...
SOUSUKE-KUN!
NAO-CHAN!
GAKU...
...LEMME INTRODUCE YOU.

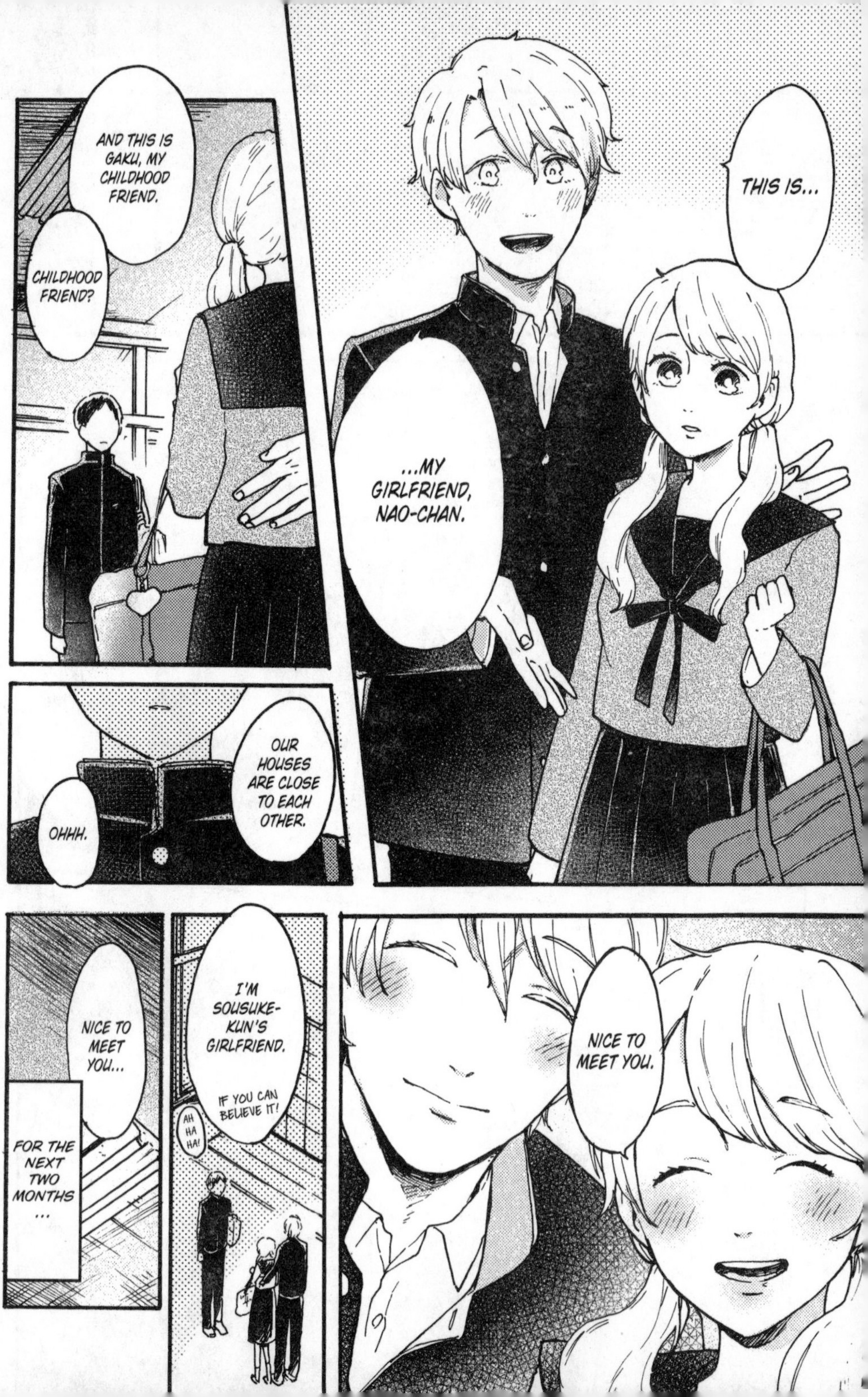
THIS IS...
...MY GIRLFRIEND, NAO-CHAN.
AND THIS IS GAKU, MY CHILDHOOD FRIEND.
CHILDHOOD FRIEND?
OUR HOUSES ARE CLOSE TO EACH OTHER.
OHHH.
NICE TO MEET YOU.
I'M SOUSUKE-KUN'S GIRLFRIEND.
IF YOU CAN BELIEVE IT!
AH HA HA!
NICE TO MEET YOU...
FOR THE NEXT TWO MONTHS...

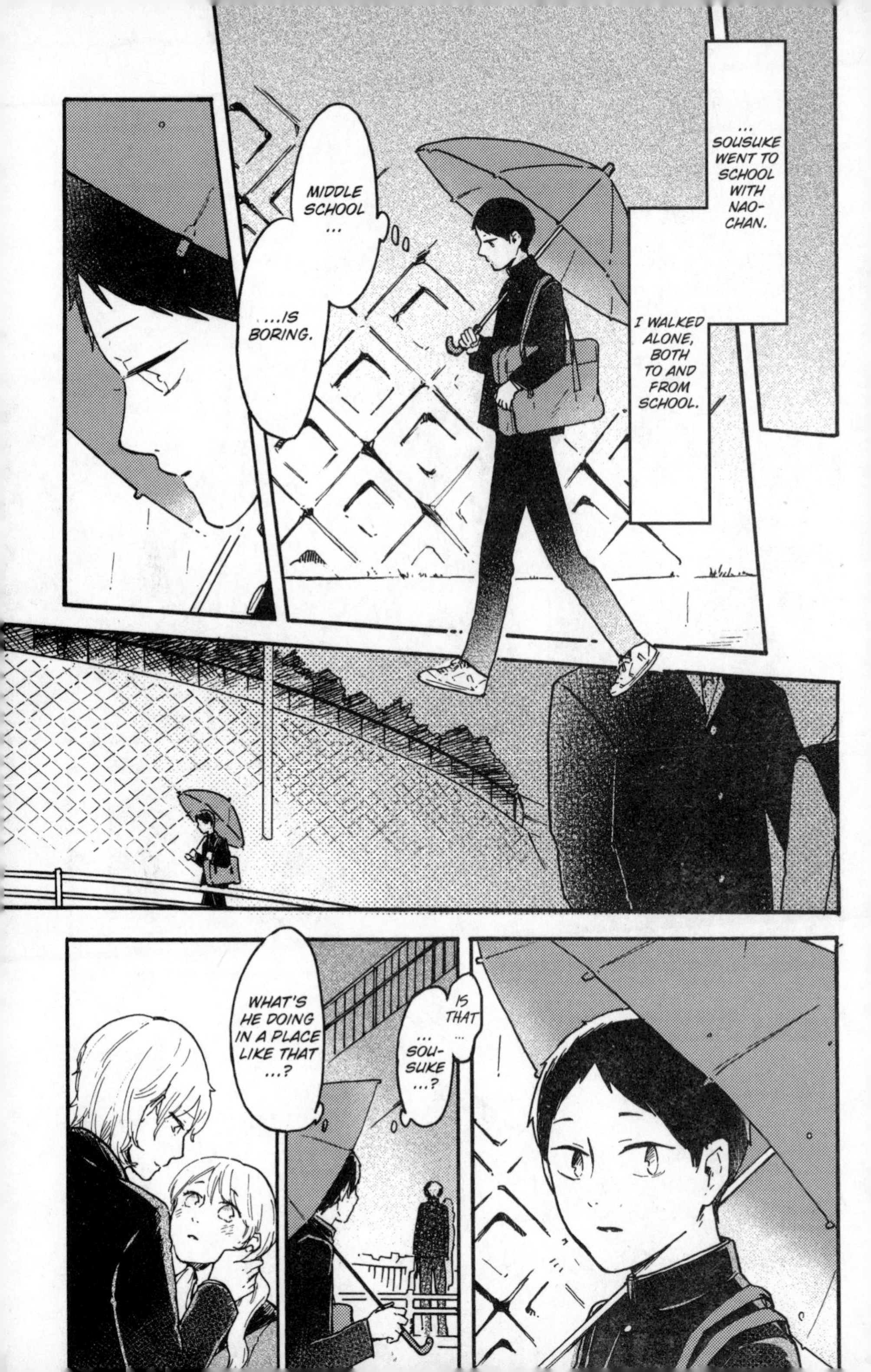
...SOUSUKE WENT TO SCHOOL WITH NAO-CHAN.
I WALKED ALONE, BOTH TO AND FROM SCHOOL.
MIDDLE SCHOOL...
...IS BORING.
IS THAT...
...SOU-SUKE...?
WHAT'S HE DOING IN A PLACE LIKE THAT...?

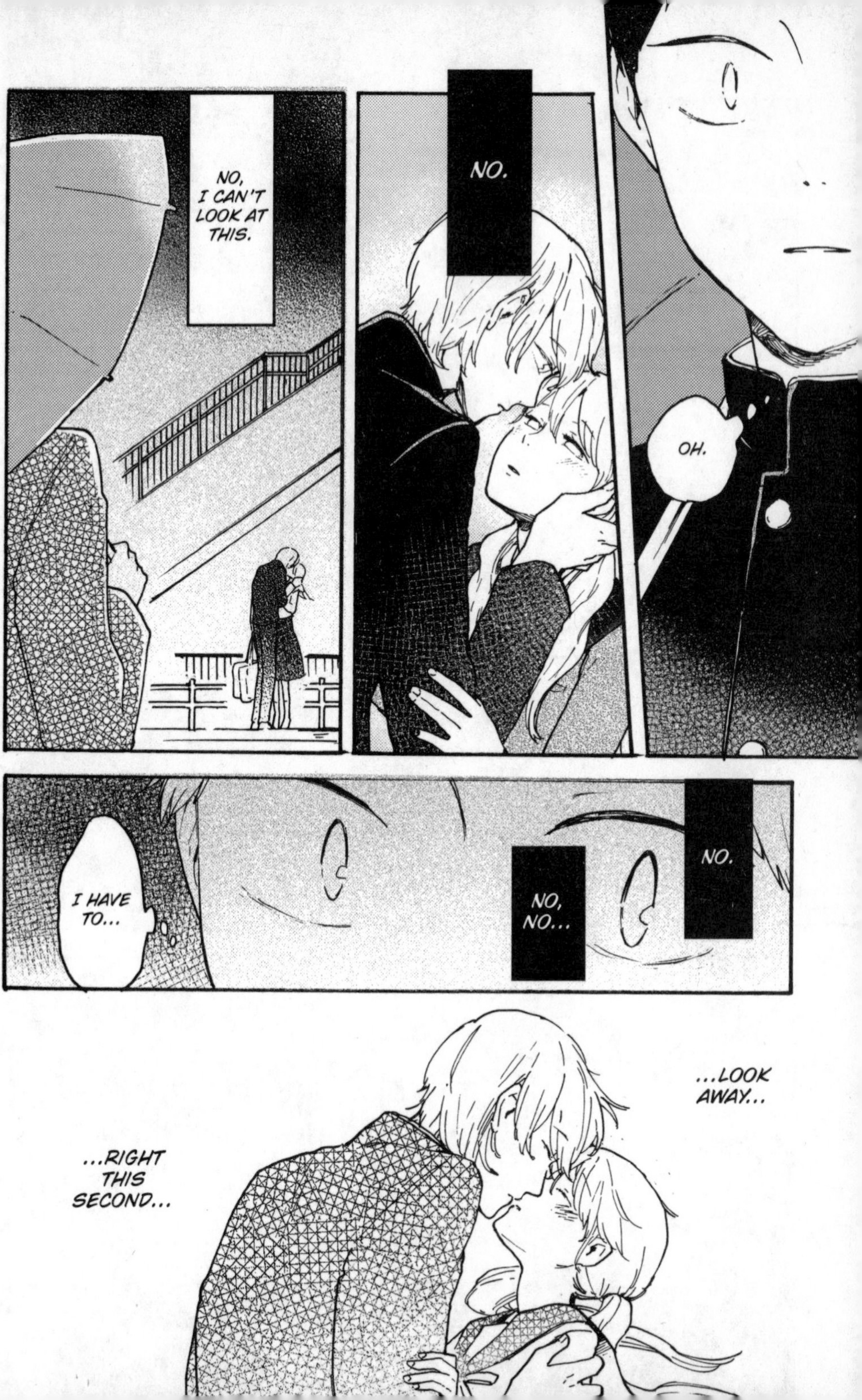
OH.
NO.
NO, I CAN'T LOOK AT THIS.
NO.
NO, NO...
I HAVE TO...
...LOOK AWAY...
...RIGHT THIS SECOND...

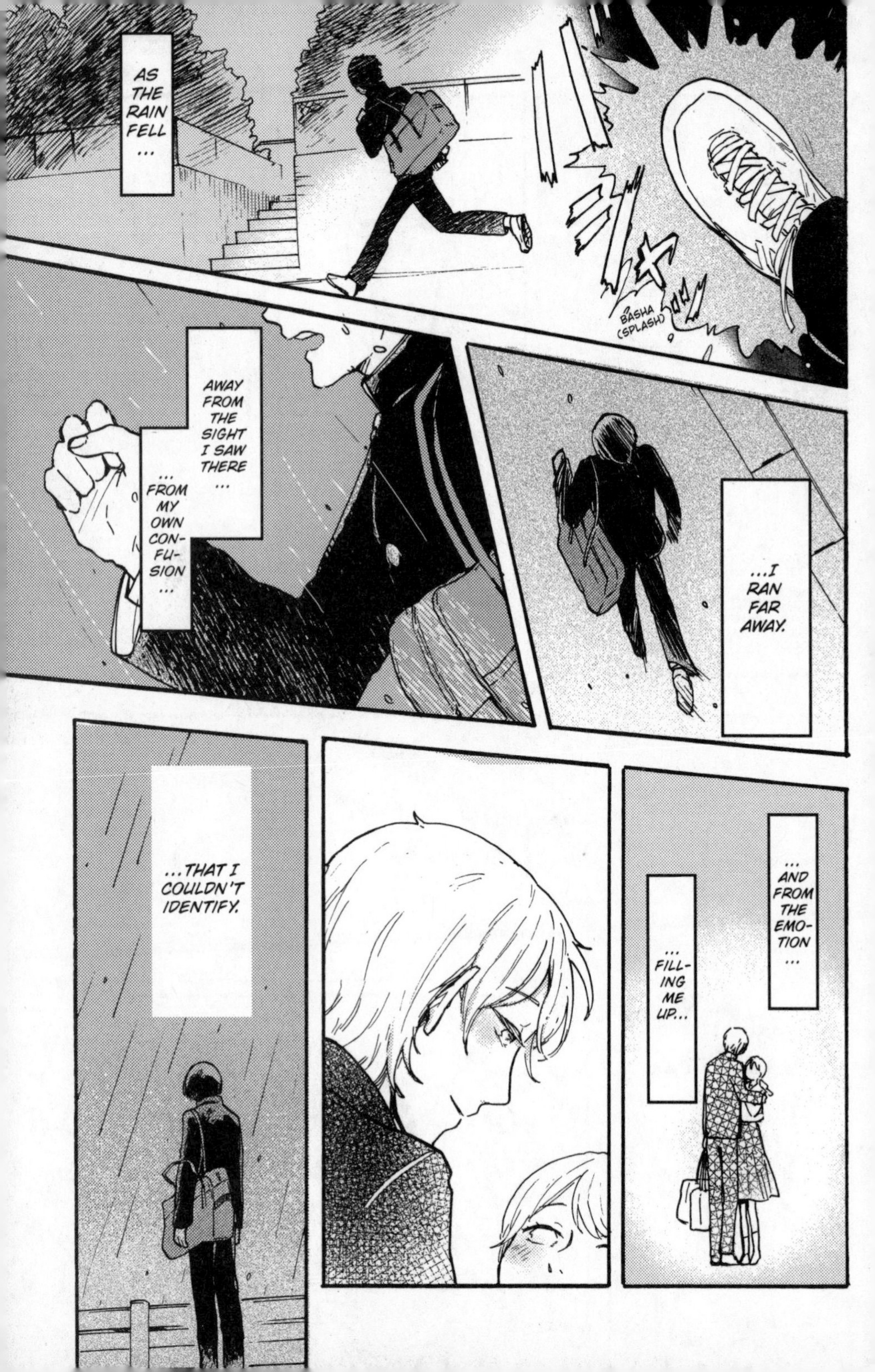
AS THE RAIN FELL...
BASHA (SPLASH)
...I RAN FAR AWAY.
AWAY FROM THE SIGHT I SAW THERE...
...FROM MY OWN CONFUSION...
...AND FROM THE EMOTION...
...FILLING ME UP...
...THAT I COULDN'T IDENTIFY.

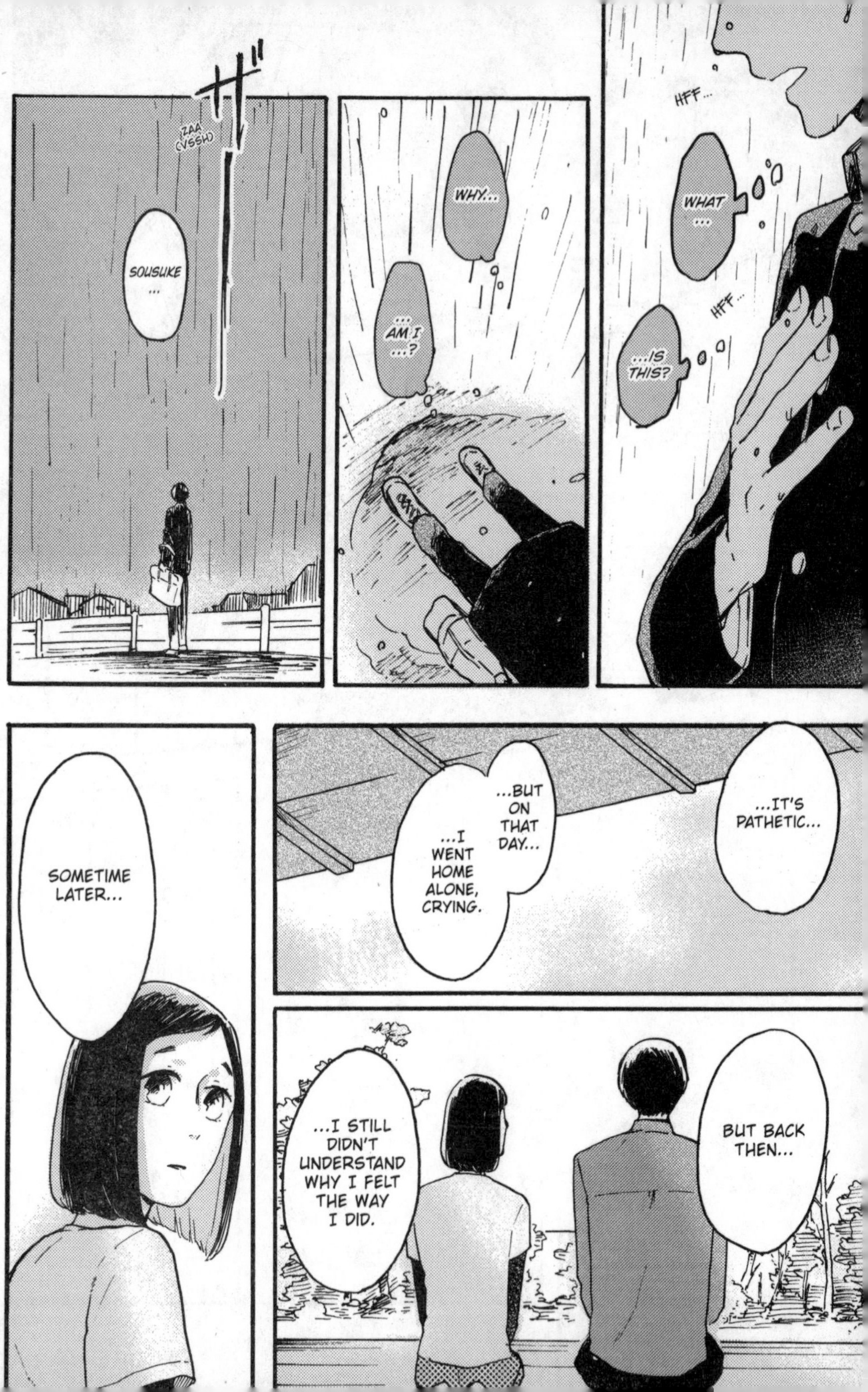
HFF...
WHAT ...
HFF...
...IS THIS?
WHY...
...AM I ...?
ZAA (VSSH)
SOUSUKE ...
...IT'S PATHETIC...
...BUT ON THAT DAY...
...I WENT HOME ALONE, CRYING.
BUT BACK THEN...
...I STILL DIDN'T UNDERSTAND WHY I FELT THE WAY I DID.
SOMETIME LATER...

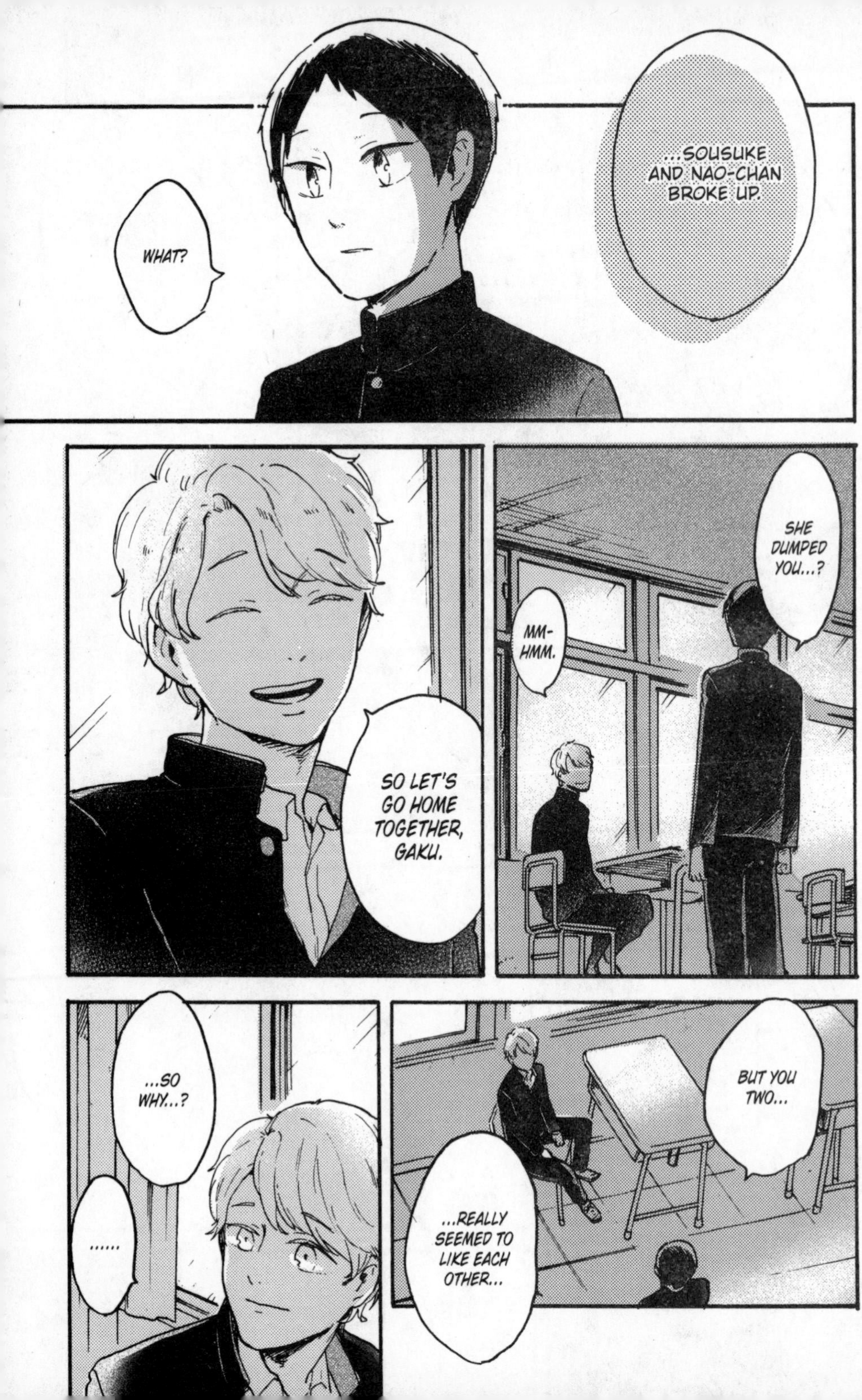
...SOUSUKE AND NAO-CHAN BROKE UP.
WHAT?
SHE DUMPED YOU...?
MM-HMM.
SO LET'S GO HOME TOGETHER, GAKU.
BUT YOU TWO...
...REALLY SEEMED TO LIKE EACH OTHER...
...SO WHY...?
......

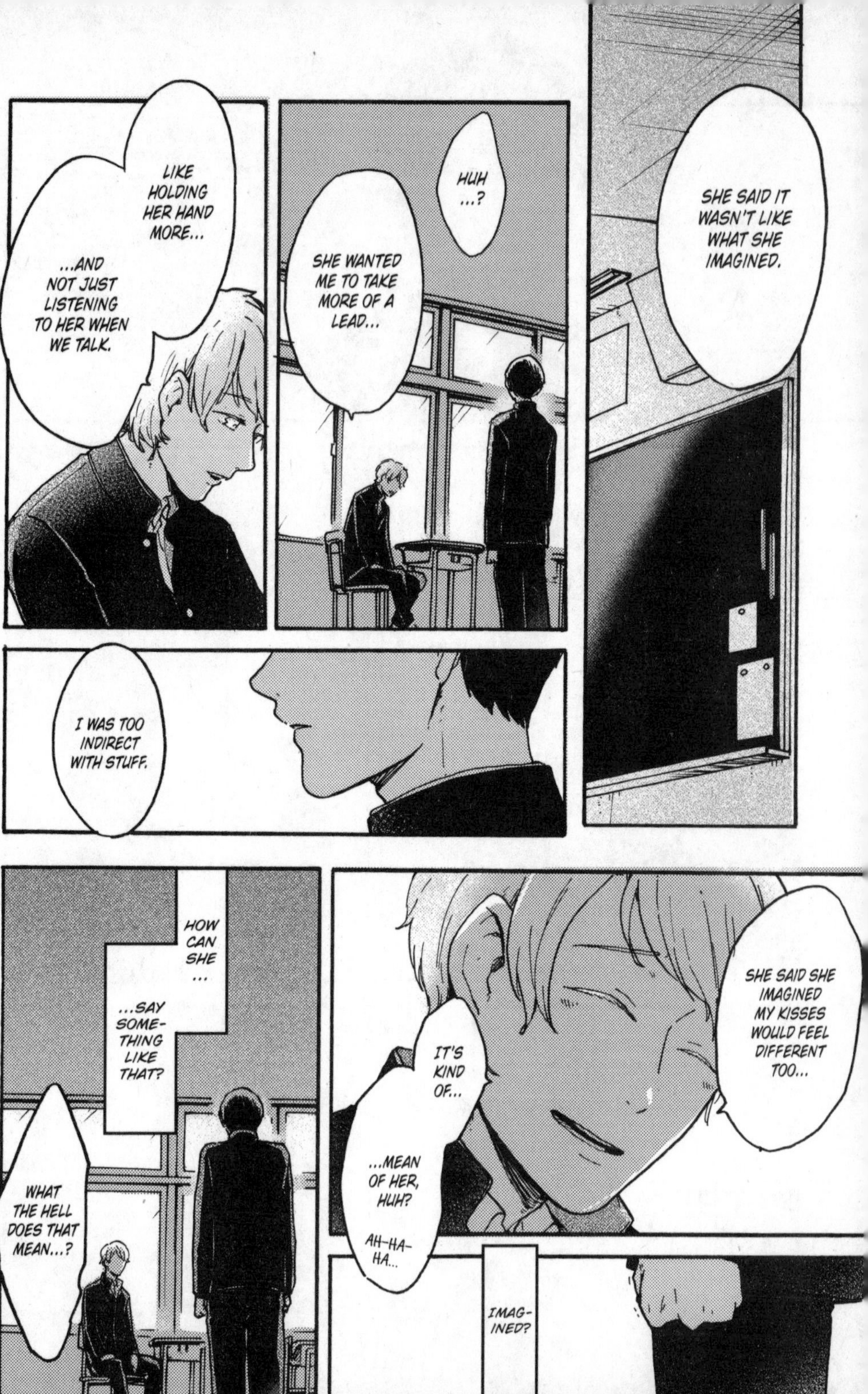
SHE SAID IT WASN'T LIKE WHAT SHE IMAGINED.
HUH ...?
SHE WANTED ME TO TAKE MORE OF A LEAD...
LIKE HOLDING HER HAND MORE...
...AND NOT JUST LISTENING TO HER WHEN WE TALK.
I WAS TOO INDIRECT WITH STUFF.
SHE SAID SHE IMAGINED MY KISSES WOULD FEEL DIFFERENT TOO...
IT'S KIND OF...
...MEAN OF HER, HUH?
AH-HA-HA...
IMAG-INED?
HOW CAN SHE ...
...SAY SOME-THING LIKE THAT?
WHAT THE HELL DOES THAT MEAN...?

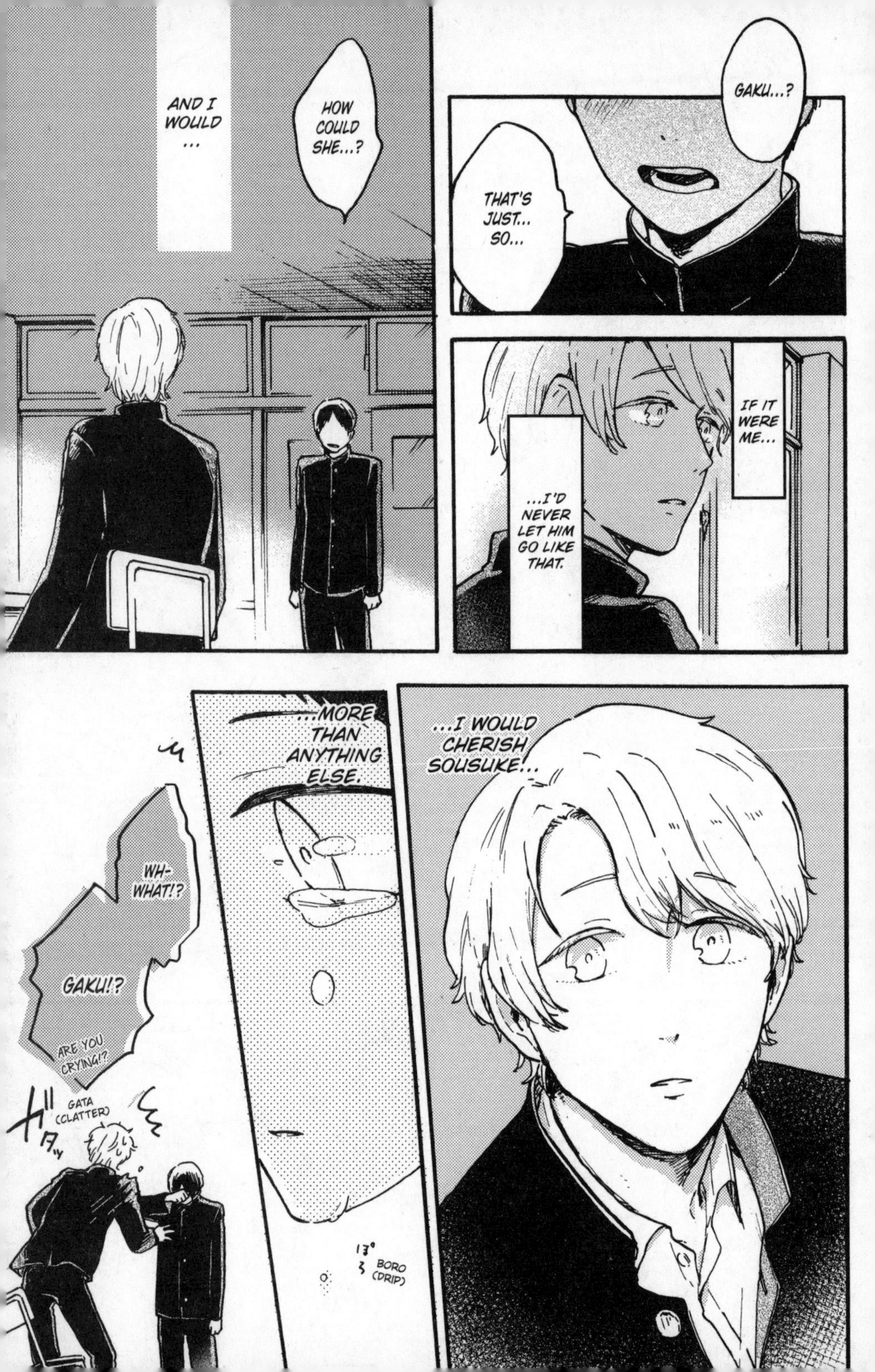
GAKU...?
THAT'S JUST... SO...
IF IT WERE ME...
...I'D NEVER LET HIM GO LIKE THAT.
HOW COULD SHE...?
AND I WOULD...
...I WOULD CHERISH SOUSUKE...
...MORE THAN ANYTHING ELSE.
BORO (DRIP)
WH-WHAT!?
GAKU!?
ARE YOU CRYING!?
GATA (CLATTER)

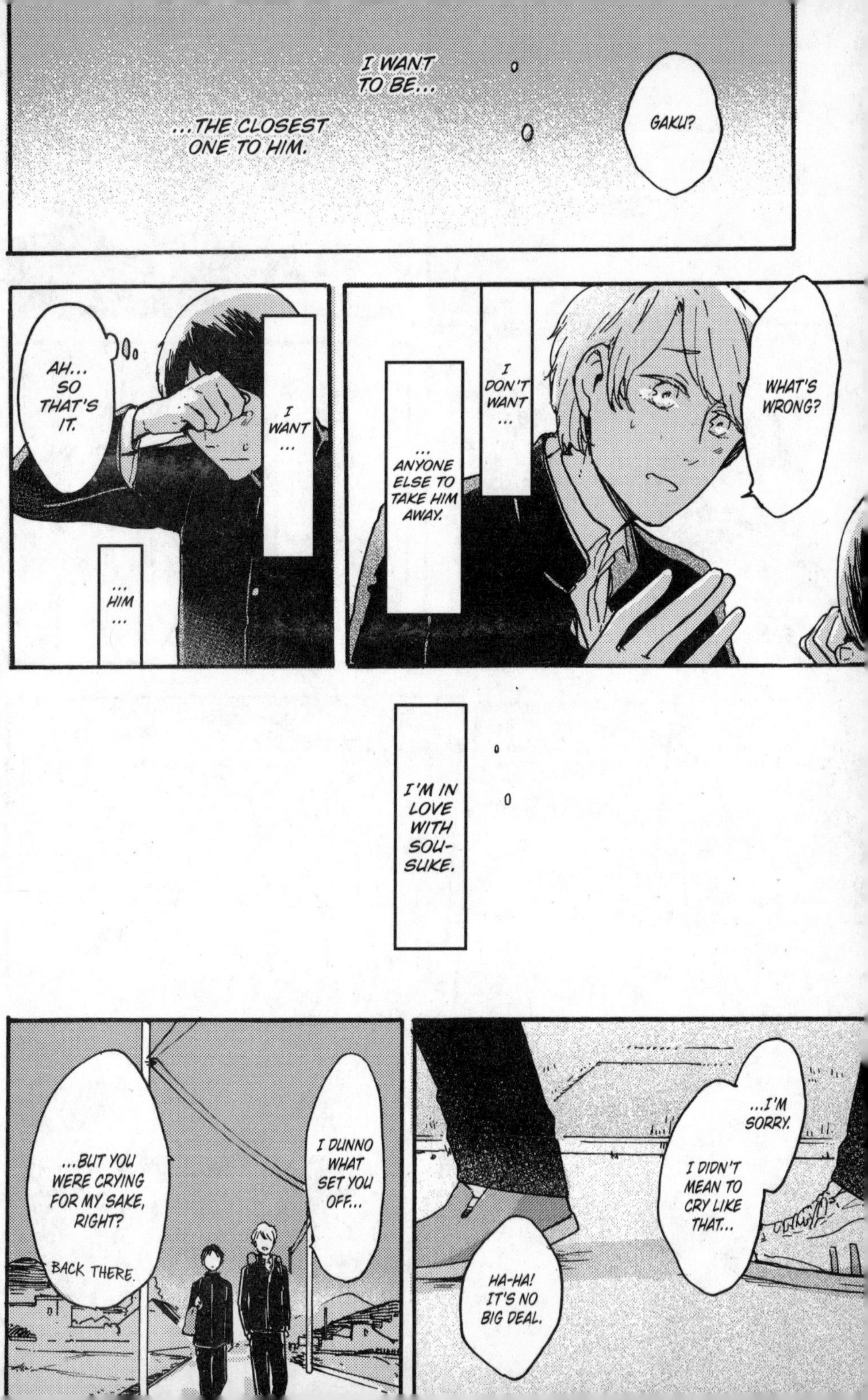
GAKU?
I WANT TO BE...
...THE CLOSEST ONE TO HIM.
WHAT'S WRONG?
I DON'T WANT...
...ANYONE ELSE TO TAKE HIM AWAY.
I WANT...
AH... SO THAT'S IT.
...HIM...
I'M IN LOVE WITH SOU-SUKE.
...I'M SORRY.
I DIDN'T MEAN TO CRY LIKE THAT...
HA-HA! IT'S NO BIG DEAL.
I DUNNO WHAT SET YOU OFF...
...BUT YOU WERE CRYING FOR MY SAKE, RIGHT?
BACK THERE.

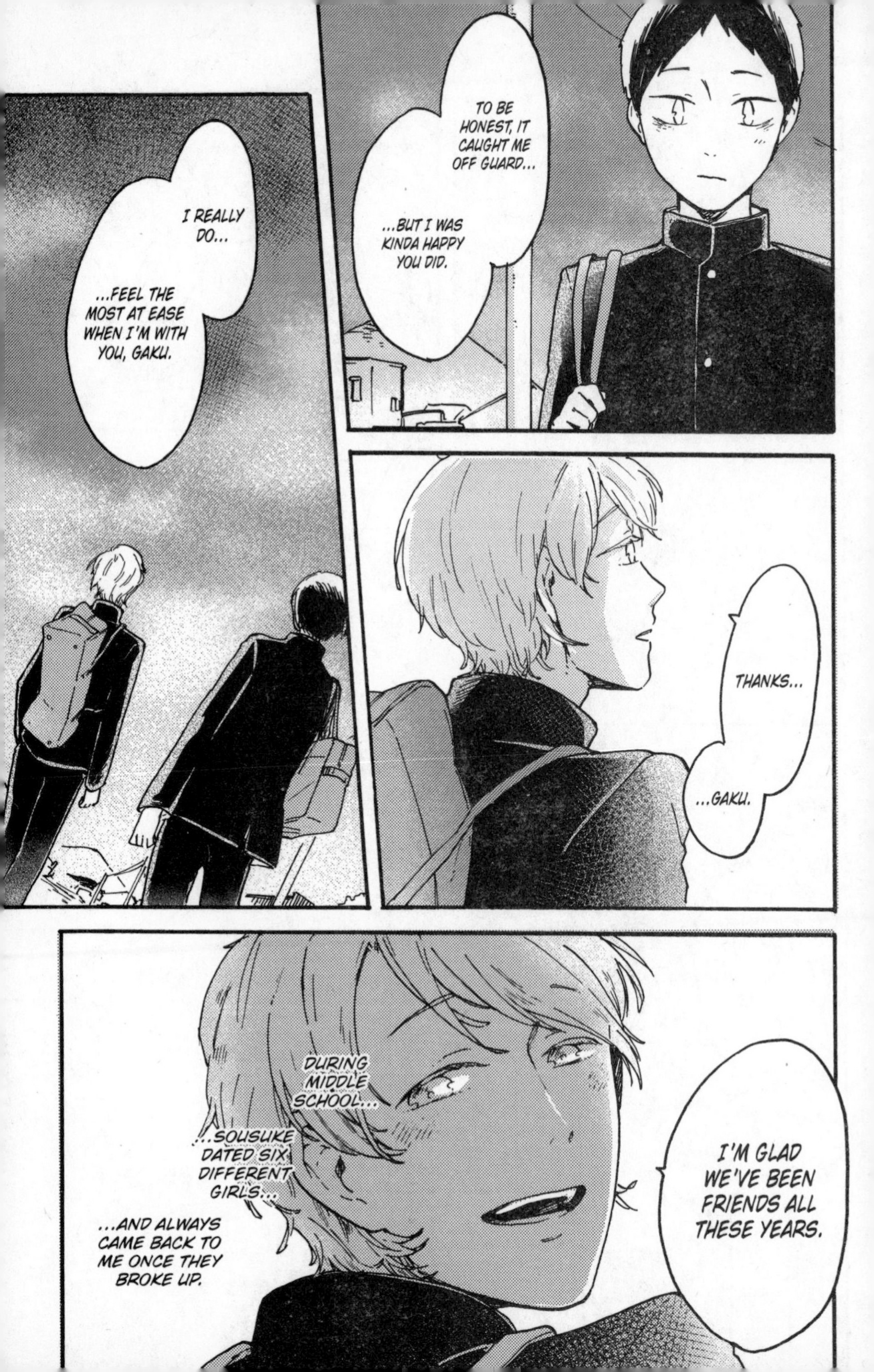
TO BE HONEST, IT CAUGHT ME OFF GUARD...
...BUT I WAS KINDA HAPPY YOU DID.
THANKS...
...GAKU.
I REALLY DO...
...FEEL THE MOST AT EASE WHEN I'M WITH YOU, GAKU.
I'M GLAD WE'VE BEEN FRIENDS ALL THESE YEARS.
DURING MIDDLE SCHOOL...
...SOUSUKE DATED SIX DIFFERENT GIRLS...
...AND ALWAYS CAME BACK TO ME ONCE THEY BROKE UP.

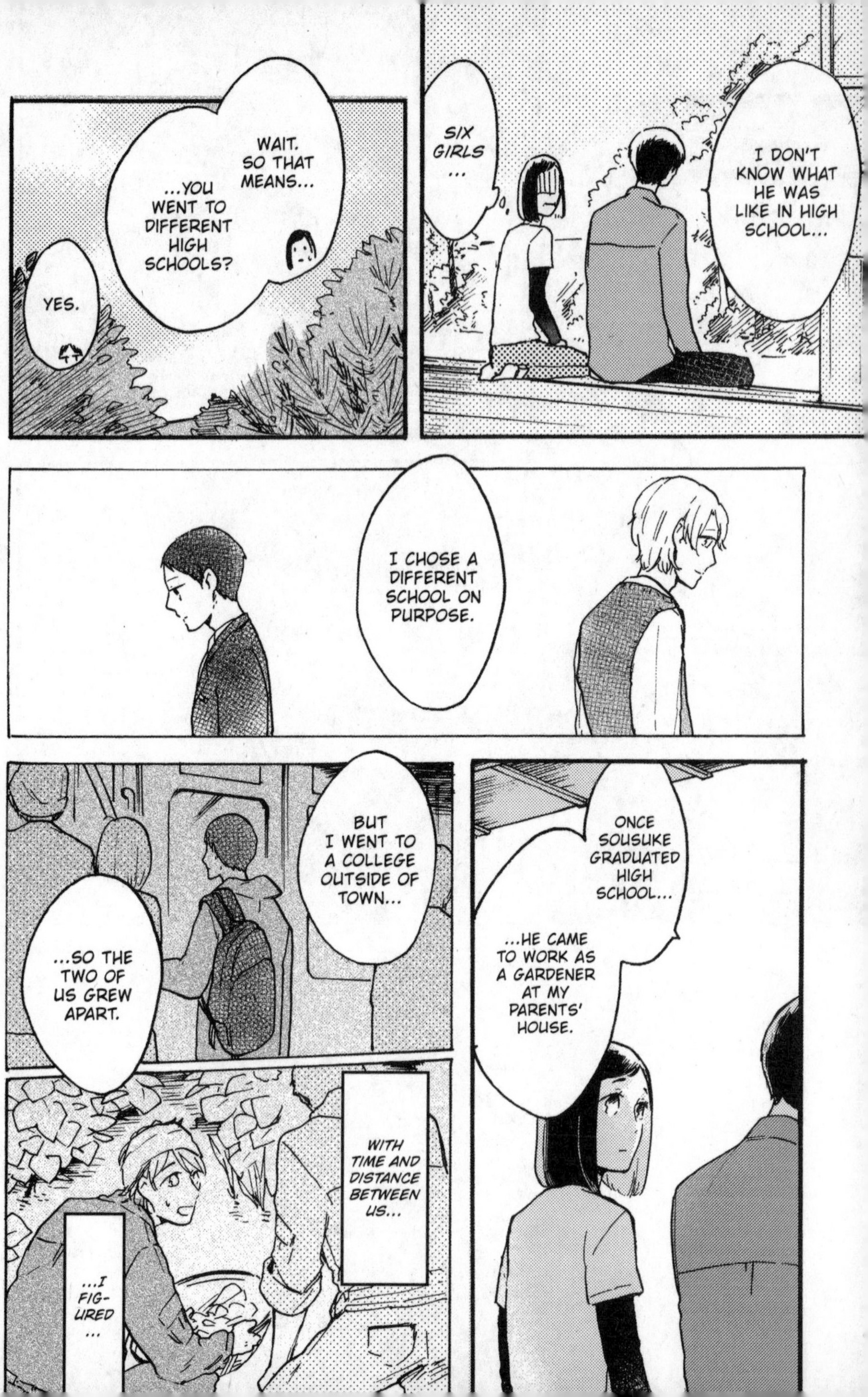
I DON'T KNOW WHAT HE WAS LIKE IN HIGH SCHOOL...
SIX GIRLS ...
WAIT. SO THAT MEANS...
...YOU WENT TO DIFFERENT HIGH SCHOOLS?
YES.
I CHOSE A DIFFERENT SCHOOL ON PURPOSE.
ONCE SOUSUKE GRADUATED HIGH SCHOOL...
...HE CAME TO WORK AS A GARDENER AT MY PARENTS' HOUSE.
BUT I WENT TO A COLLEGE OUTSIDE OF TOWN...
...SO THE TWO OF US GREW APART.
WITH TIME AND DISTANCE BETWEEN US...
...I FIG-URED ...

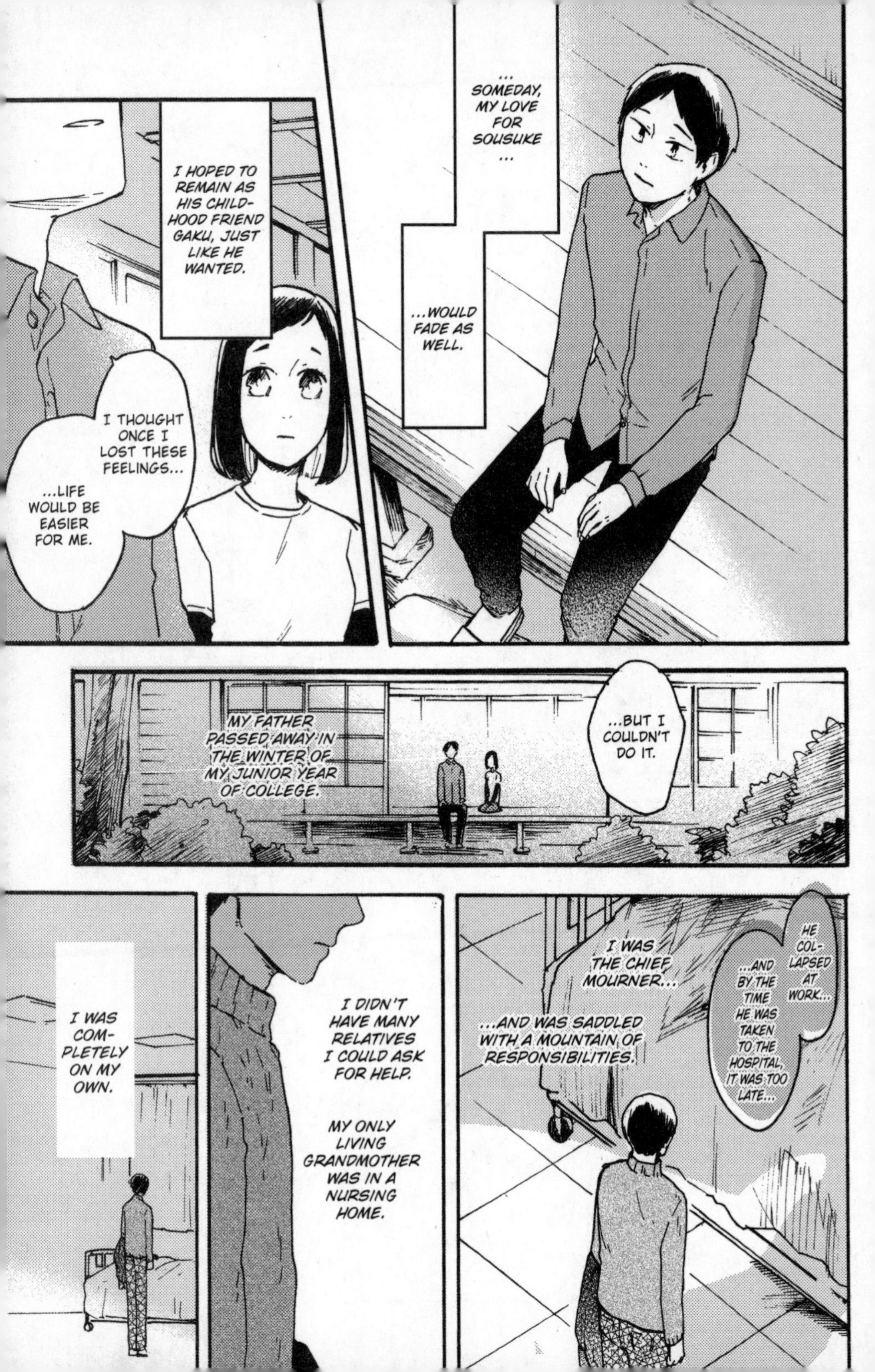

... SOMEDAY, MY LOVE FOR SOUSUKE ...
...WOULD FADE AS WELL.
I HOPED TO REMAIN AS HIS CHILDHOOD FRIEND GAKU, JUST LIKE HE WANTED.
I THOUGHT ONCE I LOST THESE FEELINGS...
...LIFE WOULD BE EASIER FOR ME.
...BUT I COULDN'T DO IT.
MY FATHER PASSED AWAY IN THE WINTER OF MY JUNIOR YEAR OF COLLEGE.
HE COLLAPSED AT WORK...
...AND BY THE TIME HE WAS TAKEN TO THE HOSPITAL, IT WAS TOO LATE...
I WAS THE CHIEF MOURNER...
...AND WAS SADDLED WITH A MOUNTAIN OF RESPONSIBILITIES.
I DIDN'T HAVE MANY RELATIVES I COULD ASK FOR HELP.
MY ONLY LIVING GRANDMOTHER WAS IN A NURSING HOME.
I WAS COMPLETELY ON MY OWN.

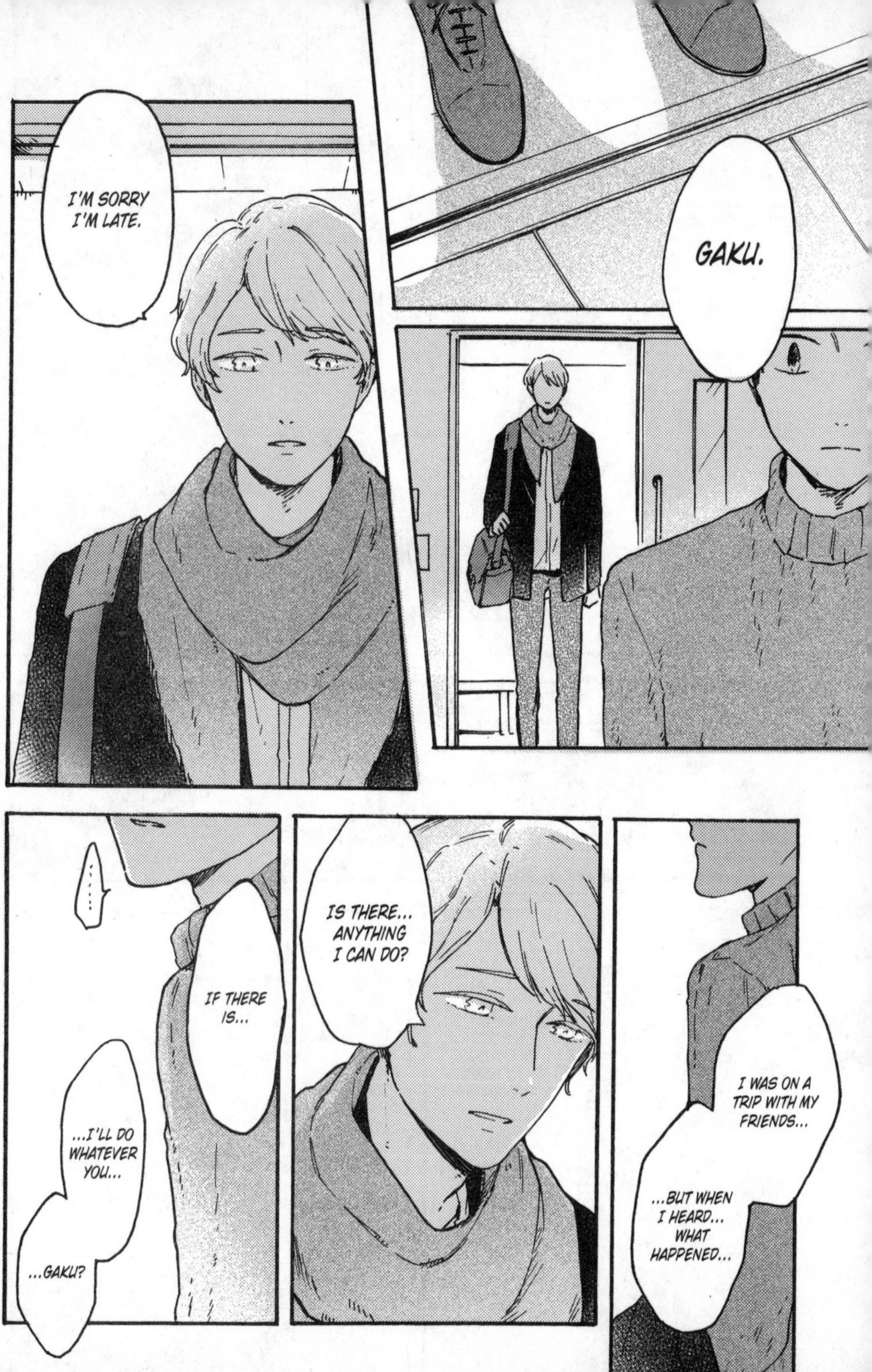
GAKU.
I'M SORRY I'M LATE.
I WAS ON A TRIP WITH MY FRIENDS...
...BUT WHEN I HEARD... WHAT HAPPENED...
IS THERE... ANYTHING I CAN DO?
...
IF THERE IS...
...I'LL DO WHATEVER YOU...
...GAKU?

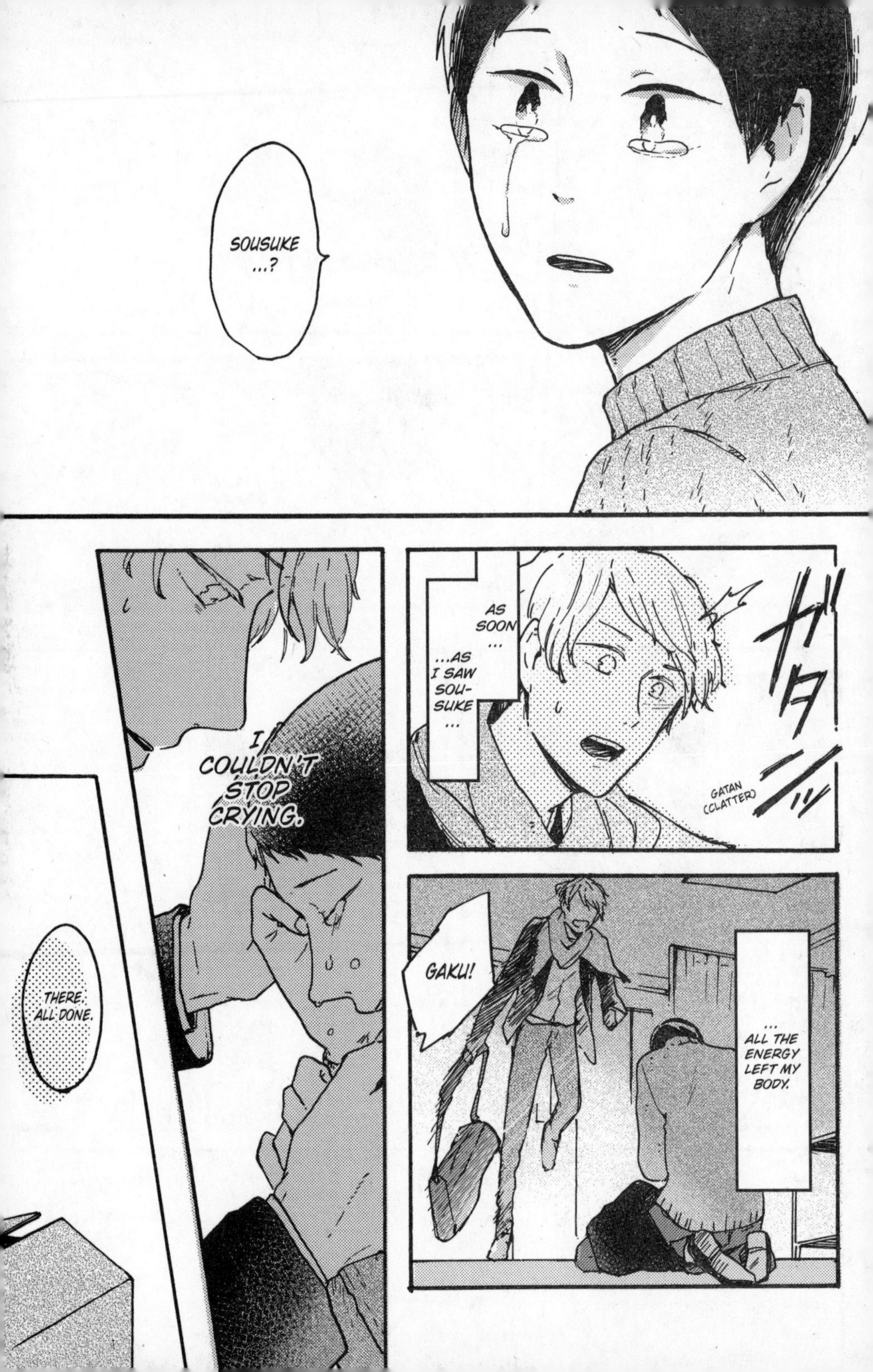
SOUSUKE ...?
AS SOON ...
...AS I SAW SOU-SUKE ...
ガタンッ
GATAN (CLATTER)
GAKU!
... ALL THE ENERGY LEFT MY BODY.
I COULDN'T STOP CRYING.
THERE. ALL DONE.

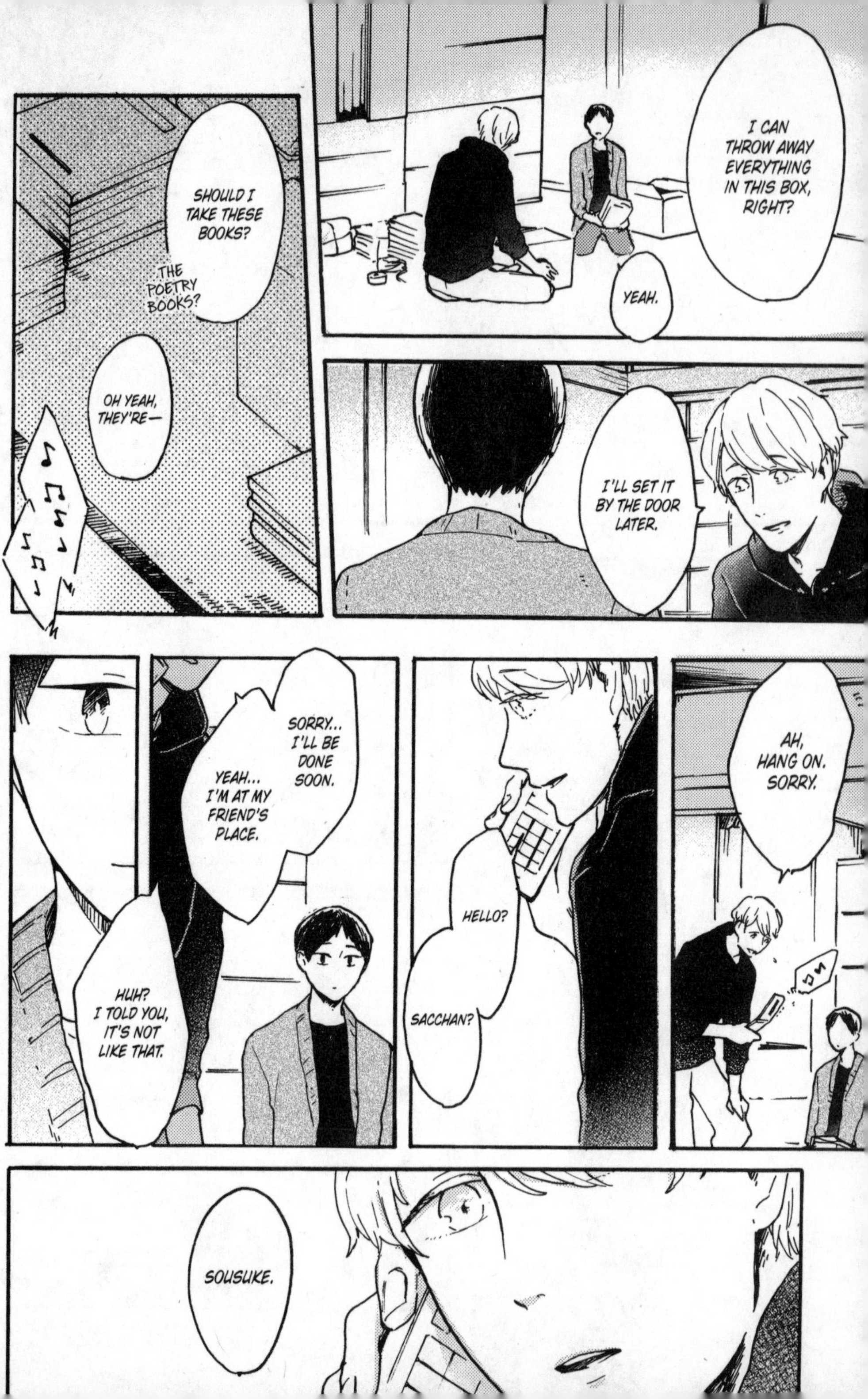
I CAN THROW AWAY EVERYTHING IN THIS BOX, RIGHT?
YEAH.
I'LL SET IT BY THE DOOR LATER.
SHOULD I TAKE THESE BOOKS?
THE POETRY BOOKS?
OH YEAH, THEY'RE—
AH, HANG ON. SORRY.
HELLO?
SACCHAN?
SORRY... I'LL BE DONE SOON.
YEAH... I'M AT MY FRIEND'S PLACE.
HUH? I TOLD YOU, IT'S NOT LIKE THAT.
SOUSUKE.

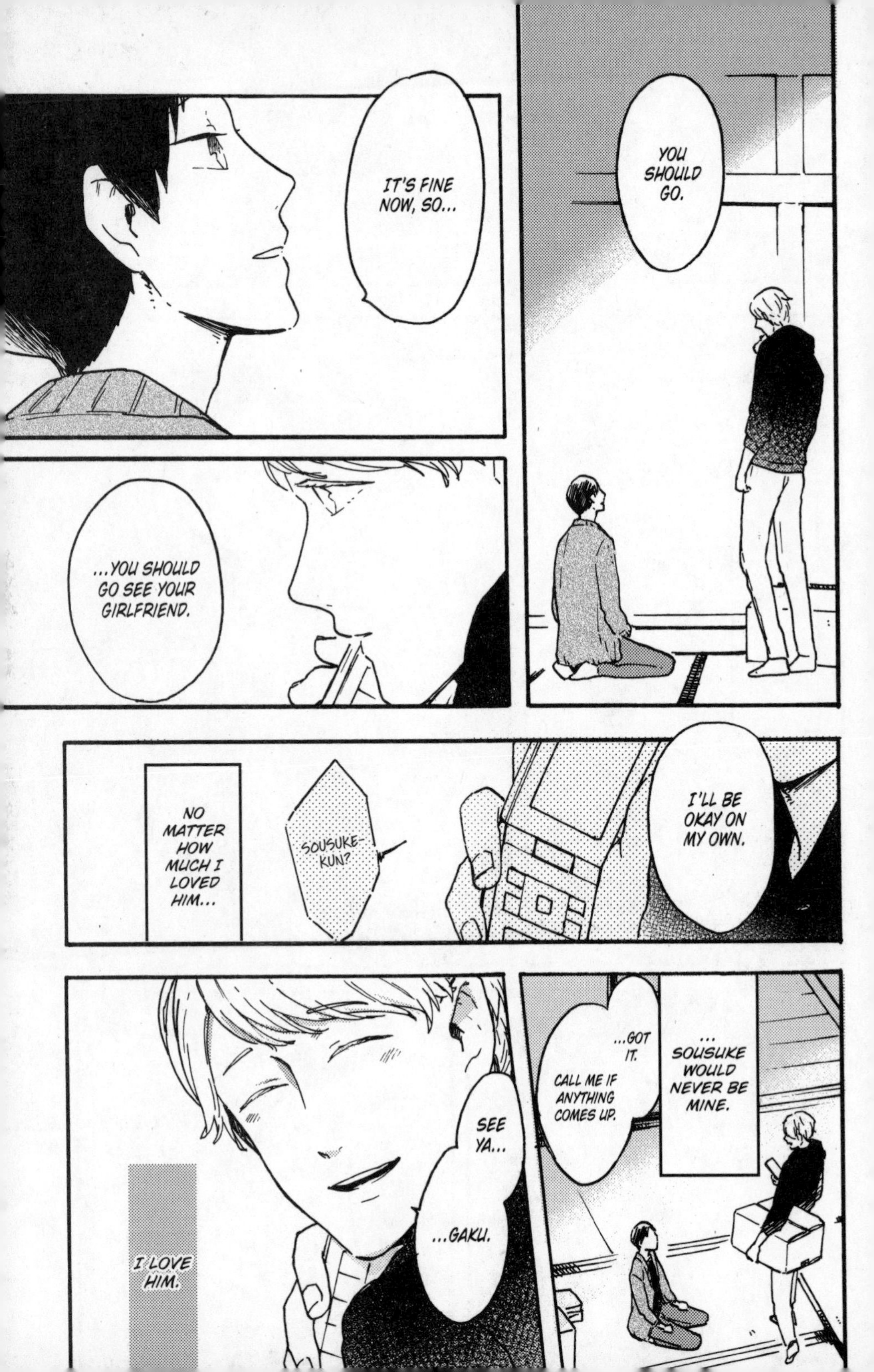
YOU SHOULD GO.
IT'S FINE NOW, SO...
...YOU SHOULD GO SEE YOUR GIRLFRIEND.
I'LL BE OKAY ON MY OWN.
SOUSUKE-KUN?
NO MATTER HOW MUCH I LOVED HIM...
...SOUSUKE WOULD NEVER BE MINE.
...GOT IT.
CALL ME IF ANYTHING COMES UP.
SEE YA...
...GAKU.
I LOVE HIM.

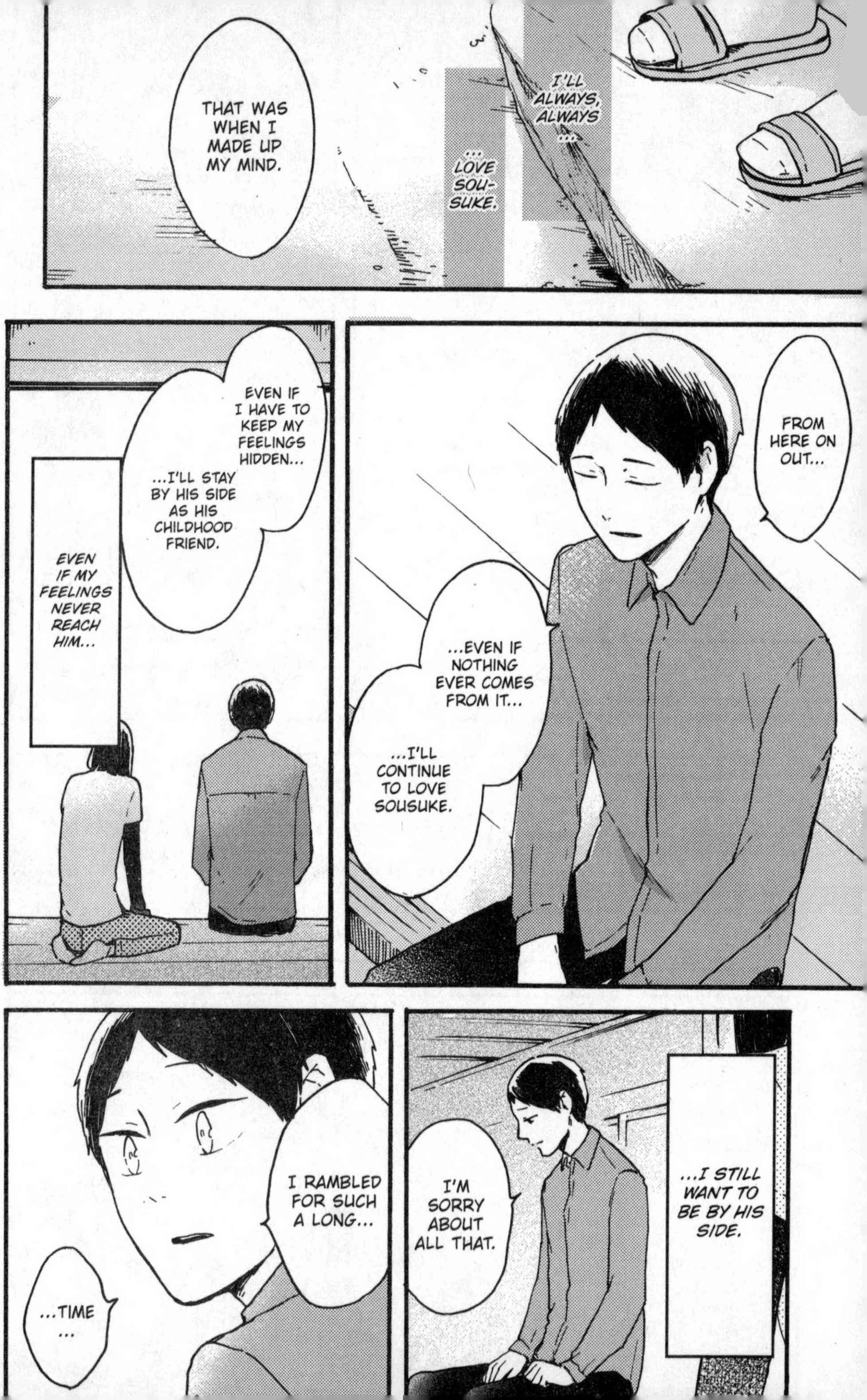
I'LL ALWAYS, ALWAYS ...
... LOVE SOU-SUKE.
THAT WAS WHEN I MADE UP MY MIND.
FROM HERE ON OUT...
...EVEN IF NOTHING EVER COMES FROM IT...
...I'LL CONTINUE TO LOVE SOUSUKE.
EVEN IF I HAVE TO KEEP MY FEELINGS HIDDEN...
...I'LL STAY BY HIS SIDE AS HIS CHILDHOOD FRIEND.
EVEN IF MY FEELINGS NEVER REACH HIM...
...I STILL WANT TO BE BY HIS SIDE.
I'M SORRY ABOUT ALL THAT.
I RAMBLED FOR SUCH A LONG...
...TIME ...

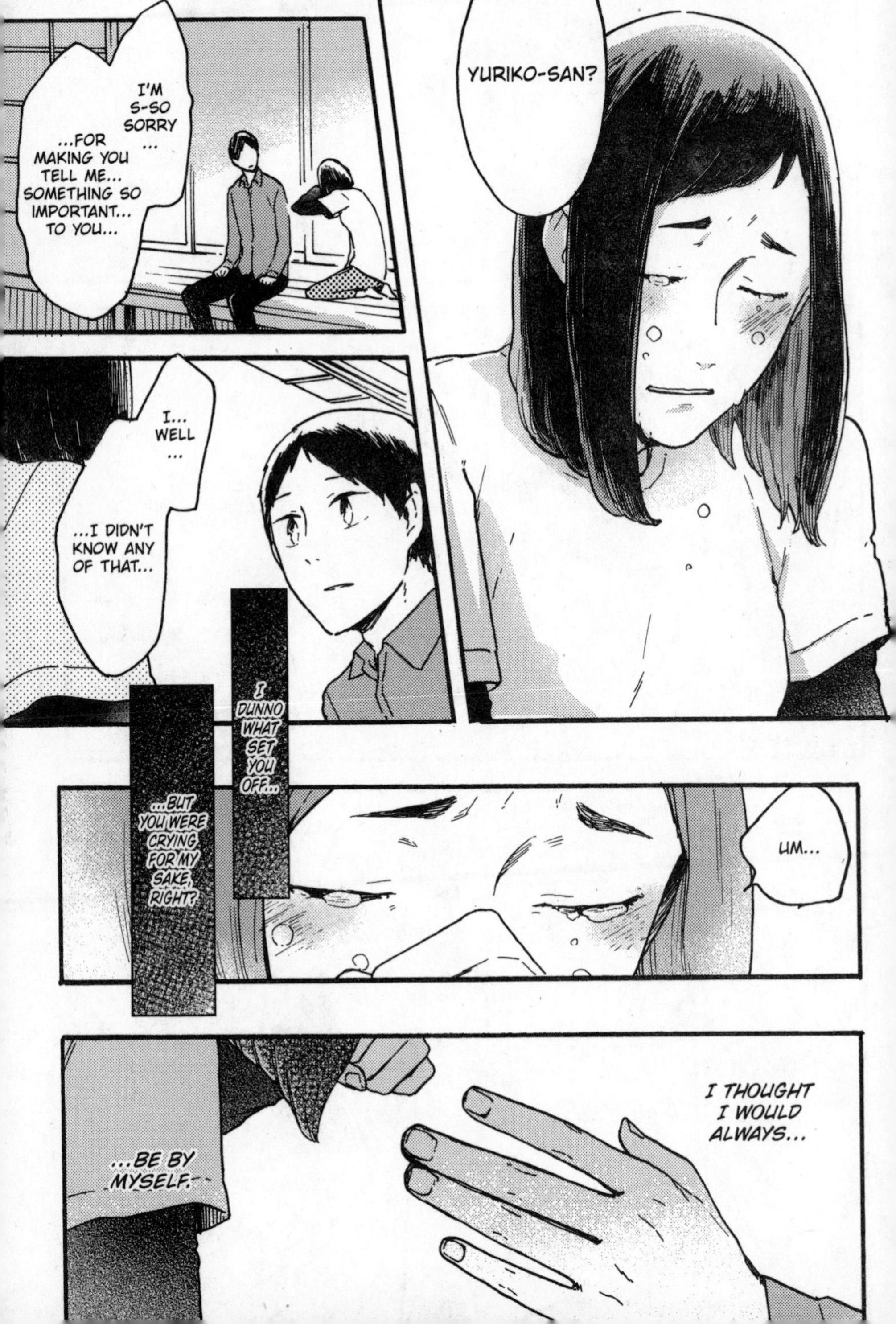
YURIKO-SAN?
I'M S-SO SORRY ...
...FOR MAKING YOU TELL ME... SOMETHING SO IMPORTANT... TO YOU...
I... WELL ...
...I DIDN'T KNOW ANY OF THAT...
I DUNNO WHAT SET YOU OFF...
...BUT YOU WERE CRYING FOR MY SAKE, RIGHT?
UM...
I THOUGHT I WOULD ALWAYS...
...BE BY MYSELF.

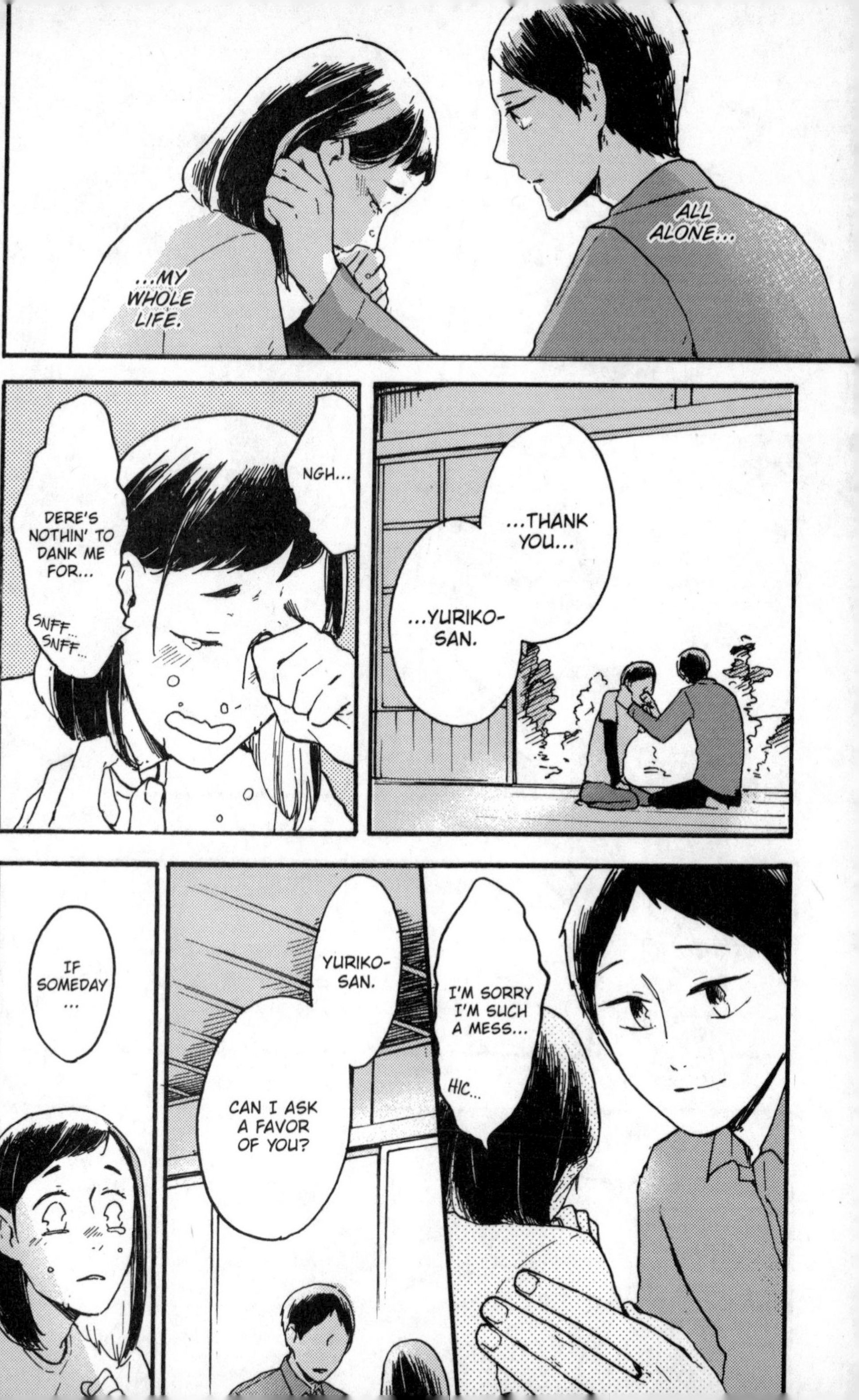
ALL ALONE...
...MY WHOLE LIFE.
...THANK YOU...
...YURIKO-SAN.
NGH...
DERE'S NOTHIN' TO DANK ME FOR...
SNFF... SNFF...
I'M SORRY I'M SUCH A MESS...
HIC...
YURIKO-SAN.
CAN I ASK A FAVOR OF YOU?
IF SOMEDAY ...

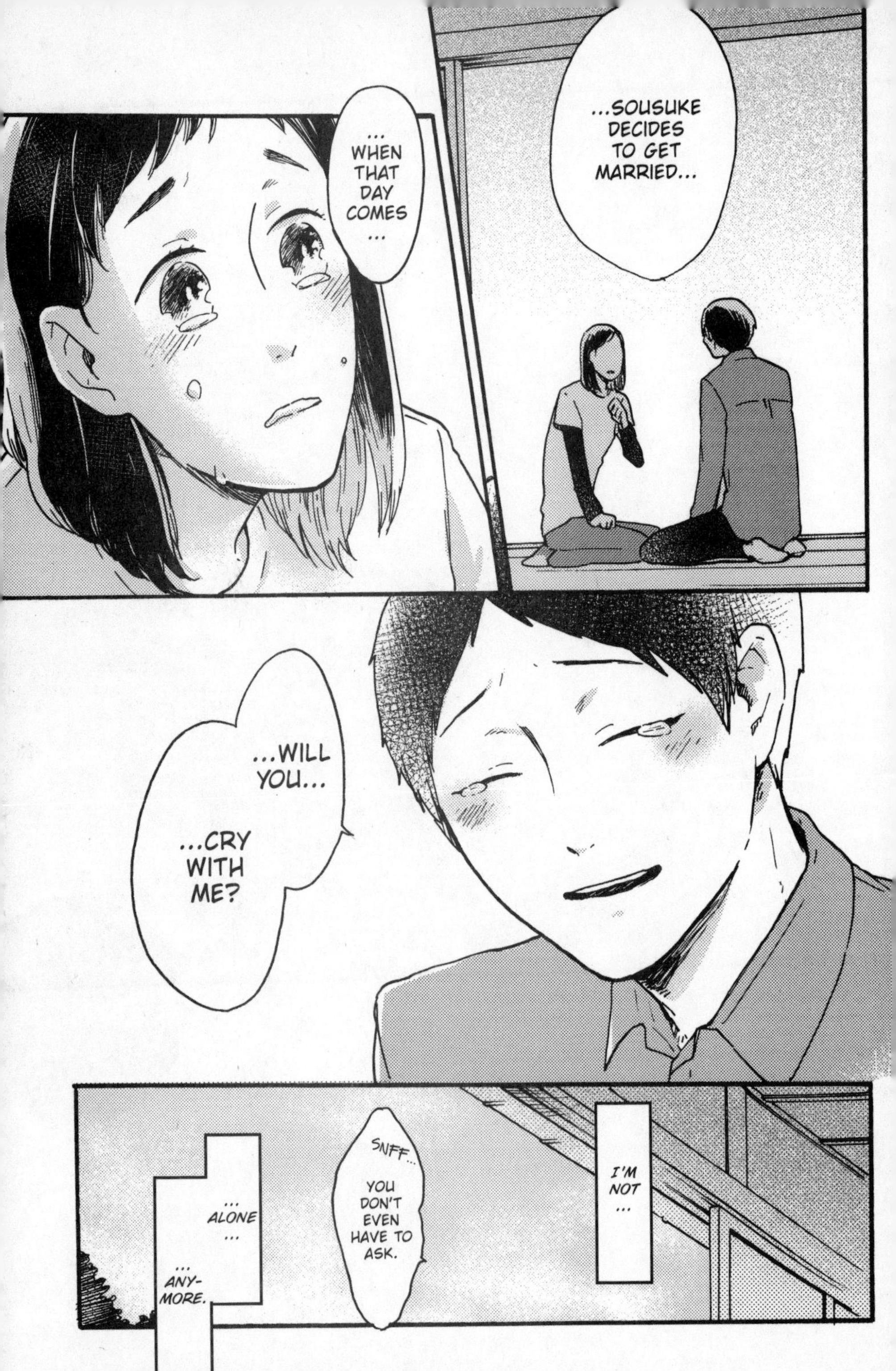
...SOUSUKE DECIDES TO GET MARRIED...
...WHEN THAT DAY COMES...
...WILL YOU...
...CRY WITH ME?
I'M NOT...
SNFF...
YOU DON'T EVEN HAVE TO ASK.
...ALONE...
...ANYMORE.

I Want
to Be a
Wall

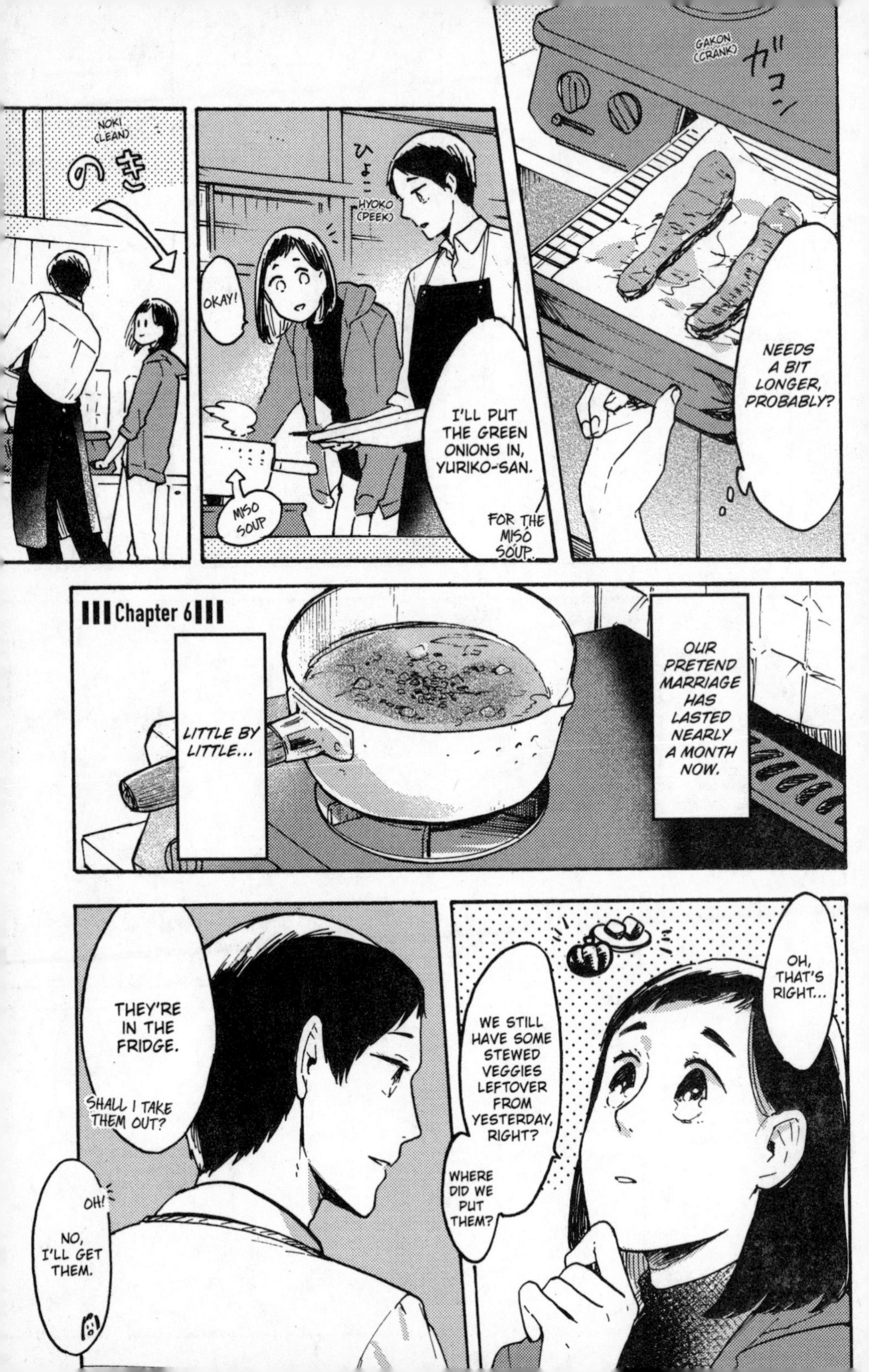
GAKON (CRANK)
ガコン
NEEDS A BIT LONGER, PROBABLY?
ひょこ
HYOKO (PEEK)
I'LL PUT THE GREEN ONIONS IN, YURIKO-SAN.
FOR THE MISO SOUP.
OKAY!
MISO SOUP
NOKI (LEAN)
のき
Chapter 6
OUR PRETEND MARRIAGE HAS LASTED NEARLY A MONTH NOW.
LITTLE BY LITTLE...
OH, THAT'S RIGHT...
WE STILL HAVE SOME STEWED VEGGIES LEFTOVER FROM YESTERDAY, RIGHT?
WHERE DID WE PUT THEM?
THEY'RE IN THE FRIDGE.
SHALL I TAKE THEM OUT?
OH!
NO, I'LL GET THEM.

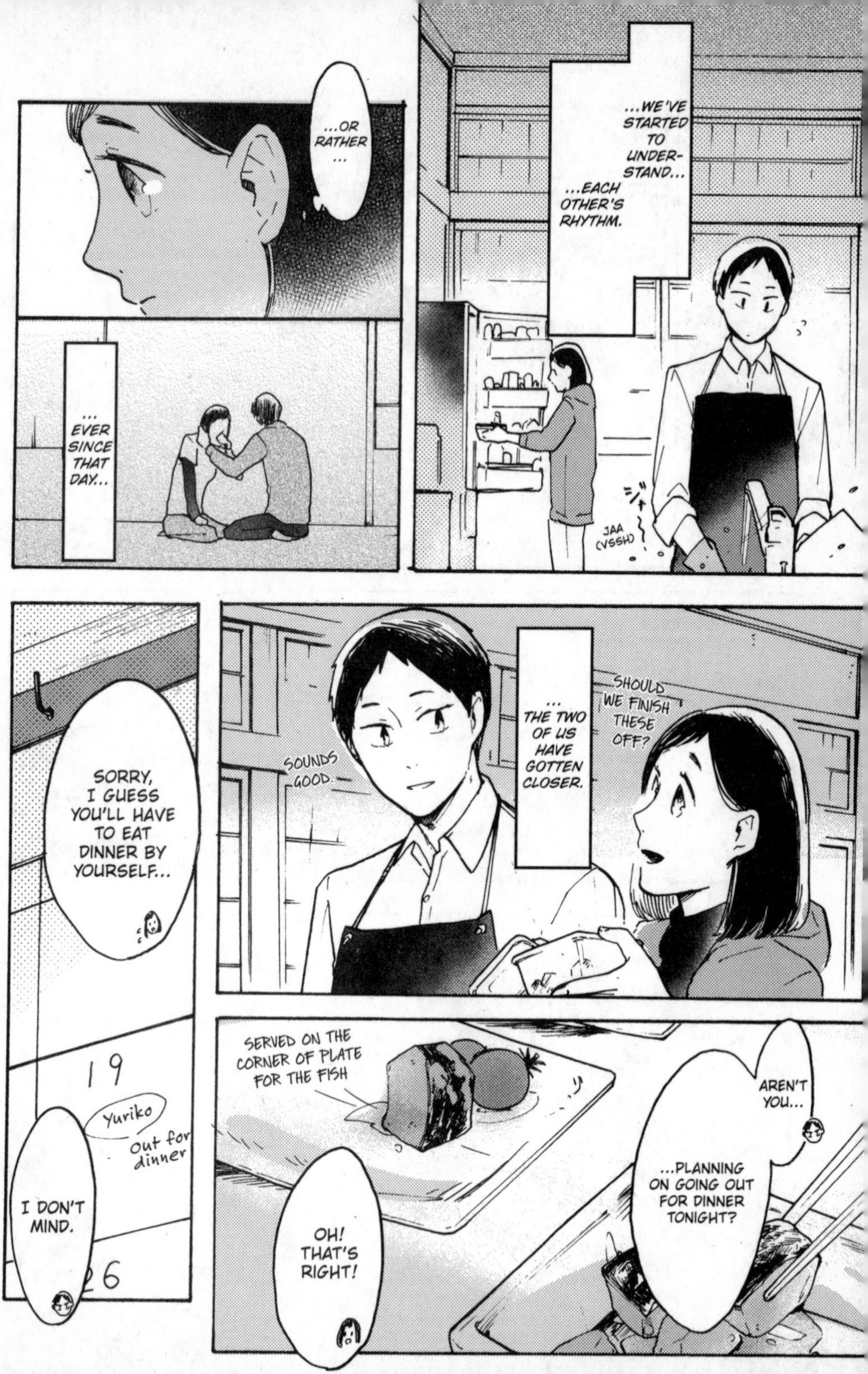
...WE'VE STARTED TO UNDER-STAND...
...EACH OTHER'S RHYTHM.
JAA (VSSH)
...OR RATHER ...
... EVER SINCE THAT DAY...
...THE TWO OF US HAVE GOTTEN CLOSER.
SHOULD WE FINISH THESE OFF?
SOUNDS GOOD.
AREN'T YOU...
...PLANNING ON GOING OUT FOR DINNER TONIGHT?
SERVED ON THE CORNER OF PLATE FOR THE FISH
OH! THAT'S RIGHT!
SORRY, I GUESS YOU'LL HAVE TO EAT DINNER BY YOURSELF...
19
Yuriko
Out for dinner
26
I DON'T MIND.

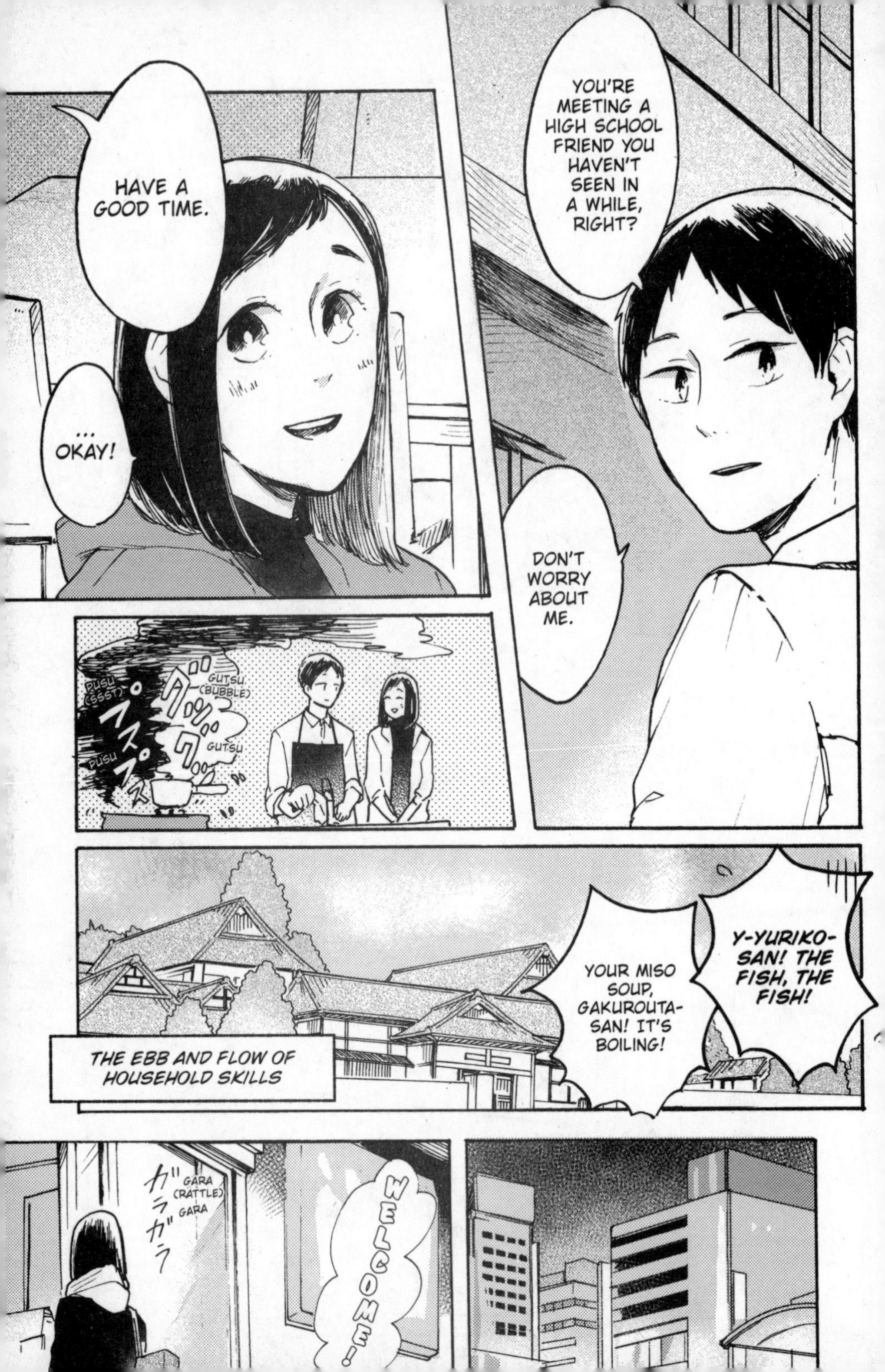
YOU'RE MEETING A HIGH SCHOOL FRIEND YOU HAVEN'T SEEN IN A WHILE, RIGHT?
DON'T WORRY ABOUT ME.
HAVE A GOOD TIME.
... OKAY!
GUTSU (BUBBLE)
GUTSU
PUSU (SSST)
PUSU
Y-YURIKO-SAN! THE FISH, THE FISH!
YOUR MISO SOUP, GAKUROUTA-SAN! IT'S BOILING!
THE EBB AND FLOW OF HOUSEHOLD SKILLS
WELCOME!
GARA (RATTLE) GARA

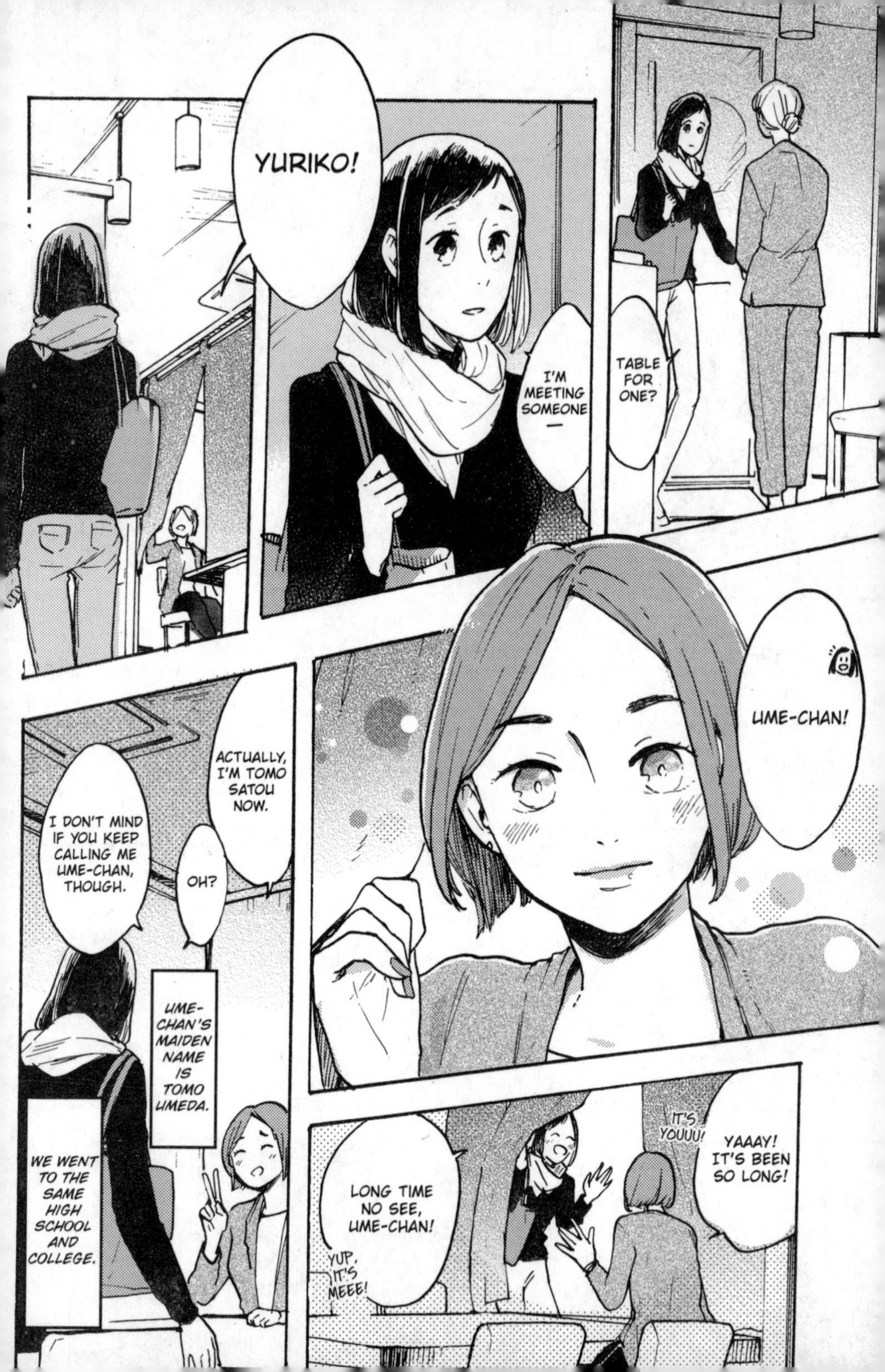

TABLE FOR ONE?
I'M MEETING SOMEONE—
YURIKO!
UME-CHAN!
YAAAY! IT'S BEEN SO LONG!
IT'S YOUUU!
LONG TIME NO SEE, UME-CHAN!
YUP, IT'S MEEE!
ACTUALLY, I'M TOMO SATOU NOW.
OH?
I DON'T MIND IF YOU KEEP CALLING ME UME-CHAN, THOUGH.
UME-CHAN'S MAIDEN NAME IS TOMO UMEDA.
WE WENT TO THE SAME HIGH SCHOOL AND COLLEGE.

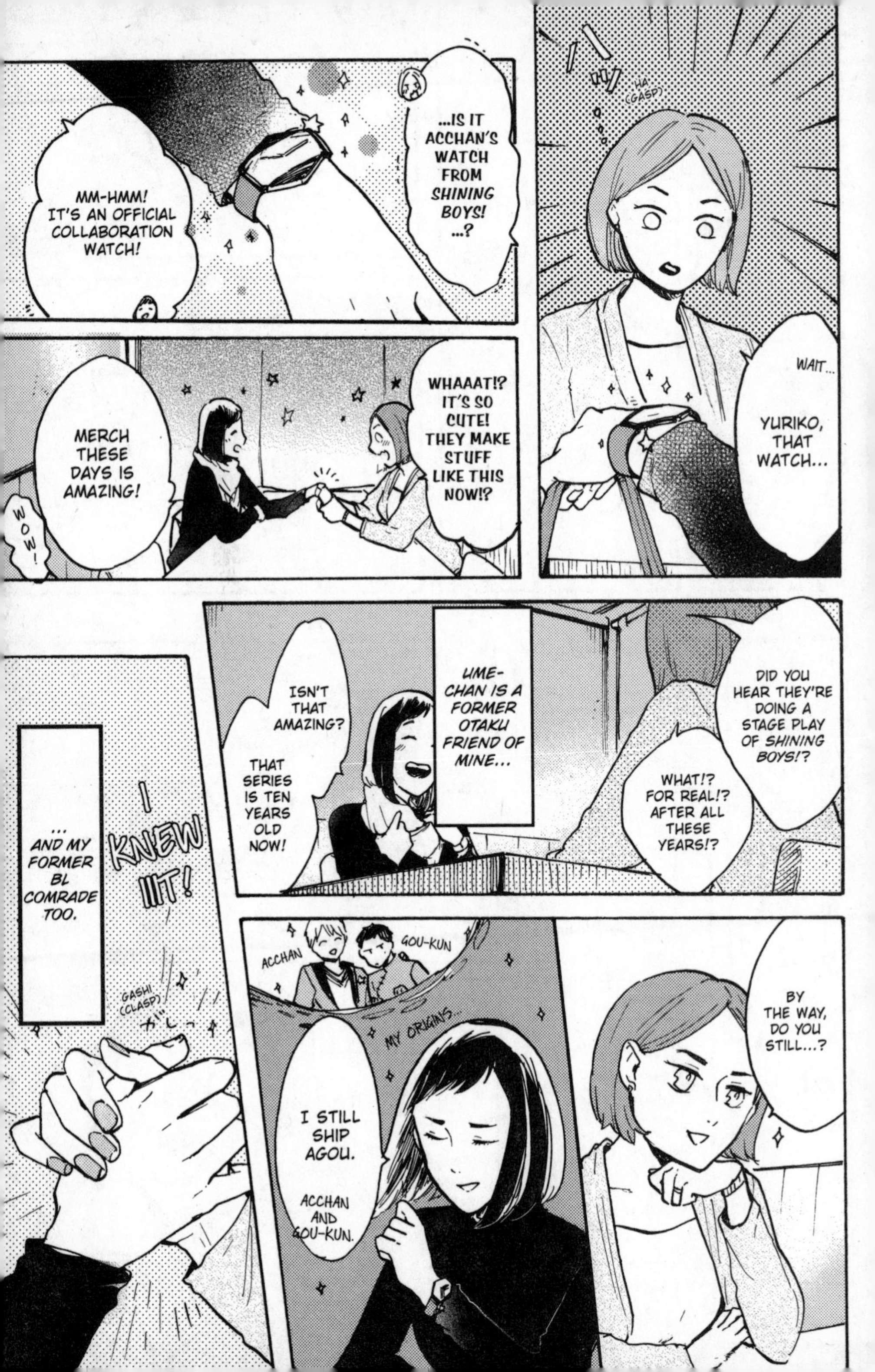
HA (GASP)
WAIT...
YURIKO, THAT WATCH...
...IS IT ACCHAN'S WATCH FROM SHINING BOYS! ...?
MM-HMM! IT'S AN OFFICIAL COLLABORATION WATCH!
WHAAAT!? IT'S SO CUTE! THEY MAKE STUFF LIKE THIS NOW!?
MERCH THESE DAYS IS AMAZING!
WOW!
DID YOU HEAR THEY'RE DOING A STAGE PLAY OF SHINING BOYS!?
WHAT!? FOR REAL!? AFTER ALL THESE YEARS!?
UME-CHAN IS A FORMER OTAKU FRIEND OF MINE...
ISN'T THAT AMAZING?
THAT SERIES IS TEN YEARS OLD NOW!
BY THE WAY, DO YOU STILL...?
ACCHAN
GOU-KUN
MY ORIGINS...
I STILL SHIP AGOU.
ACCHAN AND GOU-KUN.
...AND MY FORMER BL COMRADE TOO.
I KNEW IIIT!
GASHI (CLASP)

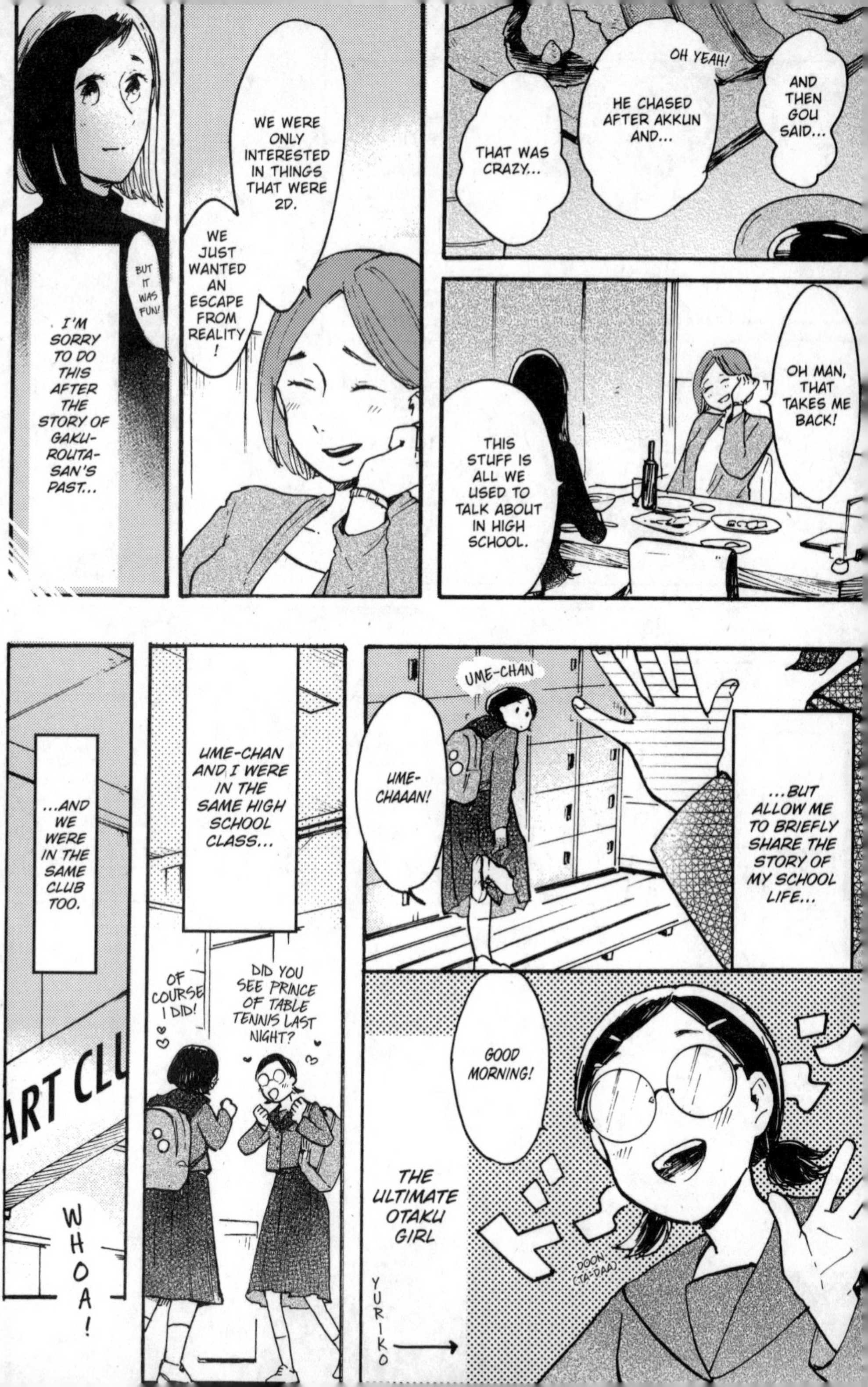
AND THEN GOU SAID...
OH YEAH!
HE CHASED AFTER AKKUN AND...
THAT WAS CRAZY...
OH MAN, THAT TAKES ME BACK!
THIS STUFF IS ALL WE USED TO TALK ABOUT IN HIGH SCHOOL.
WE WERE ONLY INTERESTED IN THINGS THAT WERE 2D.
WE JUST WANTED AN ESCAPE FROM REALITY!
BUT IT WAS FUN!
I'M SORRY TO DO THIS AFTER THE STORY OF GAKU-ROUTA-SAN'S PAST...
...BUT ALLOW ME TO BRIEFLY SHARE THE STORY OF MY SCHOOL LIFE...
UME-CHAN
UME-CHAAAN!
GOOD MORNING!
DOON (TA-DAA)
THE ULTIMATE OTAKU GIRL
YURIKO
UME-CHAN AND I WERE IN THE SAME HIGH SCHOOL CLASS...
DID YOU SEE PRINCE OF TABLE TENNIS LAST NIGHT?
OF COURSE I DID!
...AND WE WERE IN THE SAME CLUB TOO.
ART CLU
WHOA!

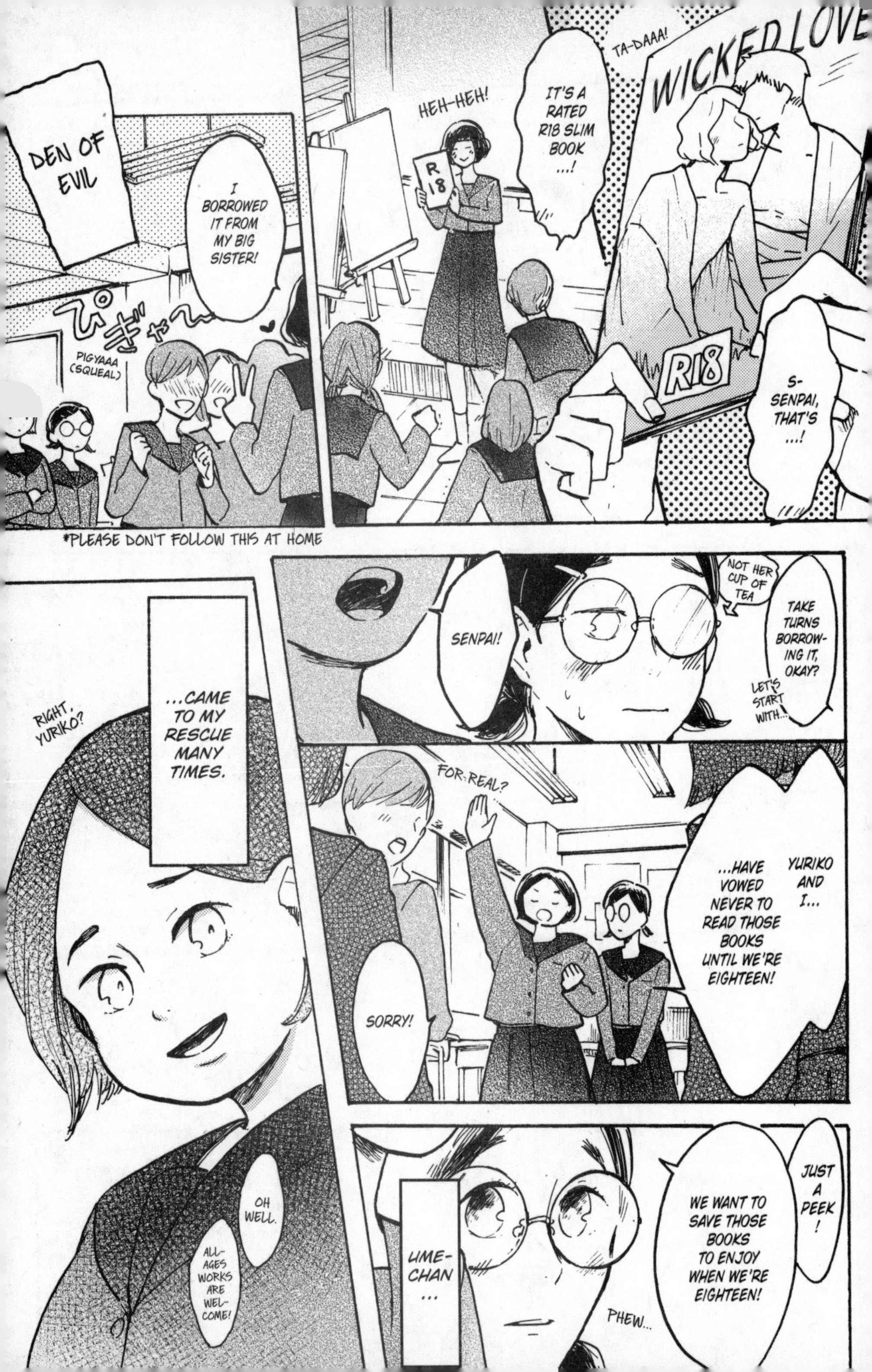
TA-DAAA!
WICKED LOVE
R18
S-SENPAI, THAT'S ...!
IT'S A RATED R18 SLIM BOOK ...!
HEH-HEH!
R 18
I BORROWED IT FROM MY BIG SISTER!
DEN OF EVIL
PIGYAAA (SQUEAL)
*PLEASE DON'T FOLLOW THIS AT HOME
TAKE TURNS BORROWING IT, OKAY?
LET'S START WITH...
NOT HER CUP OF TEA
SENPAI!
YURIKO AND I...
...HAVE VOWED NEVER TO READ THOSE BOOKS UNTIL WE'RE EIGHTEEN!
FOR REAL?
SORRY!
JUST A PEEK!
WE WANT TO SAVE THOSE BOOKS TO ENJOY WHEN WE'RE EIGHTEEN!
PHEW...
UME-CHAN ...
...CAME TO MY RESCUE MANY TIMES.
RIGHT, YURIKO?
OH WELL.
ALL-AGES WORKS ARE WEL-COME!

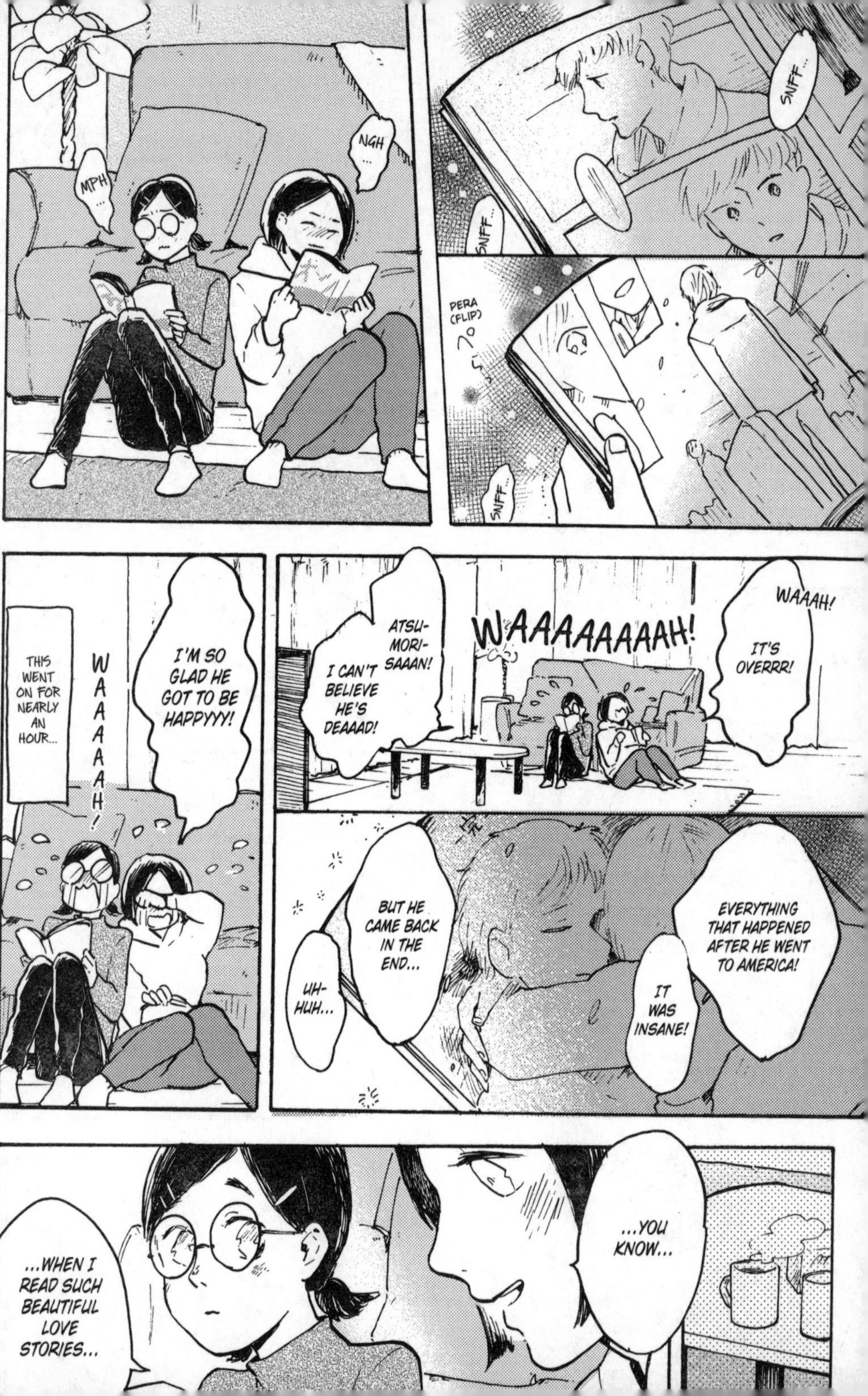
SNFF...
SNFF...
PERA (FLIP)
SNFF...
NGH...
MPH...
WAAAH! IT'S OVERRR!
WAAAAAAAAAH!
ATSU-MORI-SAAAN! I CAN'T BELIEVE HE'S DEAAAD!
EVERYTHING THAT HAPPENED AFTER HE WENT TO AMERICA!
IT WAS INSANE!
BUT HE CAME BACK IN THE END...
UH-HUH...
I'M SO GLAD HE GOT TO BE HAPPYYY!
WAAAAAAH!
THIS WENT ON FOR NEARLY AN HOUR...
...YOU KNOW...
...WHEN I READ SUCH BEAUTIFUL LOVE STORIES...

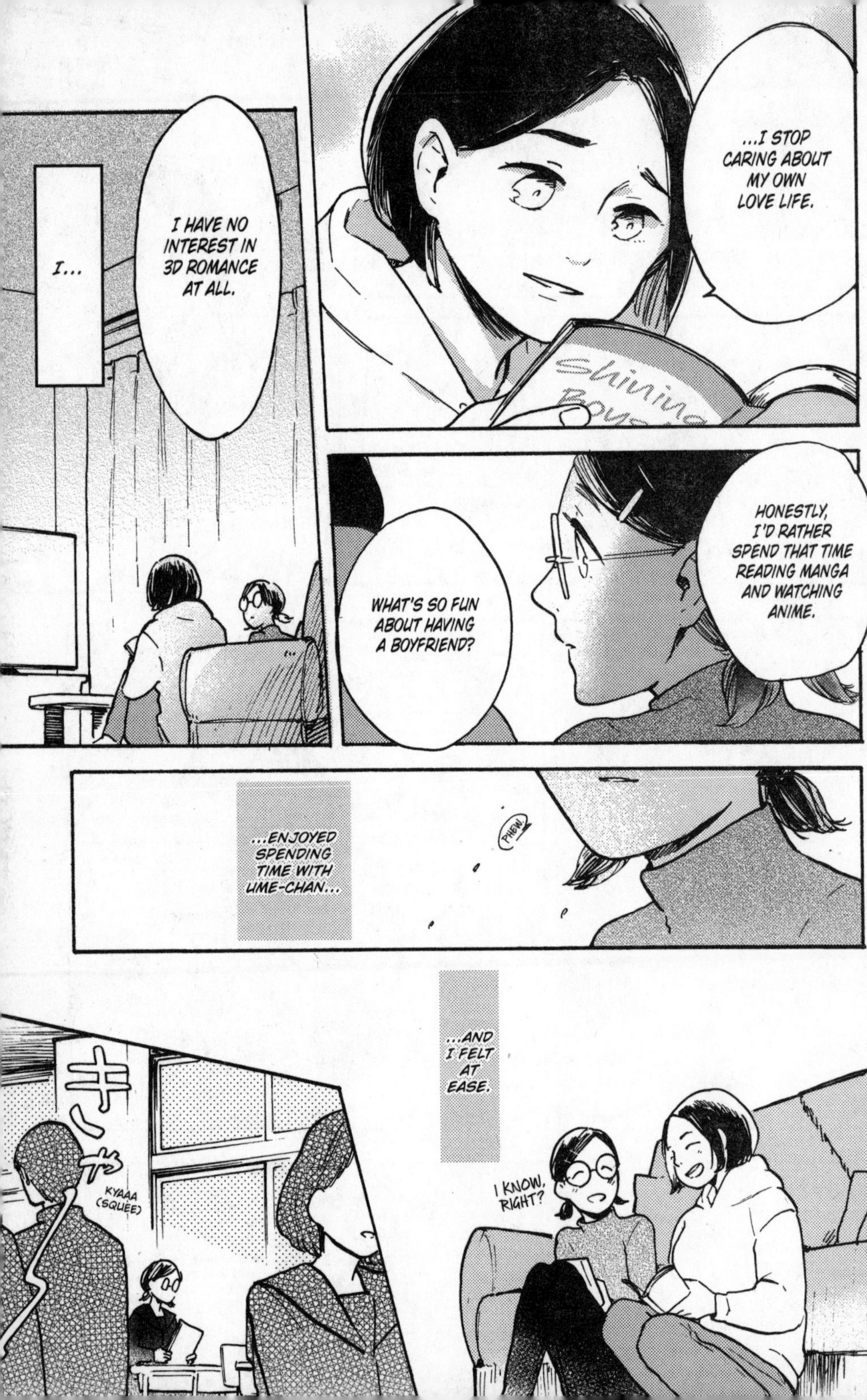
...I STOP CARING ABOUT MY OWN LOVE LIFE.
HONESTLY, I'D RATHER SPEND THAT TIME READING MANGA AND WATCHING ANIME.
WHAT'S SO FUN ABOUT HAVING A BOYFRIEND?
I HAVE NO INTEREST IN 3D ROMANCE AT ALL.
I...
PHEW
...ENJOYED SPENDING TIME WITH UME-CHAN...
...AND I FELT AT EASE.
I KNOW, RIGHT?
きゃ
KYAAA (SQUEE)

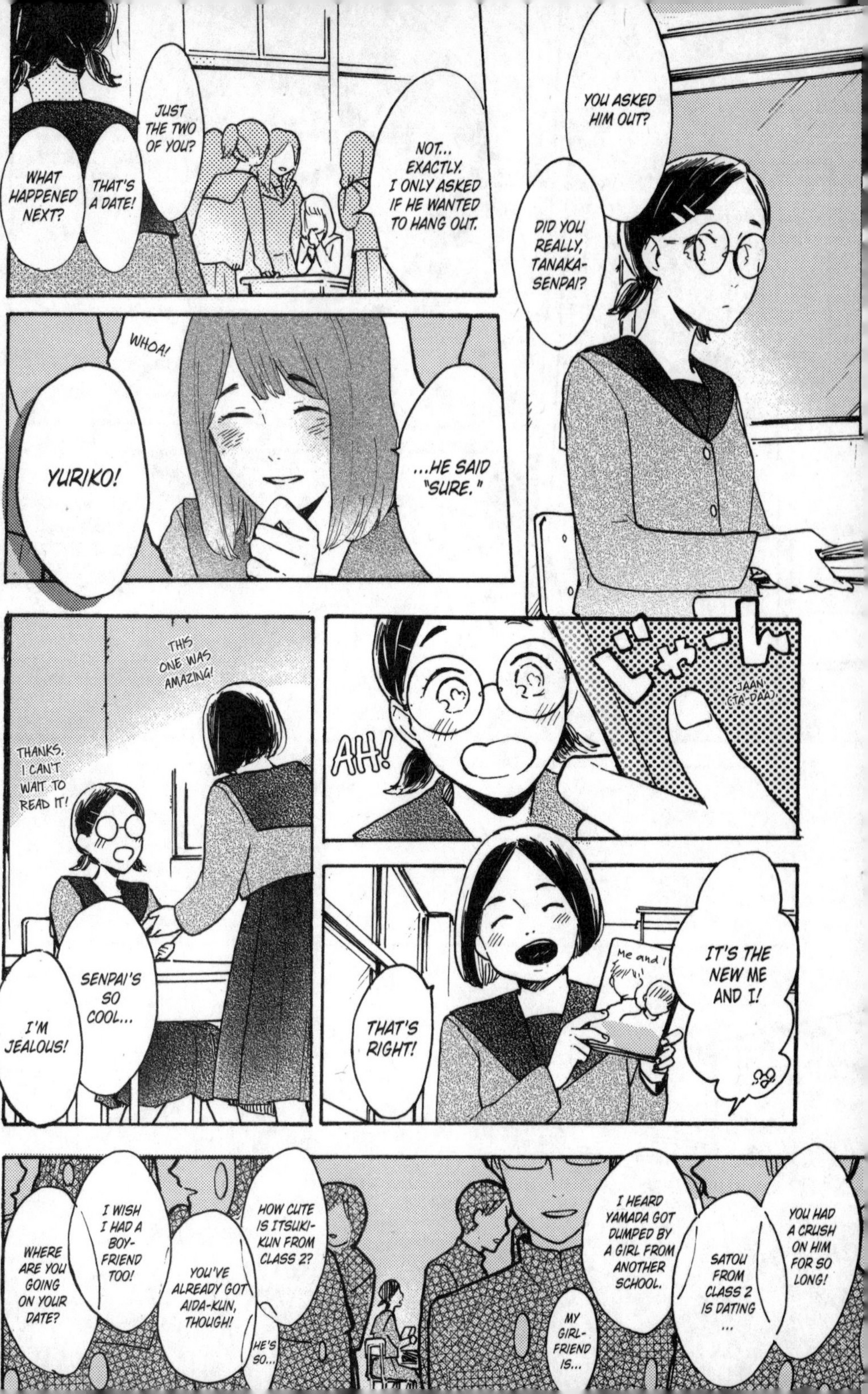
YOU ASKED HIM OUT?
DID YOU REALLY, TANAKA-SENPAI?
NOT... EXACTLY. I ONLY ASKED IF HE WANTED TO HANG OUT.
JUST THE TWO OF YOU?
THAT'S A DATE!
WHAT HAPPENED NEXT?
...HE SAID "SURE."
WHOA!
YURIKO!
じゃーん
JAAN (TA-DAA)
AH!
IT'S THE NEW ME AND I!
Me and I
THAT'S RIGHT!
THIS ONE WAS AMAZING!
THANKS, I CAN'T WAIT TO READ IT!
SENPAI'S SO COOL...
I'M JEALOUS!
YOU HAD A CRUSH ON HIM FOR SO LONG!
SATOU FROM CLASS 2 IS DATING...
I HEARD YAMADA GOT DUMPED BY A GIRL FROM ANOTHER SCHOOL.
MY GIRLFRIEND IS...
HOW CUTE IS ITSUKI-KUN FROM CLASS 2?
HE'S SO...
YOU'VE ALREADY GOT AIDA-KUN, THOUGH!
I WISH I HAD A BOYFRIEND TOO!
WHERE ARE YOU GOING ON YOUR DATE?

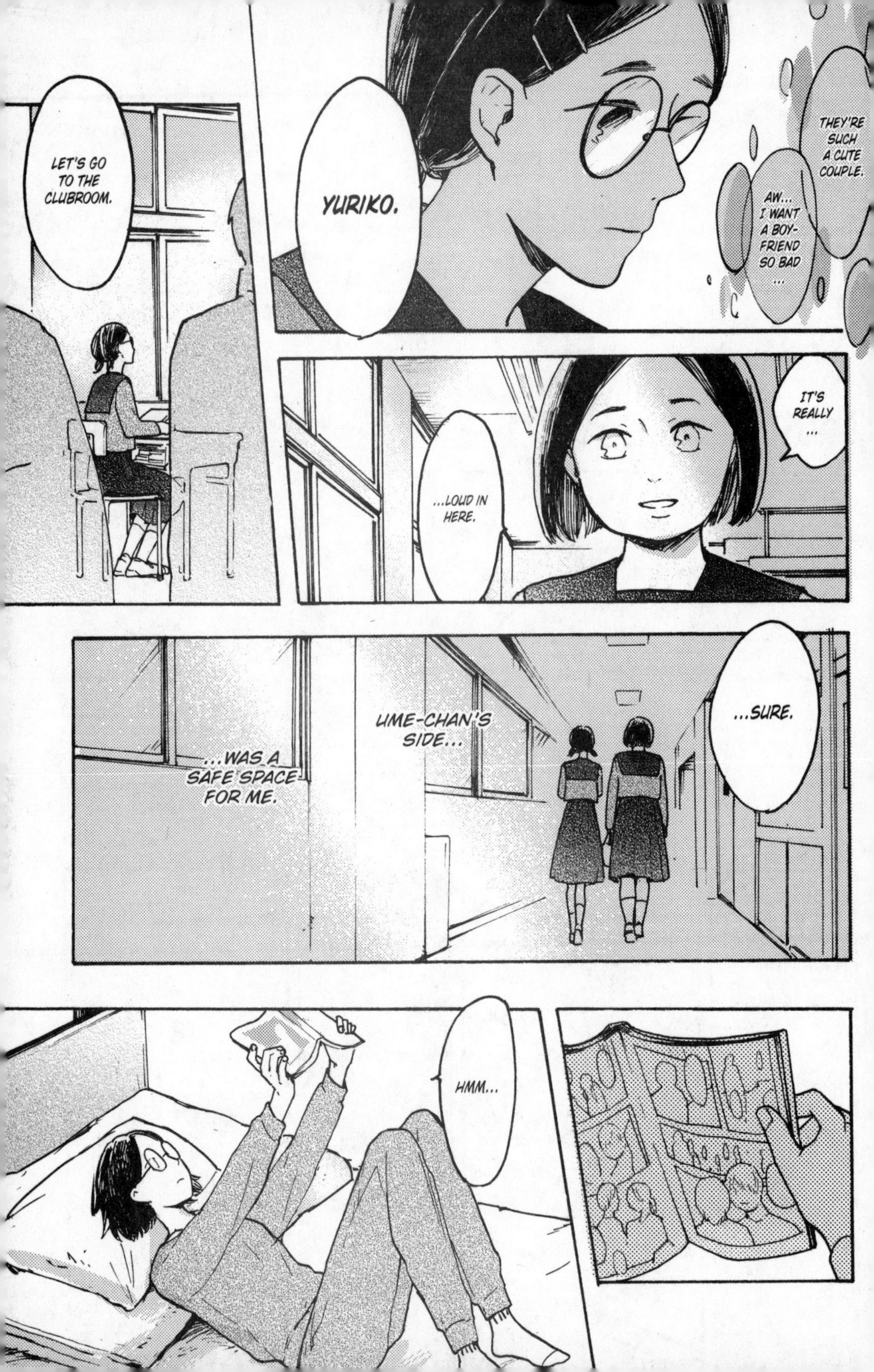
THEY'RE SUCH A CUTE COUPLE.
AW... I WANT A BOY-FRIEND SO BAD...
YURIKO.
IT'S REALLY...
...LOUD IN HERE.
LET'S GO TO THE CLUBROOM.
...SURE.
UME-CHAN'S SIDE...
...WAS A SAFE SPACE FOR ME.
HMM...

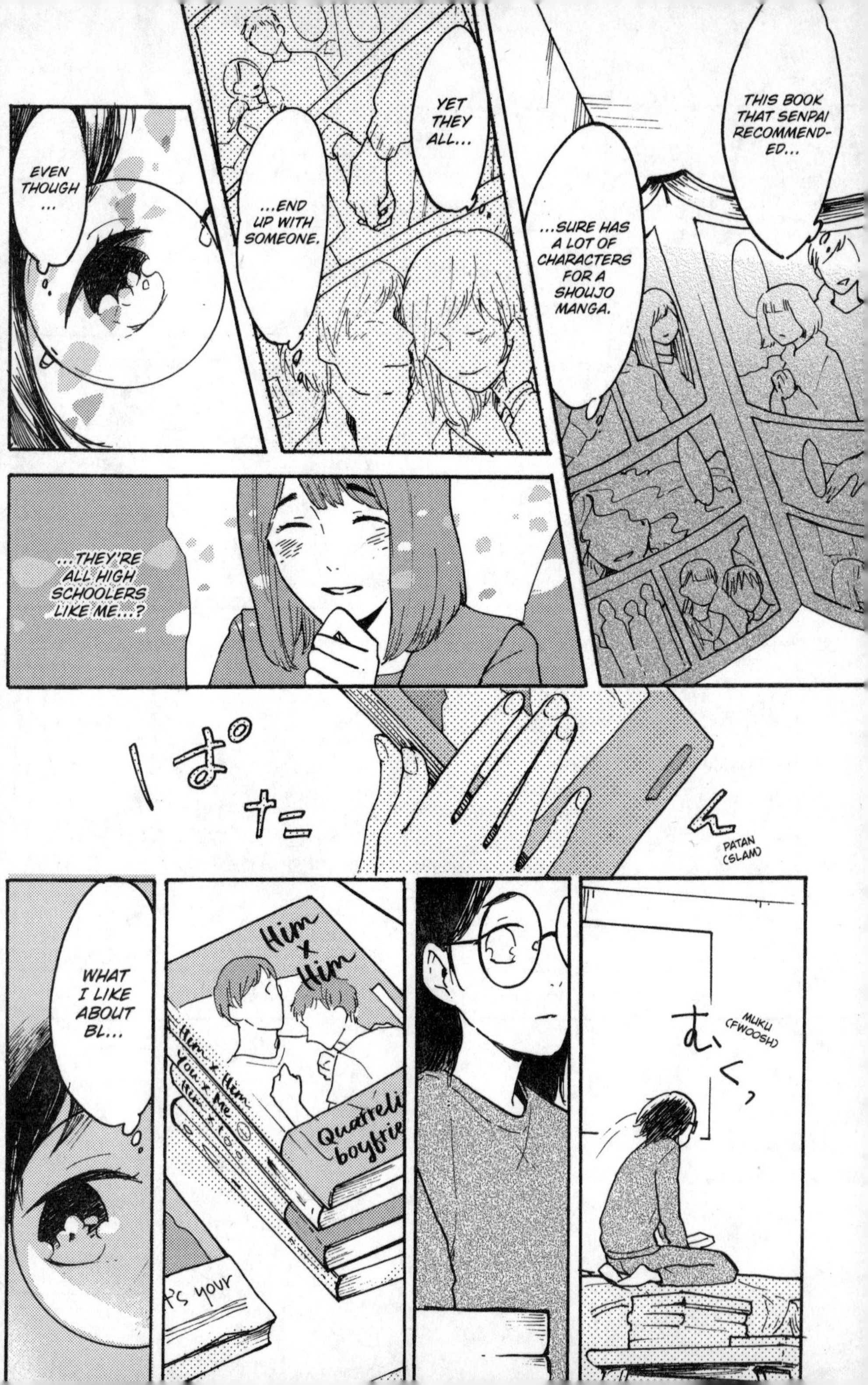
THIS BOOK THAT SENPAI RECOMMEND-ED...
...SURE HAS A LOT OF CHARACTERS FOR A SHOUJO MANGA.
YET THEY ALL...
...END UP WITH SOMEONE.
EVEN THOUGH ...
...THEY'RE ALL HIGH SCHOOLERS LIKE ME...?
ぱたん
PATAN (SLAM)
むくっ
MUKU (FWOOSH)
Him x Him
Him x Him
You x Me
WHAT I LIKE ABOUT BL...

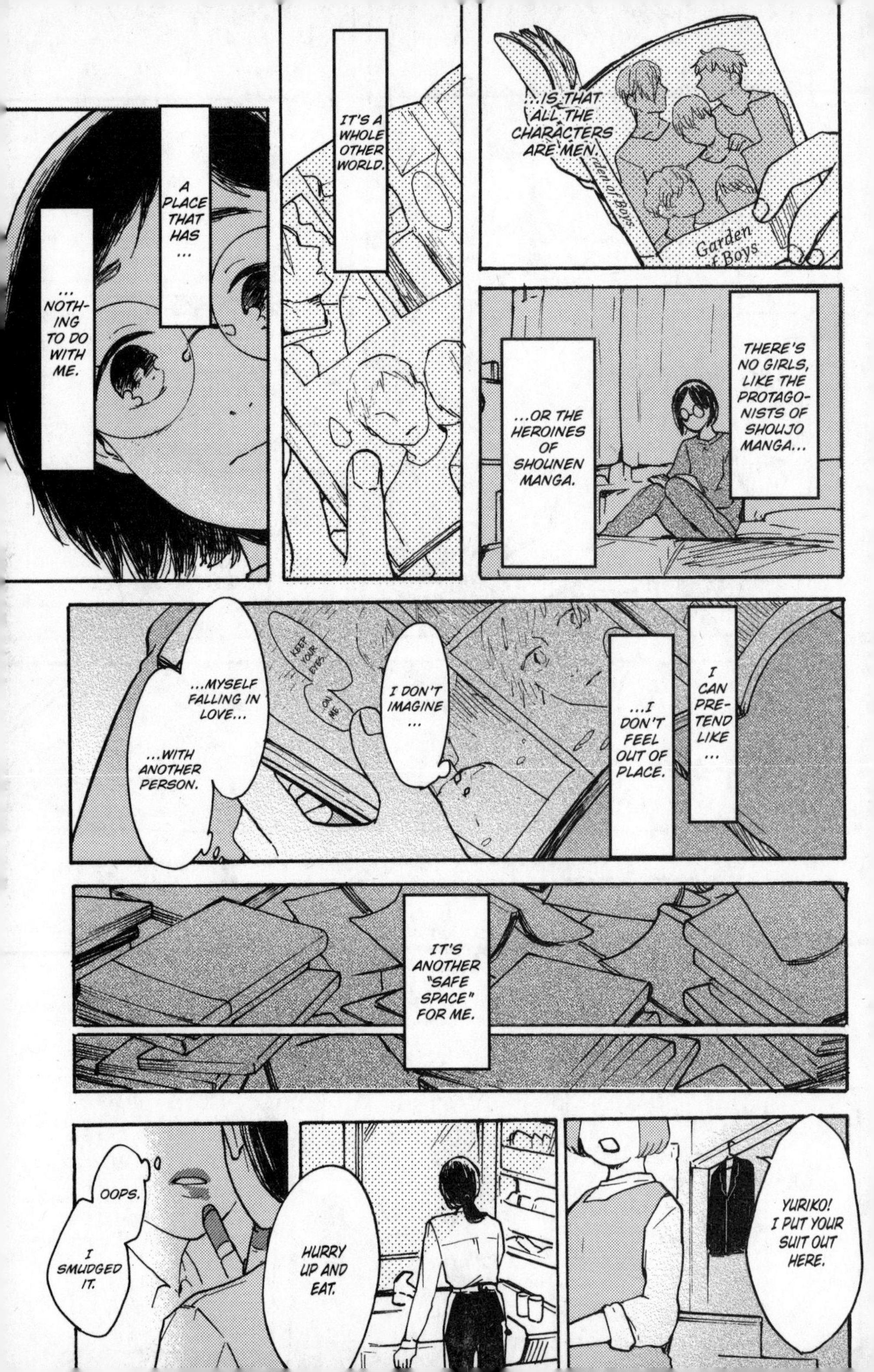

...IS THAT ALL THE CHARACTERS ARE MEN.
Garden of Boys
Garden of Boys
THERE'S NO GIRLS, LIKE THE PROTAGONISTS OF SHOUJO MANGA...
...OR THE HEROINES OF SHOUNEN MANGA.
IT'S A WHOLE OTHER WORLD.
A PLACE THAT HAS...
...NOTHING TO DO WITH ME.
I CAN PRETEND LIKE...
...I DON'T FEEL OUT OF PLACE.
I DON'T IMAGINE...
KEEP YOUR EYES ON ME
...MYSELF FALLING IN LOVE...
...WITH ANOTHER PERSON.
IT'S ANOTHER "SAFE SPACE" FOR ME.
YURIKO! I PUT YOUR SUIT OUT HERE.
HURRY UP AND EAT.
OOPS.
I SMUDGED IT.

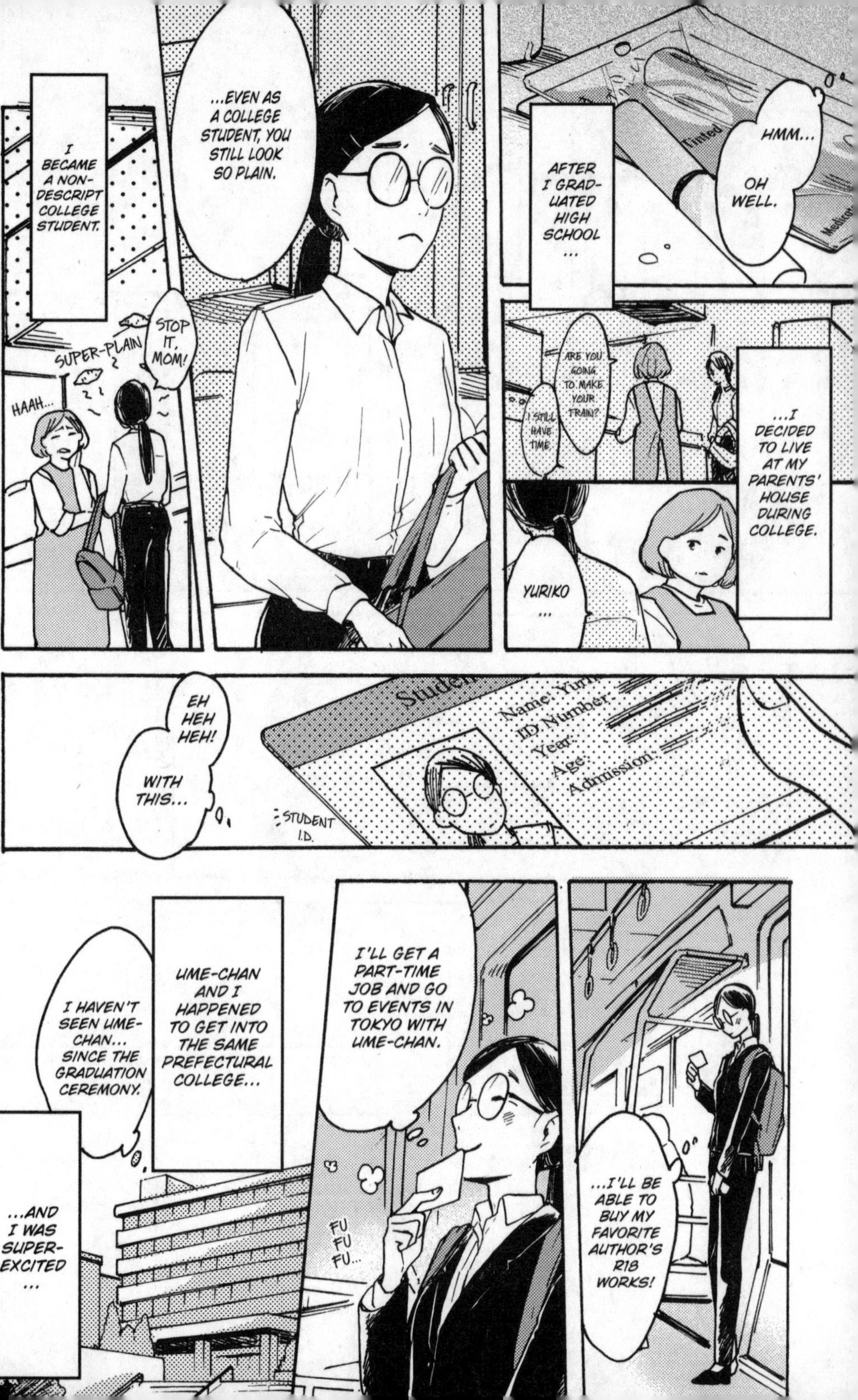
HMM... OH WELL.
AFTER I GRADUATED HIGH SCHOOL...
ARE YOU GOING TO MAKE YOUR TRAIN?
I STILL HAVE TIME.
...I DECIDED TO LIVE AT MY PARENTS' HOUSE DURING COLLEGE.
YURIKO...
...EVEN AS A COLLEGE STUDENT, YOU STILL LOOK SO PLAIN.
STOP IT, MOM!
SUPER-PLAIN
HAAH...
I BECAME A NONDESCRIPT COLLEGE STUDENT.
Name:
ID Number:
Year:
Age:
Admission:
STUDENT I.D.
EH HEH HEH!
WITH THIS...
...I'LL BE ABLE TO BUY MY FAVORITE AUTHOR'S R18 WORKS!
I'LL GET A PART-TIME JOB AND GO TO EVENTS IN TOKYO WITH UME-CHAN.
FU FU FU...
UME-CHAN AND I HAPPENED TO GET INTO THE SAME PREFECTURAL COLLEGE...
I HAVEN'T SEEN UME-CHAN... SINCE THE GRADUATION CEREMONY.
...AND I WAS SUPER-EXCITED...

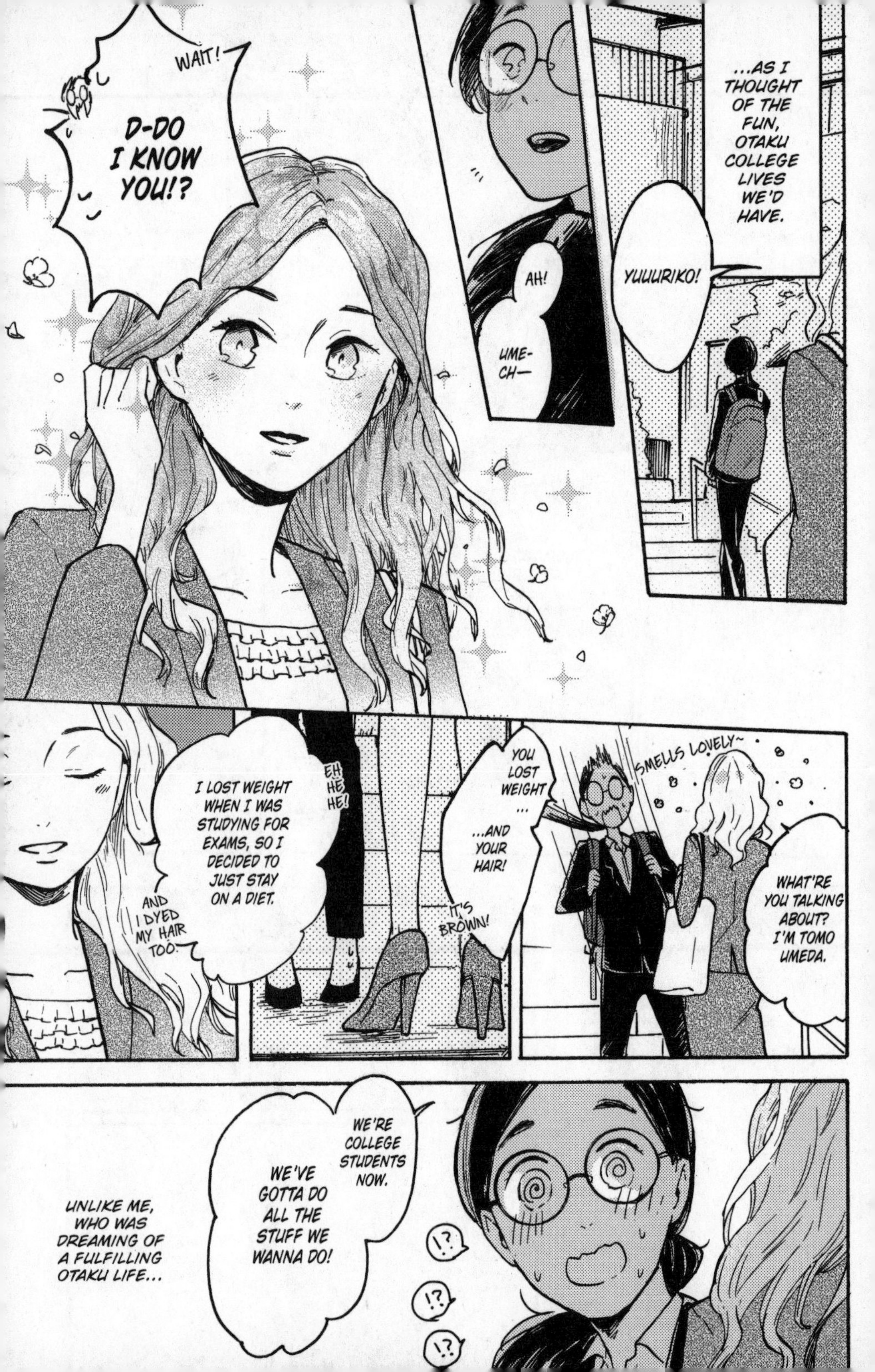
...AS I THOUGHT OF THE FUN, OTAKU COLLEGE LIVES WE'D HAVE.
YUUURIKO!
AH!
UME-CH—
WAIT!
D-DO I KNOW YOU!?
SMELLS LOVELY~
WHAT'RE YOU TALKING ABOUT? I'M TOMO UMEDA.
YOU LOST WEIGHT...
...AND YOUR HAIR!
IT'S BROWN!
EH HE HE!
I LOST WEIGHT WHEN I WAS STUDYING FOR EXAMS, SO I DECIDED TO JUST STAY ON A DIET.
AND I DYED MY HAIR TOO.
WE'RE COLLEGE STUDENTS NOW.
WE'VE GOTTA DO ALL THE STUFF WE WANNA DO!
!?
!?
!?
UNLIKE ME, WHO WAS DREAMING OF A FULFILLING OTAKU LIFE...

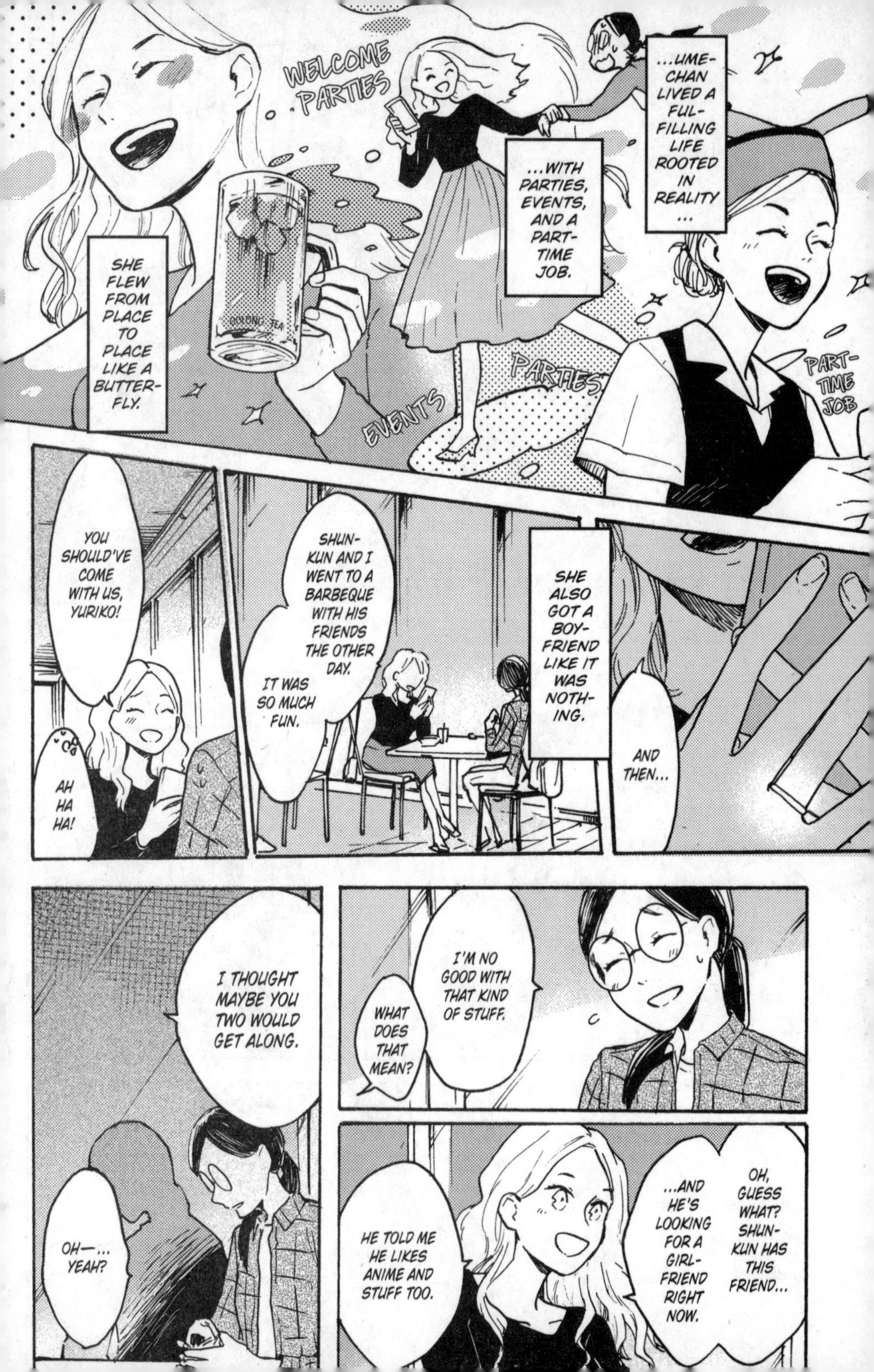
...UME-CHAN LIVED A FUL-FILLING LIFE ROOTED IN REALITY...
...WITH PARTIES, EVENTS, AND A PART-TIME JOB.
WELCOME PARTIES
SHE FLEW FROM PLACE TO PLACE LIKE A BUTTER-FLY.
PART-TIME JOB
PARTIES
EVENTS
OOLONG TEA
SHE ALSO GOT A BOY-FRIEND LIKE IT WAS NOTH-ING.
AND THEN...
SHUN-KUN AND I WENT TO A BARBEQUE WITH HIS FRIENDS THE OTHER DAY.
IT WAS SO MUCH FUN.
YOU SHOULD'VE COME WITH US, YURIKO!
AH HA HA!
I'M NO GOOD WITH THAT KIND OF STUFF.
WHAT DOES THAT MEAN?
OH, GUESS WHAT? SHUN-KUN HAS THIS FRIEND...
...AND HE'S LOOKING FOR A GIRL-FRIEND RIGHT NOW.
HE TOLD ME HE LIKES ANIME AND STUFF TOO.
I THOUGHT MAYBE YOU TWO WOULD GET ALONG.
OH—... YEAH?

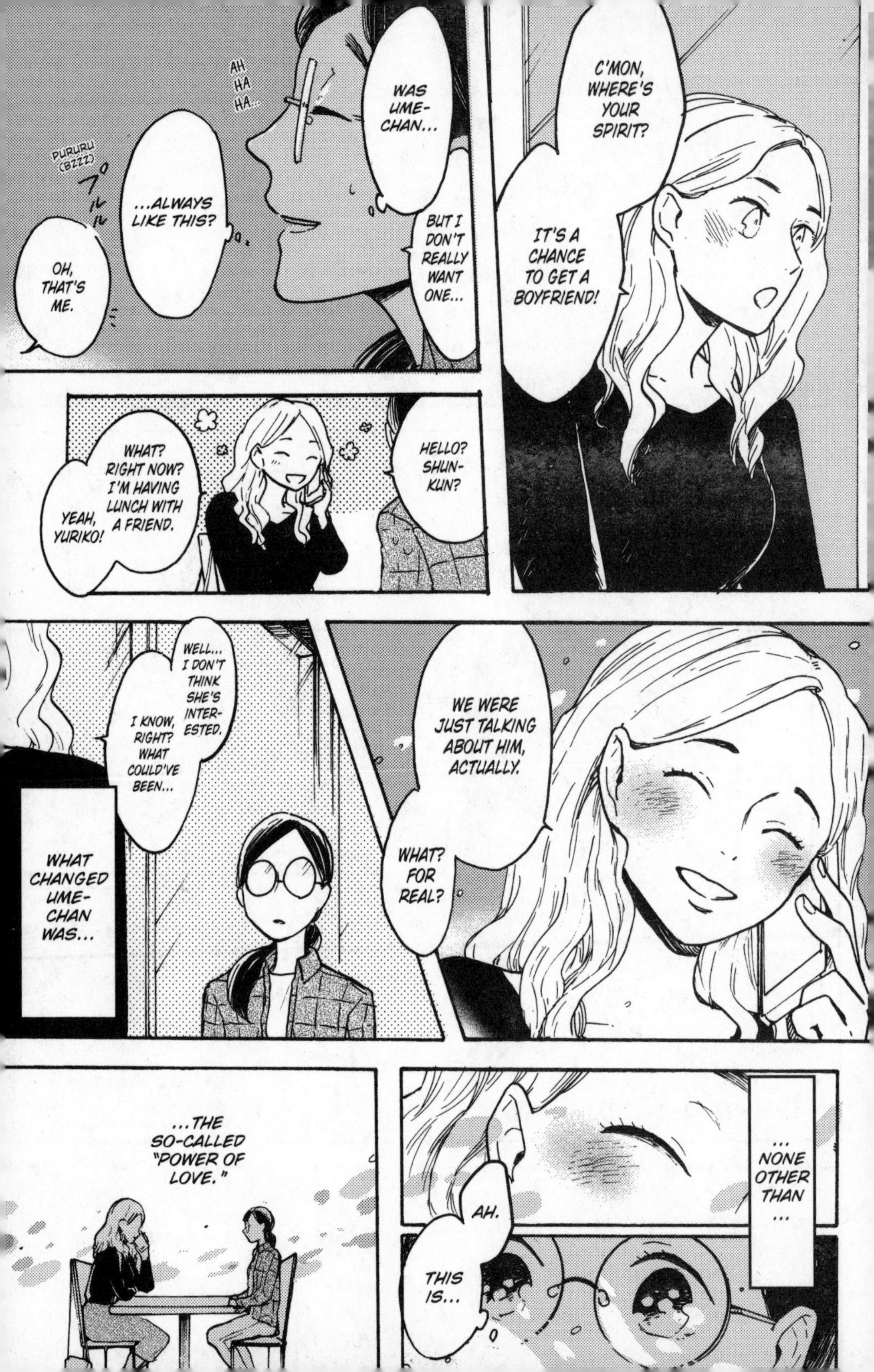
C'MON, WHERE'S YOUR SPIRIT?
IT'S A CHANCE TO GET A BOYFRIEND!
WAS UME-CHAN...
BUT I DON'T REALLY WANT ONE...
AH HA HA...
...ALWAYS LIKE THIS?
プルル
PURURU (BZZZ)
OH, THAT'S ME.
HELLO? SHUN-KUN?
YEAH, YURIKO!
WHAT? RIGHT NOW? I'M HAVING LUNCH WITH A FRIEND.
WE WERE JUST TALKING ABOUT HIM, ACTUALLY.
WHAT? FOR REAL?
WELL... I DON'T THINK SHE'S INTER-ESTED.
I KNOW, RIGHT? WHAT COULD'VE BEEN...
WHAT CHANGED UME-CHAN WAS...
...NONE OTHER THAN...
AH.
THIS IS...
...THE SO-CALLED "POWER OF LOVE."

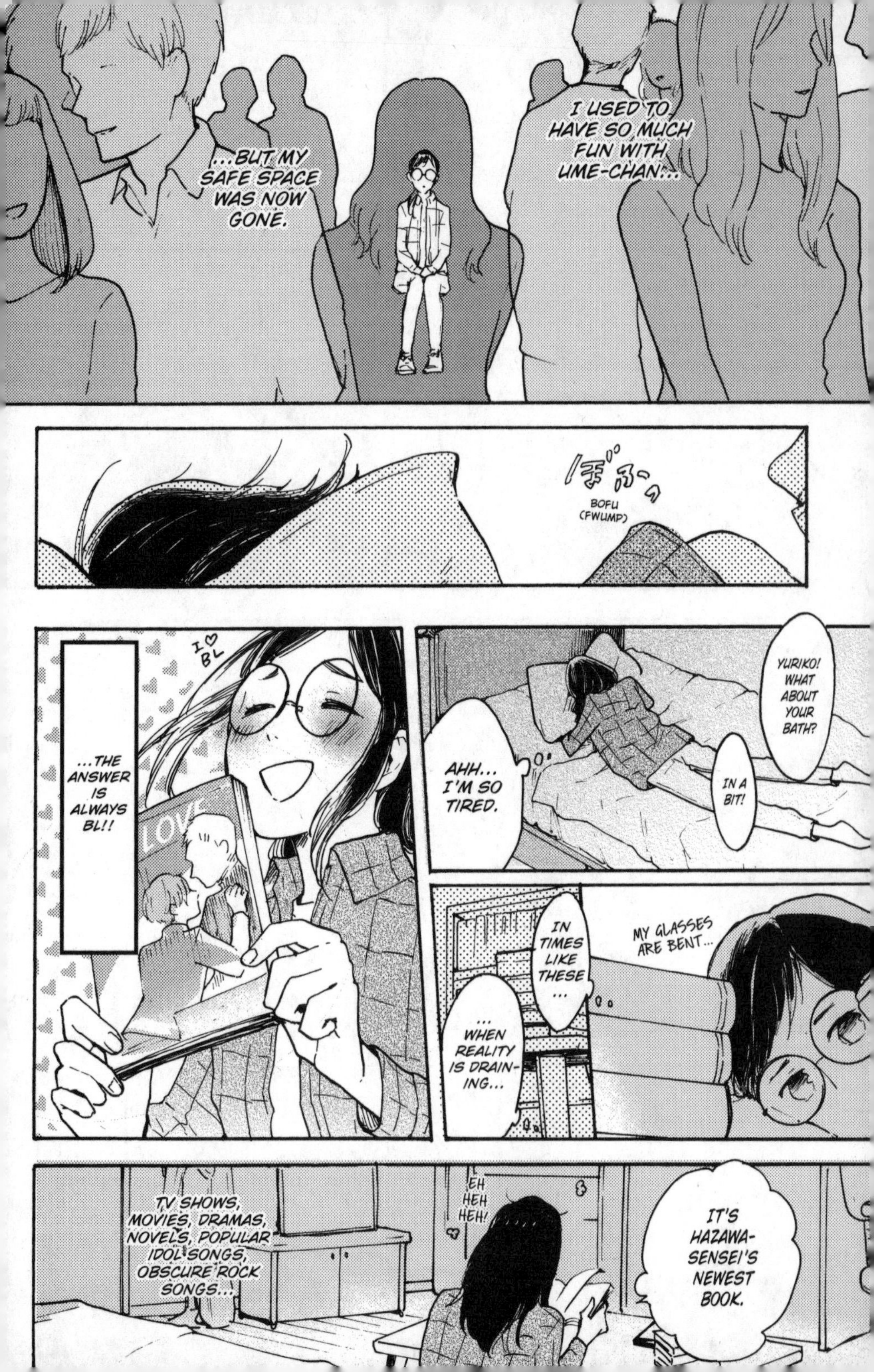
I USED TO HAVE SO MUCH FUN WITH UME-CHAN...
...BUT MY SAFE SPACE WAS NOW GONE.
ぼふっ
BOFU (FWUMP)
YURIKO! WHAT ABOUT YOUR BATH?
IN A BIT!
AHH... I'M SO TIRED.
MY GLASSES ARE BENT...
IN TIMES LIKE THESE...
...WHEN REALITY IS DRAINING...
I ♡ BL
...THE ANSWER IS ALWAYS BL!!
LOVE
IT'S HAZAWA-SENSEI'S NEWEST BOOK.
EH HEH HEH!
TV SHOWS, MOVIES, DRAMAS, NOVELS, POPULAR IDOL SONGS, OBSCURE ROCK SONGS...

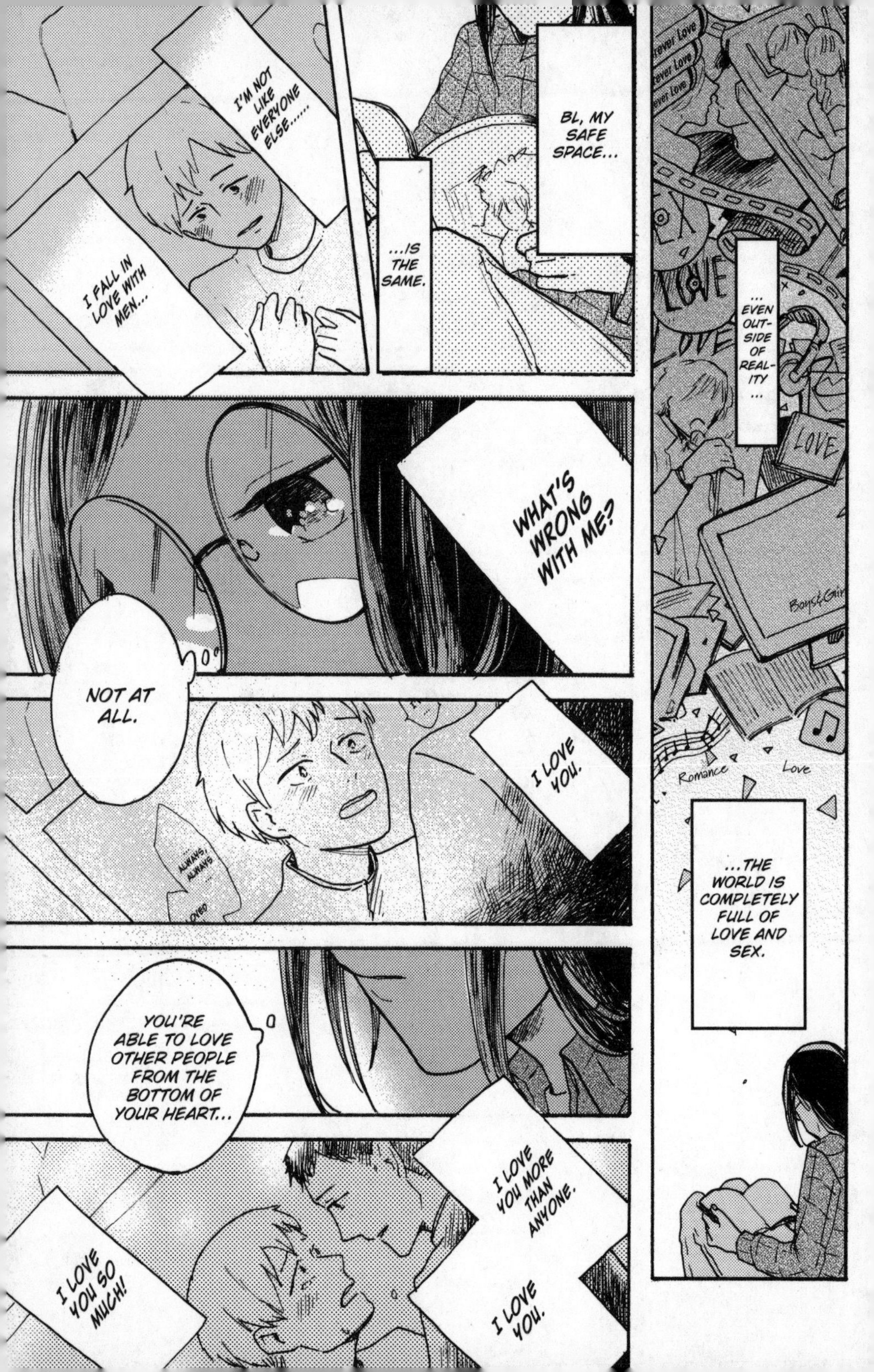
LOVE
LOVE
LOVE
...EVEN OUTSIDE OF REALITY...
Romance
Love
...THE WORLD IS COMPLETELY FULL OF LOVE AND SEX.
BL, MY SAFE SPACE...
...IS THE SAME.
I'M NOT LIKE EVERYONE ELSE......
I FALL IN LOVE WITH MEN...
WHAT'S WRONG WITH ME?
NOT AT ALL.
I LOVE YOU.
ALWAYS, ALWAYS
YOU'RE ABLE TO LOVE OTHER PEOPLE FROM THE BOTTOM OF YOUR HEART...
I LOVE YOU MORE THAN ANYONE.
I LOVE YOU.
I LOVE YOU SO MUCH!

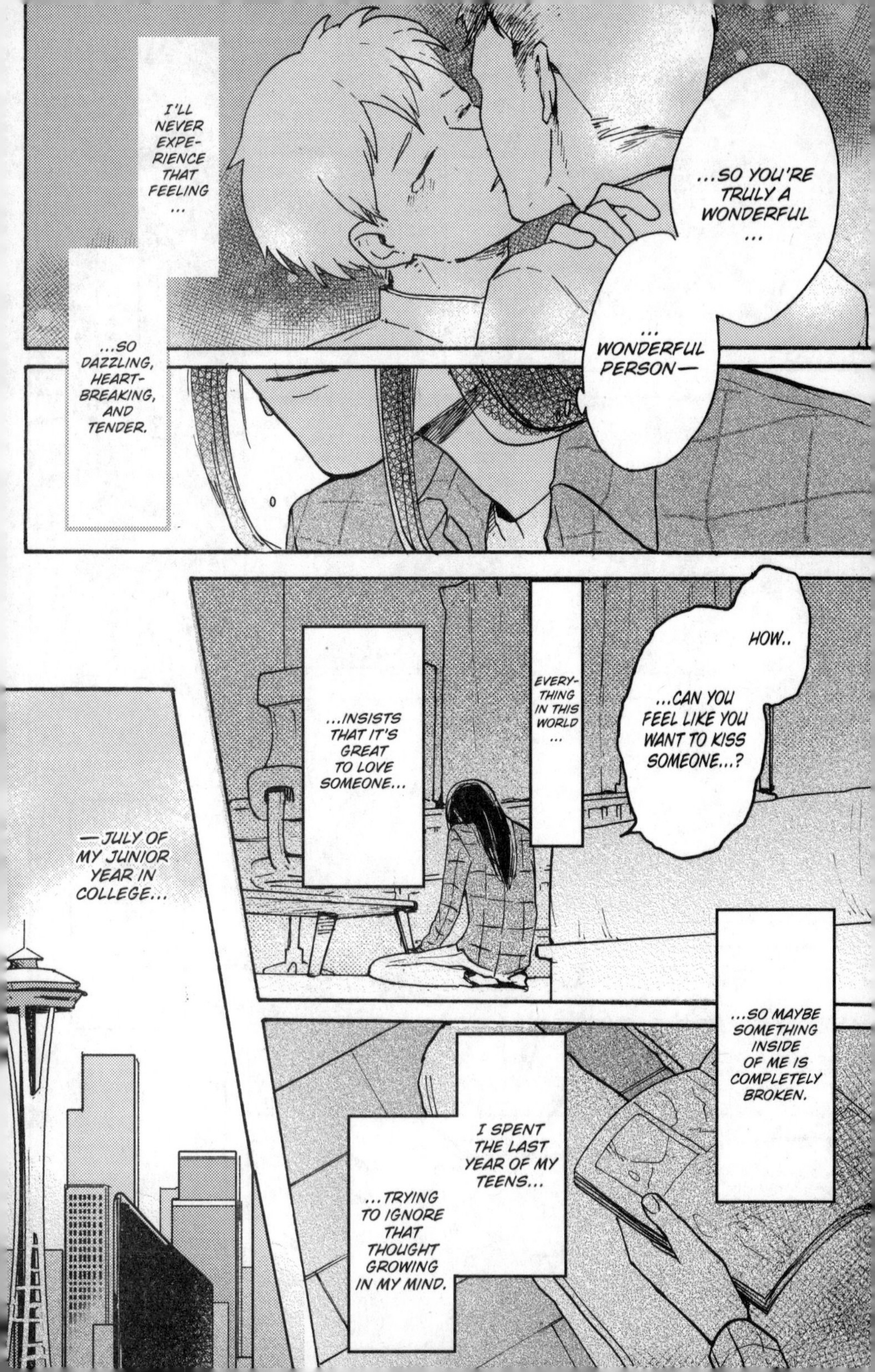
...SO YOU'RE TRULY A WONDERFUL ...
I'LL NEVER EXPERIENCE THAT FEELING ...
... WONDERFUL PERSON—
...SO DAZZLING, HEART-BREAKING, AND TENDER.
HOW..
...CAN YOU FEEL LIKE YOU WANT TO KISS SOMEONE...?
EVERYTHING IN THIS WORLD ...
...INSISTS THAT IT'S GREAT TO LOVE SOMEONE...
...SO MAYBE SOMETHING INSIDE OF ME IS COMPLETELY BROKEN.
I SPENT THE LAST YEAR OF MY TEENS...
...TRYING TO IGNORE THAT THOUGHT GROWING IN MY MIND.
—JULY OF MY JUNIOR YEAR IN COLLEGE...

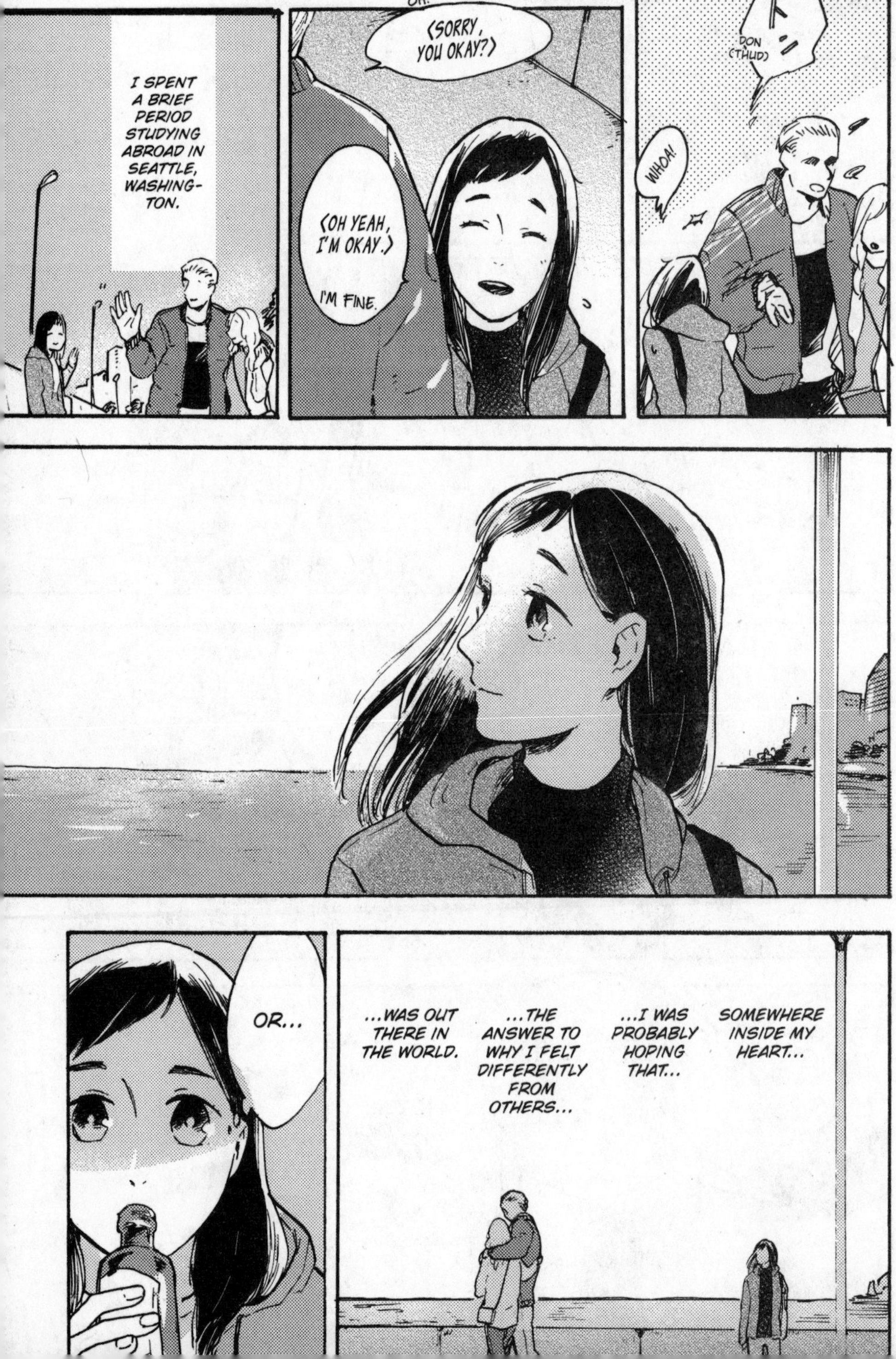
DON (THUD)
WHOA!
OH!
<SORRY, YOU OKAY?>
<OH YEAH, I'M OKAY.>
I'M FINE.
I SPENT A BRIEF PERIOD STUDYING ABROAD IN SEATTLE, WASHINGTON.
SOMEWHERE INSIDE MY HEART...
...I WAS PROBABLY HOPING THAT...
...THE ANSWER TO WHY I FELT DIFFERENTLY FROM OTHERS...
...WAS OUT THERE IN THE WORLD.
OR...

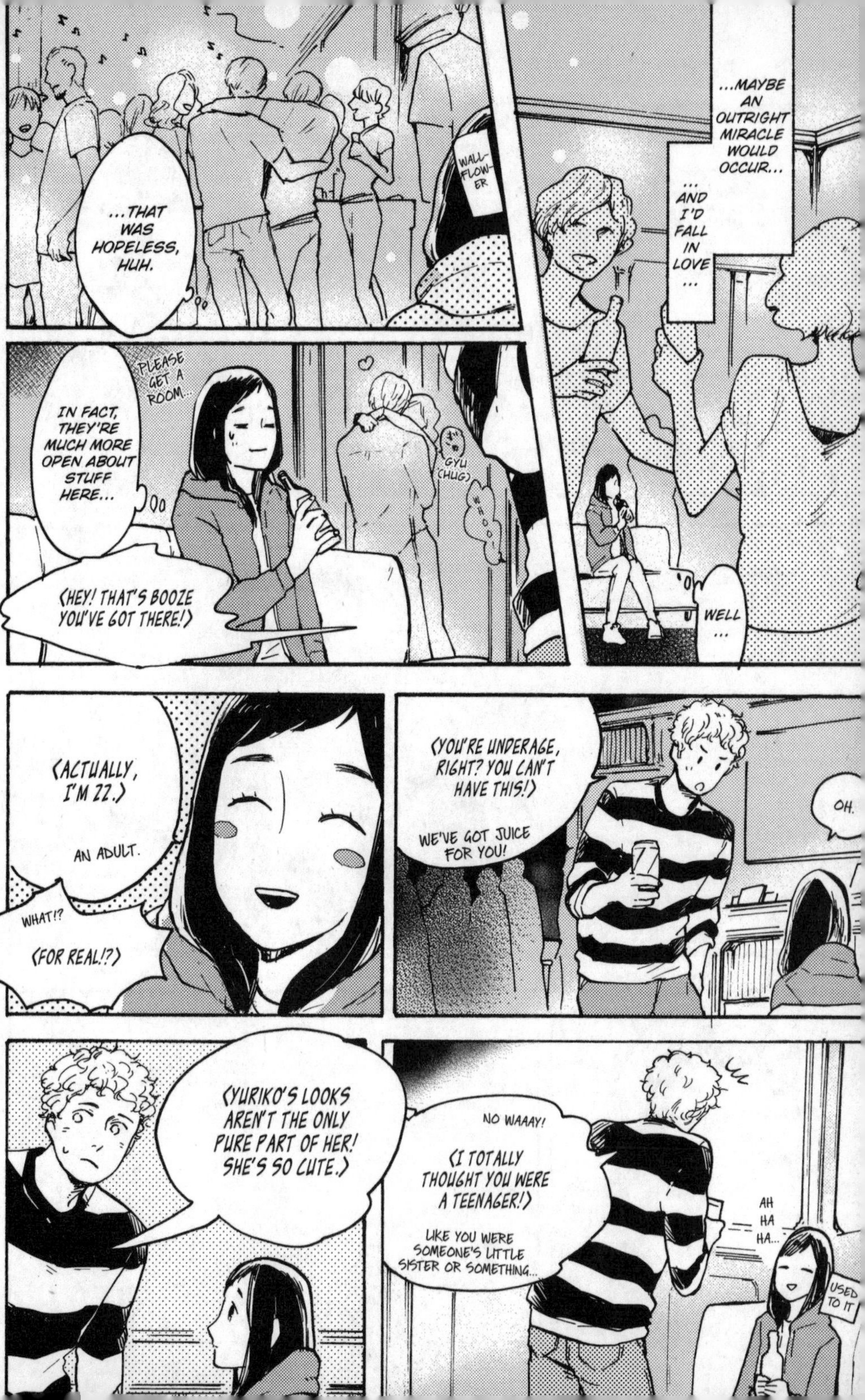

...MAYBE AN OUTRIGHT MIRACLE WOULD OCCUR...
...AND I'D FALL IN LOVE...
WELL...
WALL-FLOWER
...THAT WAS HOPELESS, HUH.
GYU (HUG)
WHOO
PLEASE GET A ROOM...
IN FACT, THEY'RE MUCH MORE OPEN ABOUT STUFF HERE...
〈HEY! THAT'S BOOZE YOU'VE GOT THERE!〉
OH.
〈YOU'RE UNDERAGE, RIGHT? YOU CAN'T HAVE THIS!〉
WE'VE GOT JUICE FOR YOU!
〈ACTUALLY, I'M 22.〉
AN ADULT.
WHAT!?
〈FOR REAL!?〉
NO WAAAY!
〈I TOTALLY THOUGHT YOU WERE A TEENAGER!〉
AH HA HA...
LIKE YOU WERE SOMEONE'S LITTLE SISTER OR SOMETHING...
USED TO IT
〈YURIKO'S LOOKS AREN'T THE ONLY PURE PART OF HER! SHE'S SO CUTE.〉

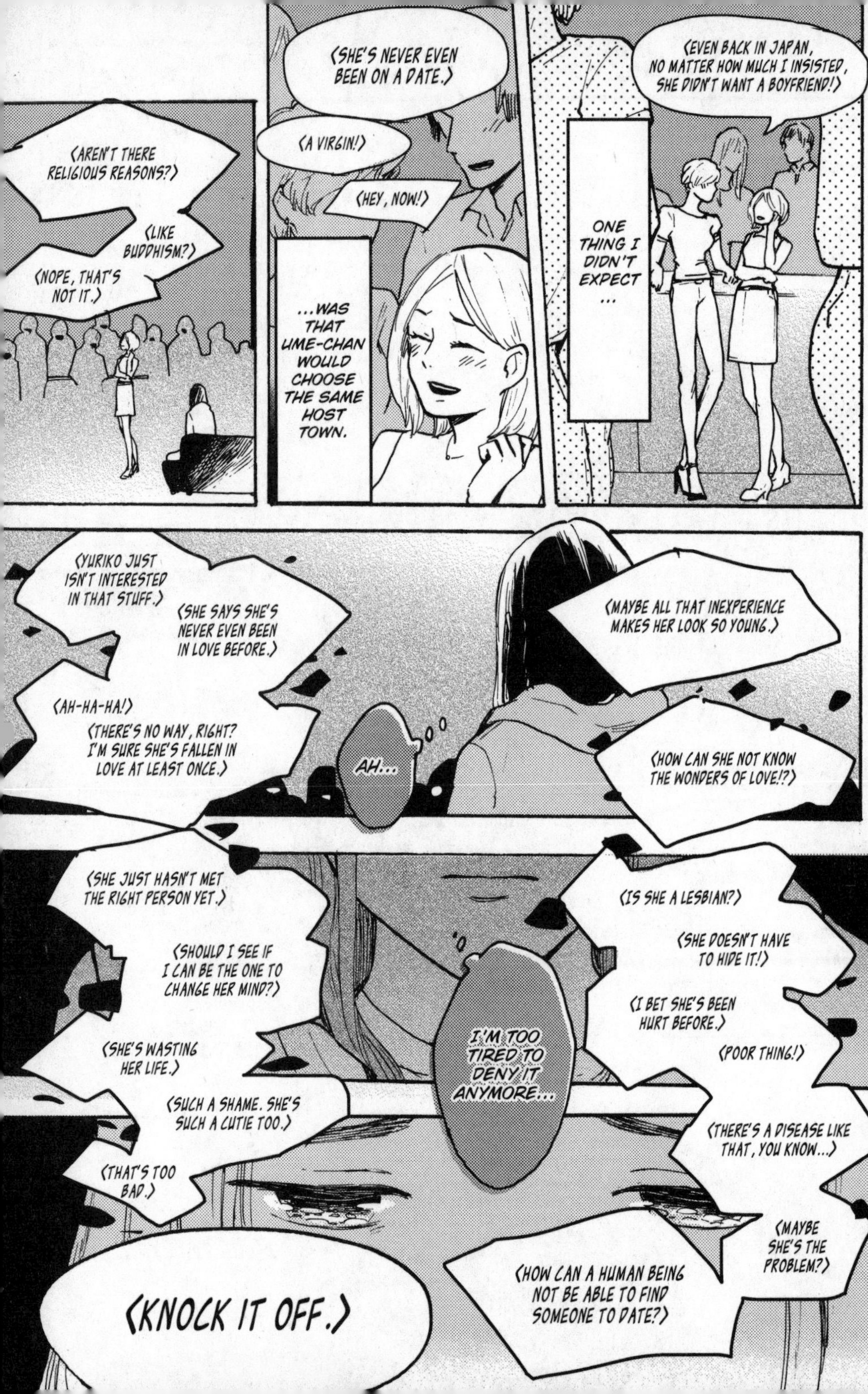
⟨EVEN BACK IN JAPAN, NO MATTER HOW MUCH I INSISTED, SHE DIDN'T WANT A BOYFRIEND!⟩
ONE THING I DIDN'T EXPECT ...
⟨SHE'S NEVER EVEN BEEN ON A DATE.⟩
⟨A VIRGIN!⟩
⟨HEY, NOW!⟩
...WAS THAT UME-CHAN WOULD CHOOSE THE SAME HOST TOWN.
⟨AREN'T THERE RELIGIOUS REASONS?⟩
⟨LIKE BUDDHISM?⟩
⟨NOPE, THAT'S NOT IT.⟩
⟨MAYBE ALL THAT INEXPERIENCE MAKES HER LOOK SO YOUNG.⟩
⟨HOW CAN SHE NOT KNOW THE WONDERS OF LOVE!?⟩
AH...
⟨YURIKO JUST ISN'T INTERESTED IN THAT STUFF.⟩
⟨SHE SAYS SHE'S NEVER EVEN BEEN IN LOVE BEFORE.⟩
⟨AH-HA-HA!⟩
⟨THERE'S NO WAY, RIGHT? I'M SURE SHE'S FALLEN IN LOVE AT LEAST ONCE.⟩
⟨IS SHE A LESBIAN?⟩
⟨SHE DOESN'T HAVE TO HIDE IT!⟩
⟨I BET SHE'S BEEN HURT BEFORE.⟩
⟨POOR THING!⟩
⟨THERE'S A DISEASE LIKE THAT, YOU KNOW...⟩
⟨MAYBE SHE'S THE PROBLEM?⟩
⟨HOW CAN A HUMAN BEING NOT BE ABLE TO FIND SOMEONE TO DATE?⟩
I'M TOO TIRED TO DENY IT ANYMORE...
⟨SHE JUST HASN'T MET THE RIGHT PERSON YET.⟩
⟨SHOULD I SEE IF I CAN BE THE ONE TO CHANGE HER MIND?⟩
⟨SHE'S WASTING HER LIFE.⟩
⟨SUCH A SHAME. SHE'S SUCH A CUTIE TOO.⟩
⟨THAT'S TOO BAD.⟩
⟨KNOCK IT OFF.⟩

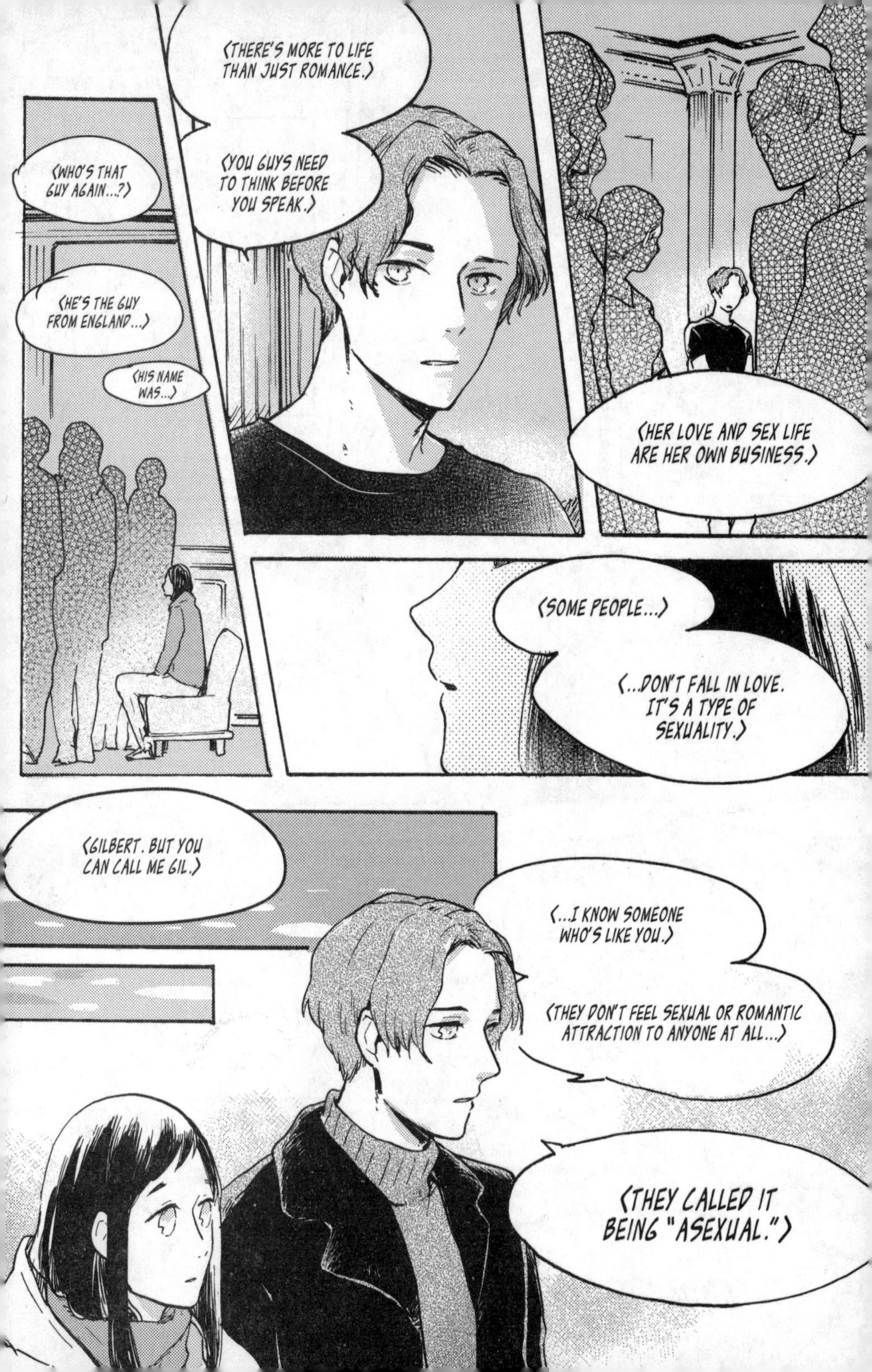

〈HER LOVE AND SEX LIFE ARE HER OWN BUSINESS.〉
〈THERE'S MORE TO LIFE THAN JUST ROMANCE.〉
〈YOU GUYS NEED TO THINK BEFORE YOU SPEAK.〉
〈SOME PEOPLE...〉
〈...DON'T FALL IN LOVE. IT'S A TYPE OF SEXUALITY.〉
〈WHO'S THAT GUY AGAIN...?〉
〈HE'S THE GUY FROM ENGLAND...〉
〈HIS NAME WAS...〉
〈GILBERT. BUT YOU CAN CALL ME GIL.〉
〈...I KNOW SOMEONE WHO'S LIKE YOU.〉
〈THEY DON'T FEEL SEXUAL OR ROMANTIC ATTRACTION TO ANYONE AT ALL...〉
〈THEY CALLED IT BEING "ASEXUAL."〉

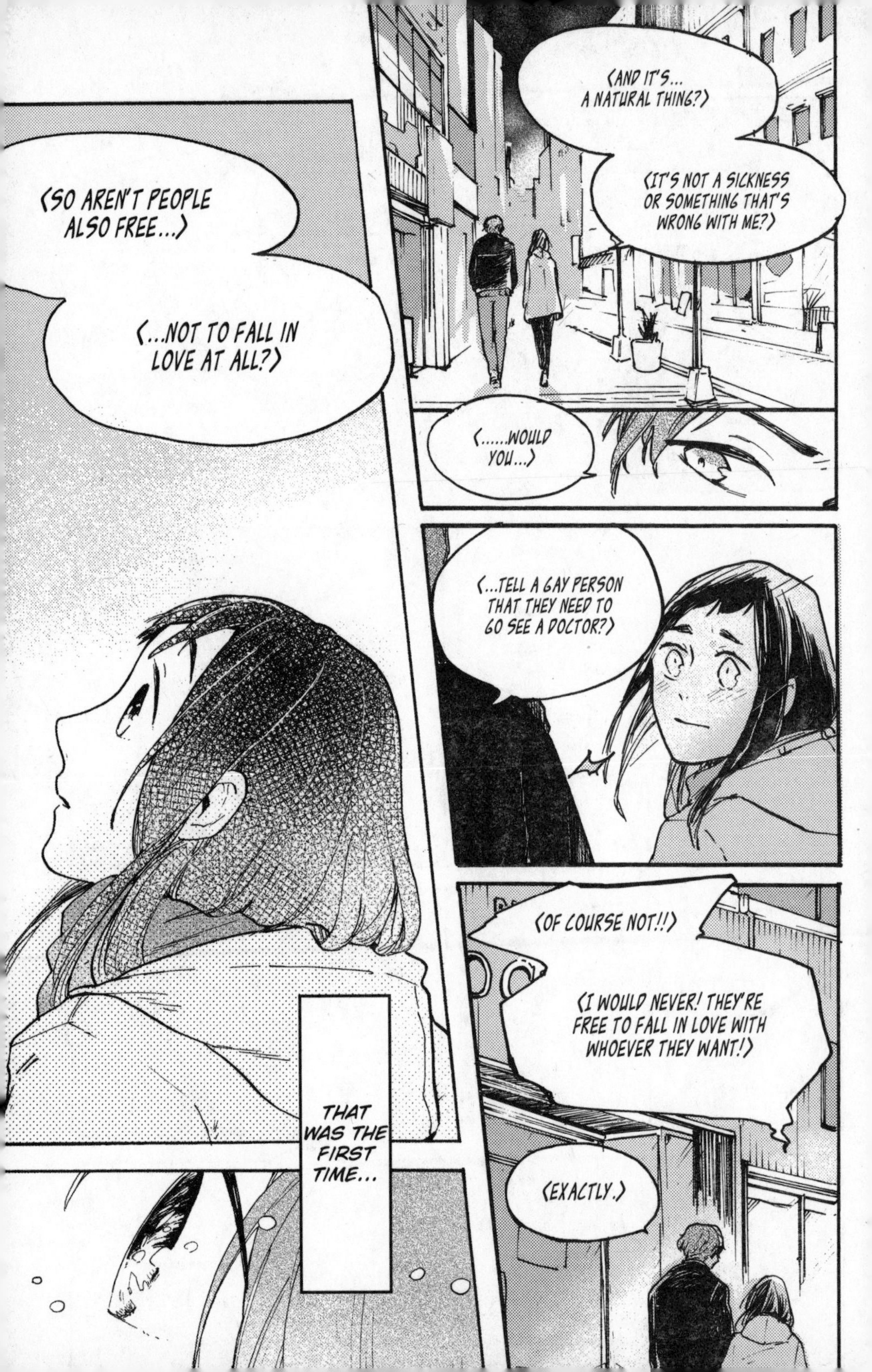
‹AND IT'S... A NATURAL THING?›
‹IT'S NOT A SICKNESS OR SOMETHING THAT'S WRONG WITH ME?›
‹......WOULD YOU...›
‹...TELL A GAY PERSON THAT THEY NEED TO GO SEE A DOCTOR?›
‹OF COURSE NOT!!›
‹I WOULD NEVER! THEY'RE FREE TO FALL IN LOVE WITH WHOEVER THEY WANT!›
‹EXACTLY.›
‹SO AREN'T PEOPLE ALSO FREE...›
‹...NOT TO FALL IN LOVE AT ALL?›
THAT WAS THE FIRST TIME...

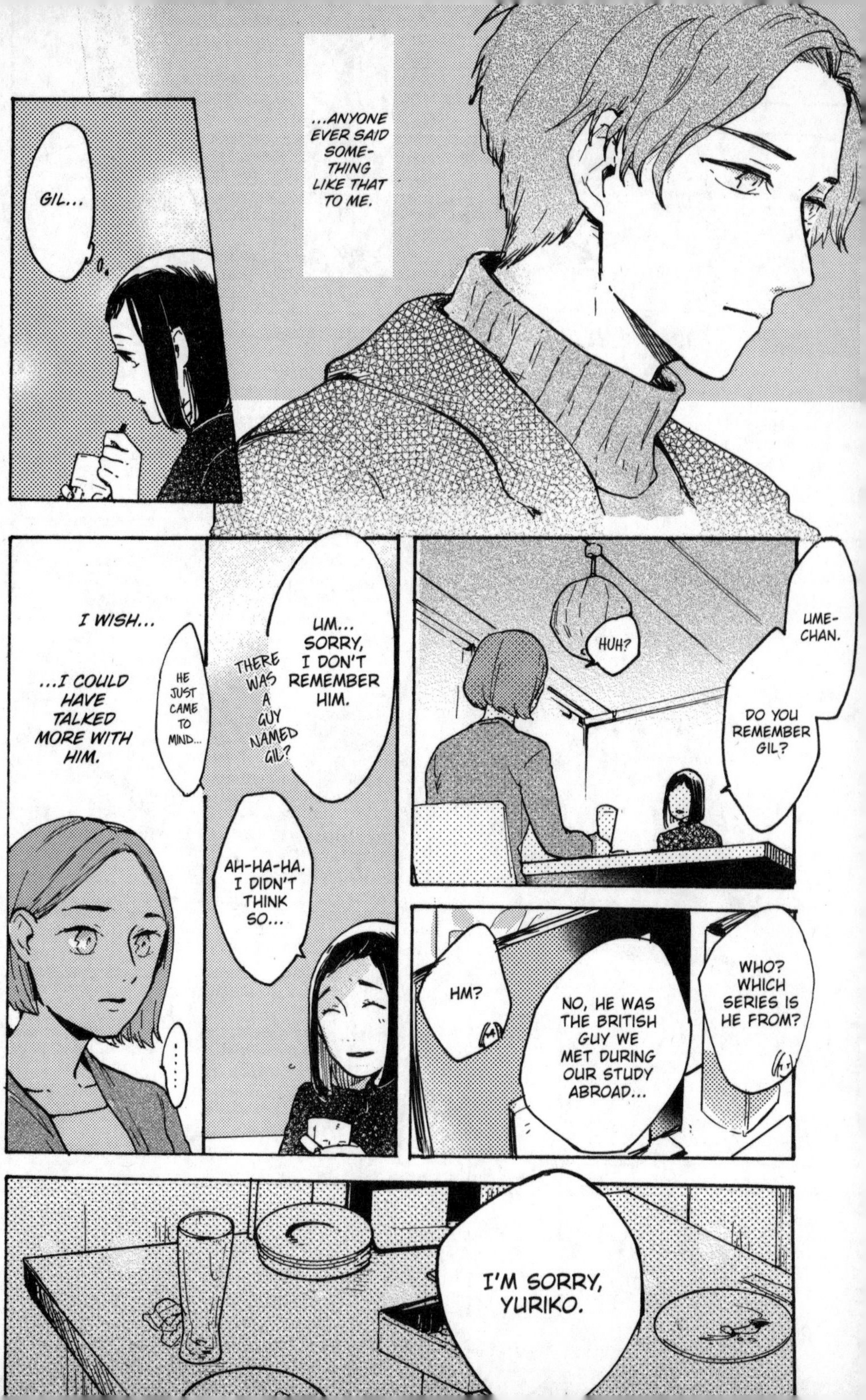
...ANYONE EVER SAID SOMETHING LIKE THAT TO ME.
GIL...
UME-CHAN.
HUH?
DO YOU REMEMBER GIL?
WHO? WHICH SERIES IS HE FROM?
HM?
NO, HE WAS THE BRITISH GUY WE MET DURING OUR STUDY ABROAD...
UM... SORRY, I DON'T REMEMBER HIM.
THERE WAS A GUY NAMED GIL?
AH-HA-HA. I DIDN'T THINK SO...
I WISH...
HE JUST CAME TO MIND...
...I COULD HAVE TALKED MORE WITH HIM.
......
I'M SORRY, YURIKO.

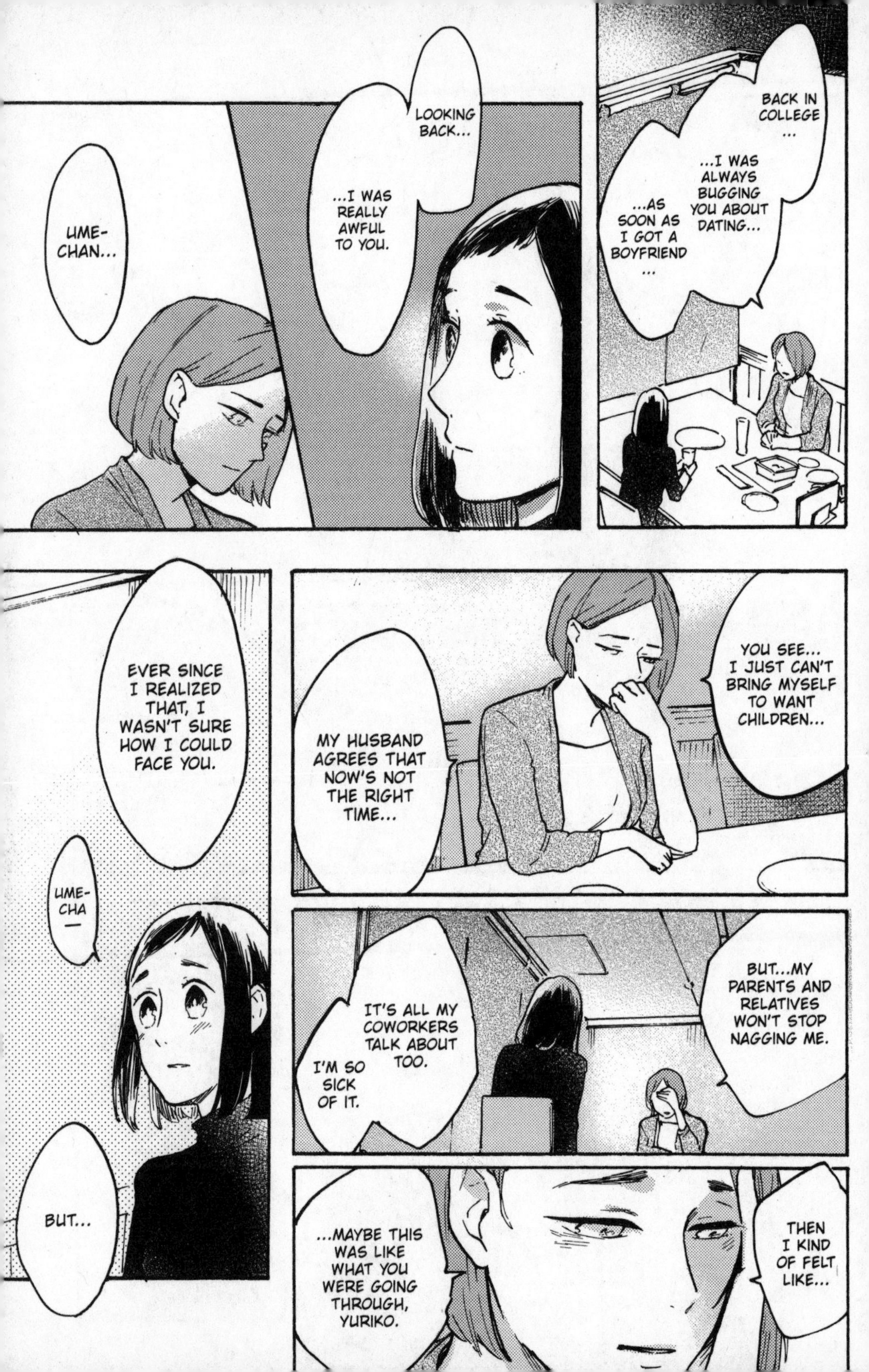
BACK IN COLLEGE...
...I WAS ALWAYS BUGGING YOU ABOUT DATING...
...AS SOON AS I GOT A BOYFRIEND...
LOOKING BACK...
...I WAS REALLY AWFUL TO YOU.
UME-CHAN...
YOU SEE... I JUST CAN'T BRING MYSELF TO WANT CHILDREN...
MY HUSBAND AGREES THAT NOW'S NOT THE RIGHT TIME...
BUT...MY PARENTS AND RELATIVES WON'T STOP NAGGING ME.
IT'S ALL MY COWORKERS TALK ABOUT TOO.
I'M SO SICK OF IT.
THEN I KIND OF FELT LIKE...
...MAYBE THIS WAS LIKE WHAT YOU WERE GOING THROUGH, YURIKO.
EVER SINCE I REALIZED THAT, I WASN'T SURE HOW I COULD FACE YOU.
UME-CHA—
BUT...

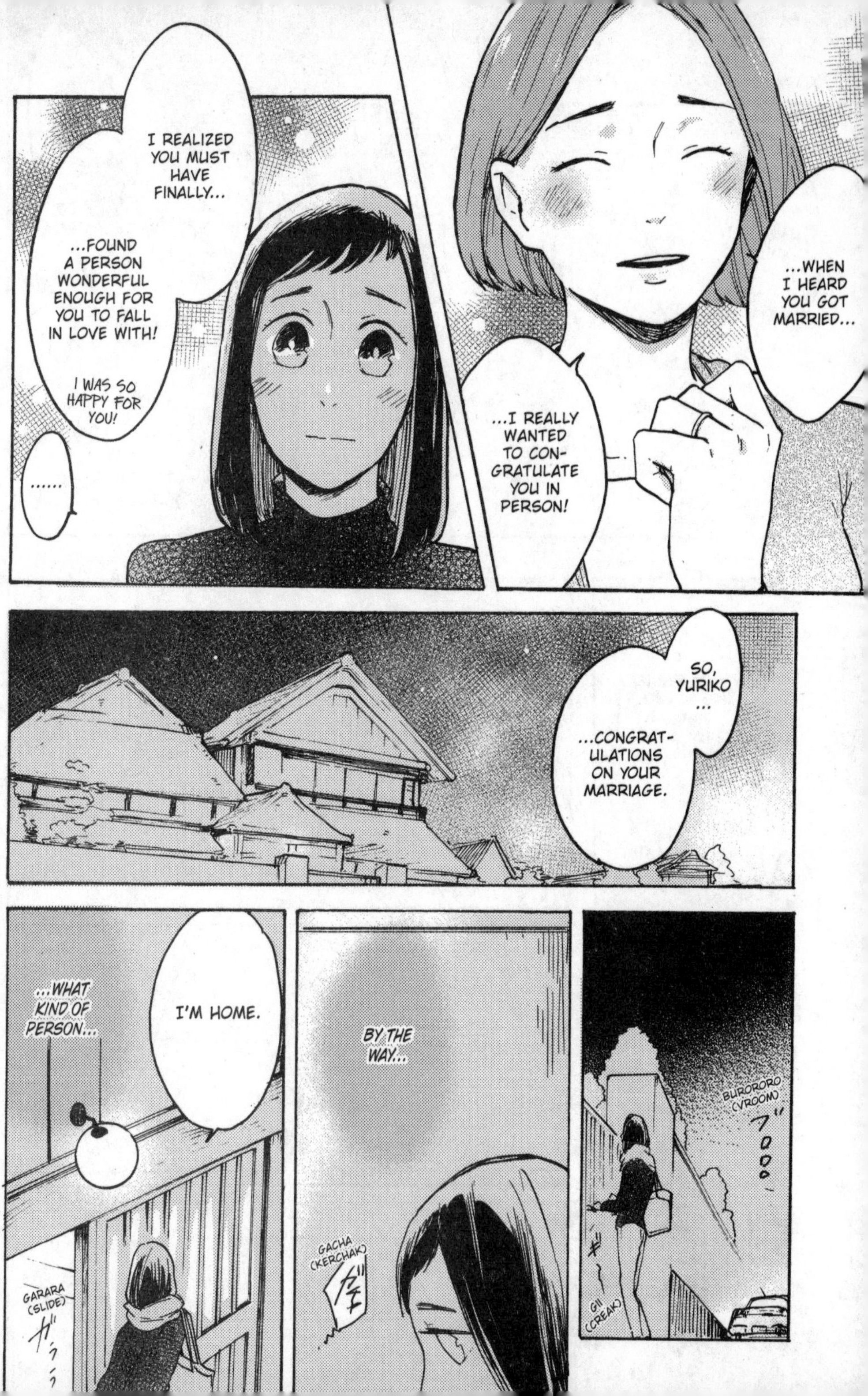
...WHEN I HEARD YOU GOT MARRIED...
...I REALLY WANTED TO CON-GRATULATE YOU IN PERSON!
I REALIZED YOU MUST HAVE FINALLY...
...FOUND A PERSON WONDERFUL ENOUGH FOR YOU TO FALL IN LOVE WITH!
I WAS SO HAPPY FOR YOU!
......
SO, YURIKO ...
...CONGRAT-ULATIONS ON YOUR MARRIAGE.
BURORORO (VROOM)
GII (CREAK)
BY THE WAY...
GACHA (KERCHAK)
...WHAT KIND OF PERSON...
I'M HOME.
GARARA (SLIDE)

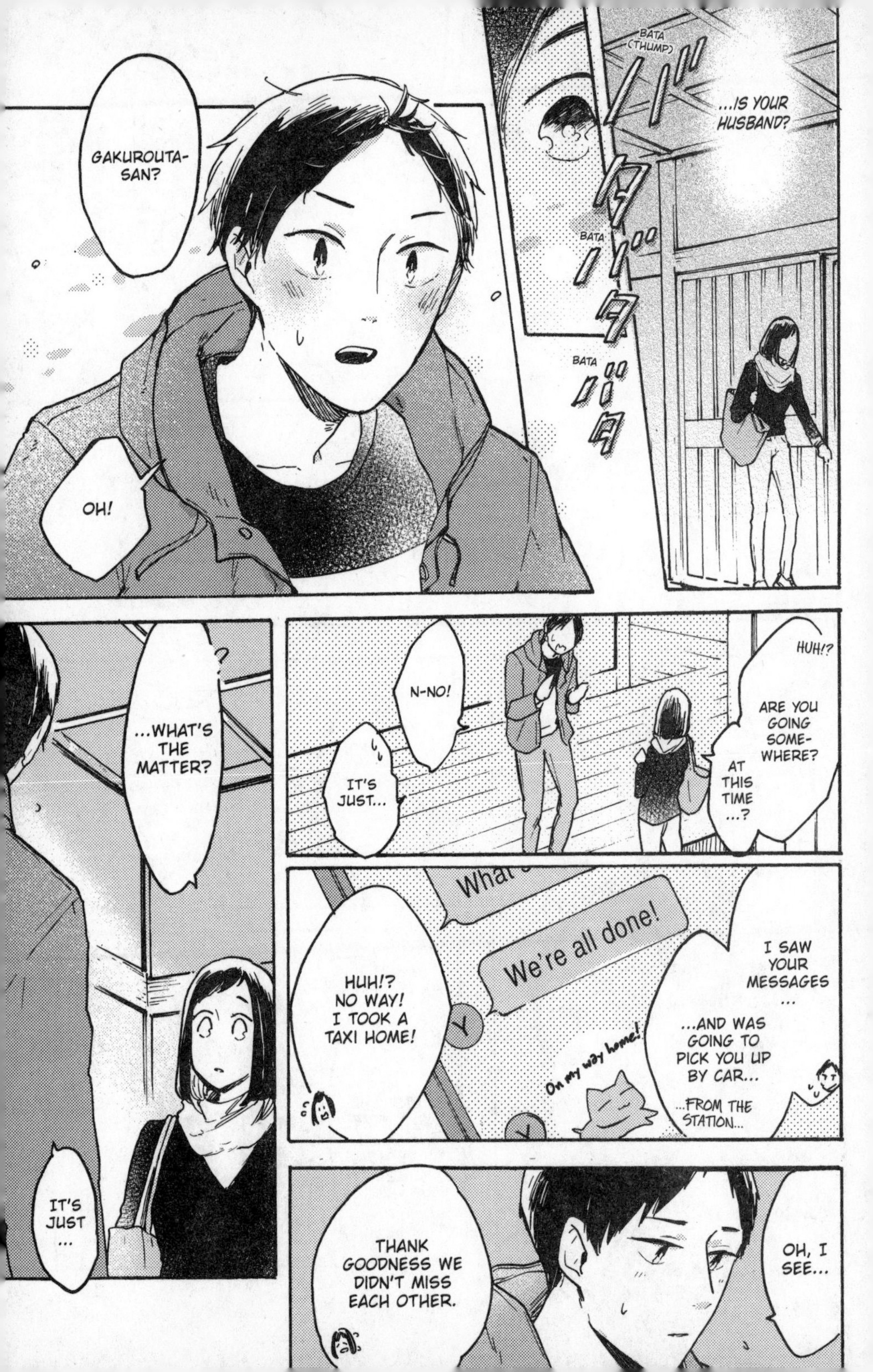
BATA (THUMP)
BATA
BATA
...IS YOUR HUSBAND?
GAKUROUTA-SAN?
OH!
HUH!?
ARE YOU GOING SOME-WHERE?
AT THIS TIME ...?
N-NO!
IT'S JUST...
I SAW YOUR MESSAGES ...
...AND WAS GOING TO PICK YOU UP BY CAR...
...FROM THE STATION...
We're all done!
On my way home!
HUH!? NO WAY! I TOOK A TAXI HOME!
OH, I SEE...
THANK GOODNESS WE DIDN'T MISS EACH OTHER.
...WHAT'S THE MATTER?
IT'S JUST ...

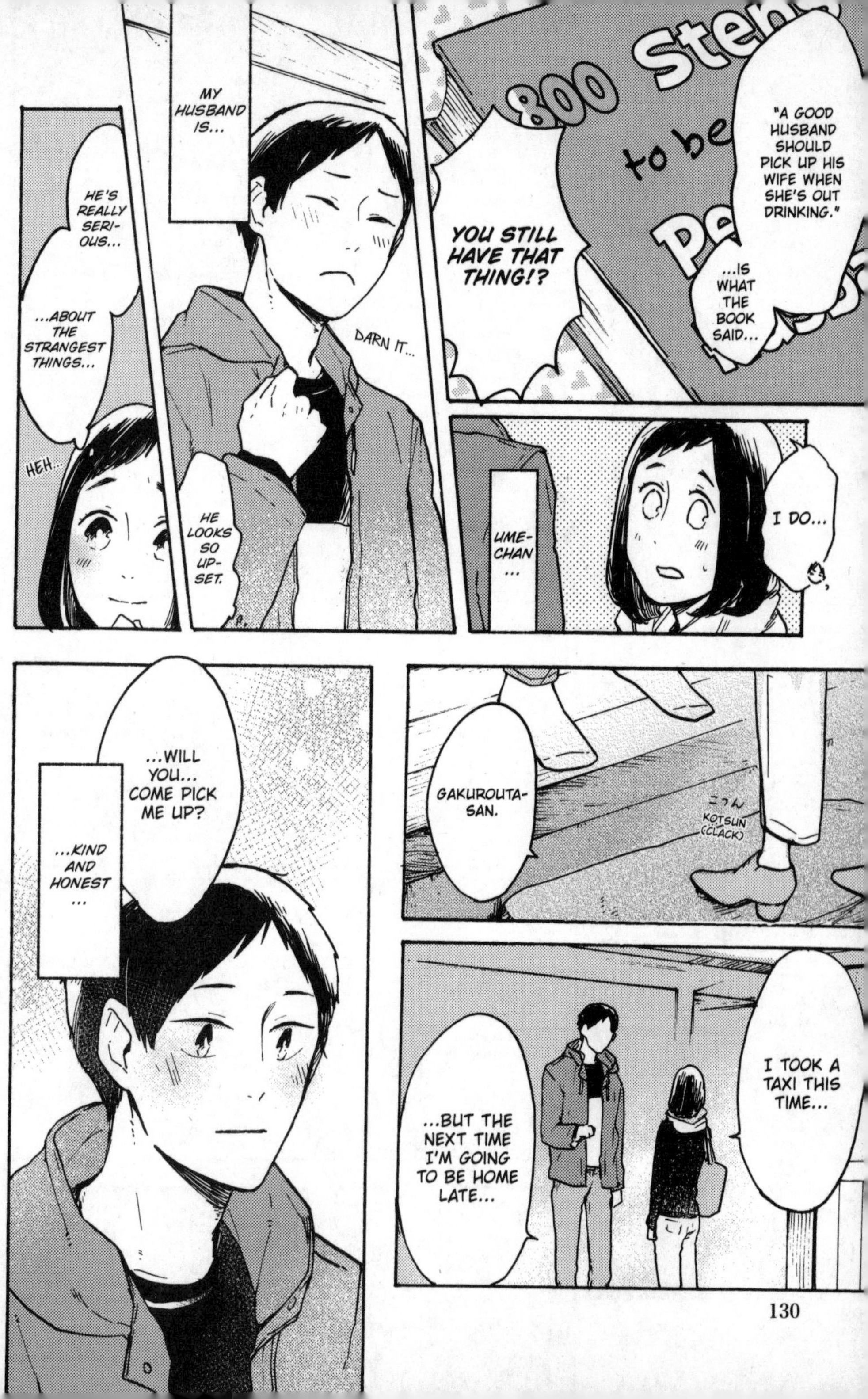
"A GOOD HUSBAND SHOULD PICK UP HIS WIFE WHEN SHE'S OUT DRINKING."
...IS WHAT THE BOOK SAID...
YOU STILL HAVE THAT THING!?
I DO...
UME-CHAN...
MY HUSBAND IS...
DARN IT...
HE LOOKS SO UP-SET.
HE'S REALLY SERI-OUS...
...ABOUT THE STRANGEST THINGS...
HEH...
GAKUROUTA-SAN.
こつん
KOTSUN (CLACK)
I TOOK A TAXI THIS TIME...
...BUT THE NEXT TIME I'M GOING TO BE HOME LATE...
...WILL YOU... COME PICK ME UP?
...KIND AND HONEST...

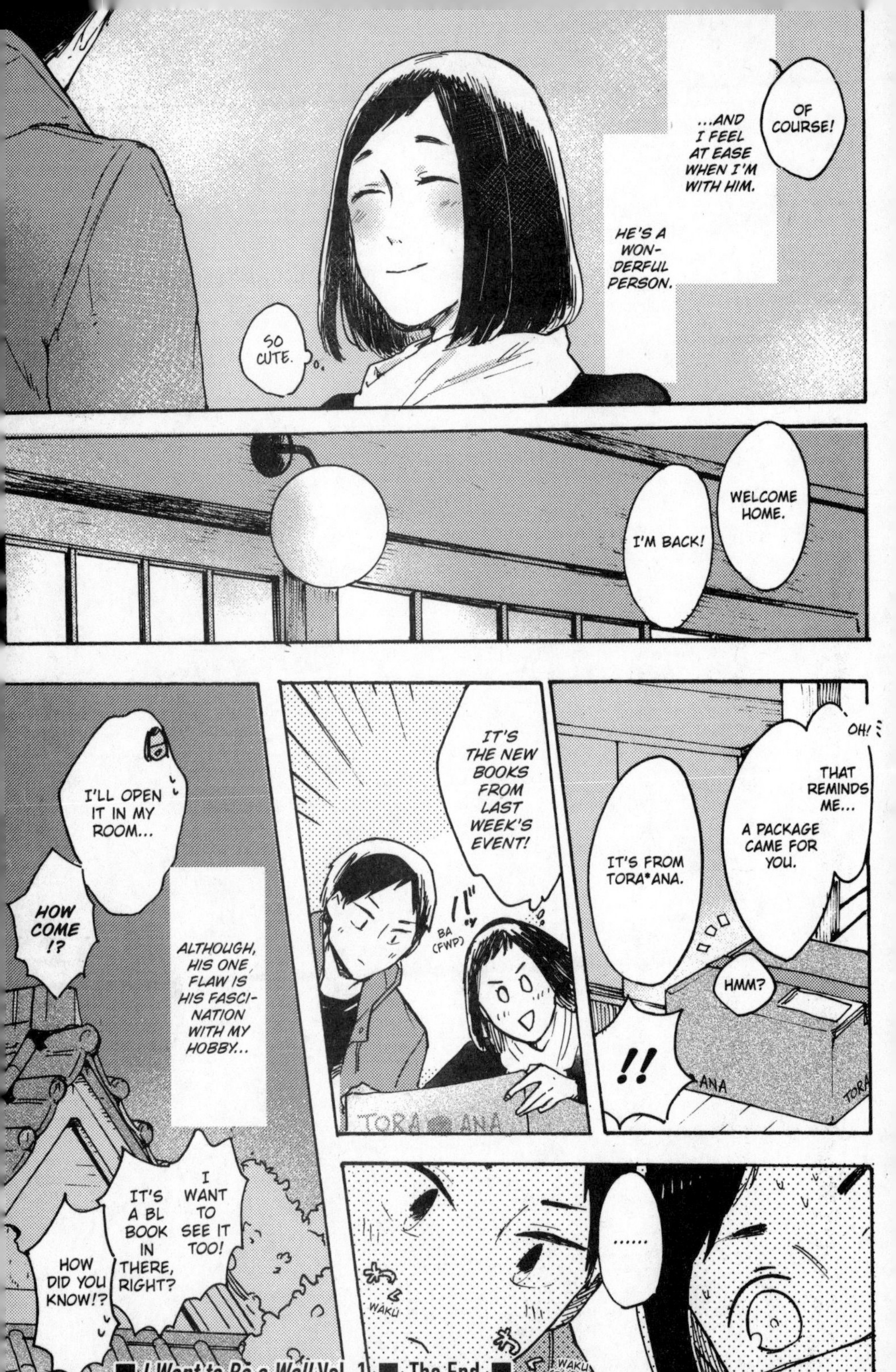
OF COURSE!
...AND I FEEL AT EASE WHEN I'M WITH HIM.
HE'S A WON-DERFUL PERSON.
SO CUTE.
WELCOME HOME.
I'M BACK!
OH!
THAT REMINDS ME...
A PACKAGE CAME FOR YOU.
IT'S FROM TORA*ANA.
HMM?
!!
ANA
TORA
IT'S THE NEW BOOKS FROM LAST WEEK'S EVENT!
BA (FWP)
TORA ANA
......
WAKU
WAKU (EAGER)
I'LL OPEN IT IN MY ROOM...
HOW COME !?
ALTHOUGH, HIS ONE FLAW IS HIS FASCI-NATION WITH MY HOBBY...
I WANT TO SEE IT TOO!
IT'S A BL BOOK IN THERE, RIGHT?
HOW DID YOU KNOW!?

■ *I Want to Be a Wall* Vol. 1 ■ The End ■

I Want
to Be a
Wall

I Want
to Be a
Wall

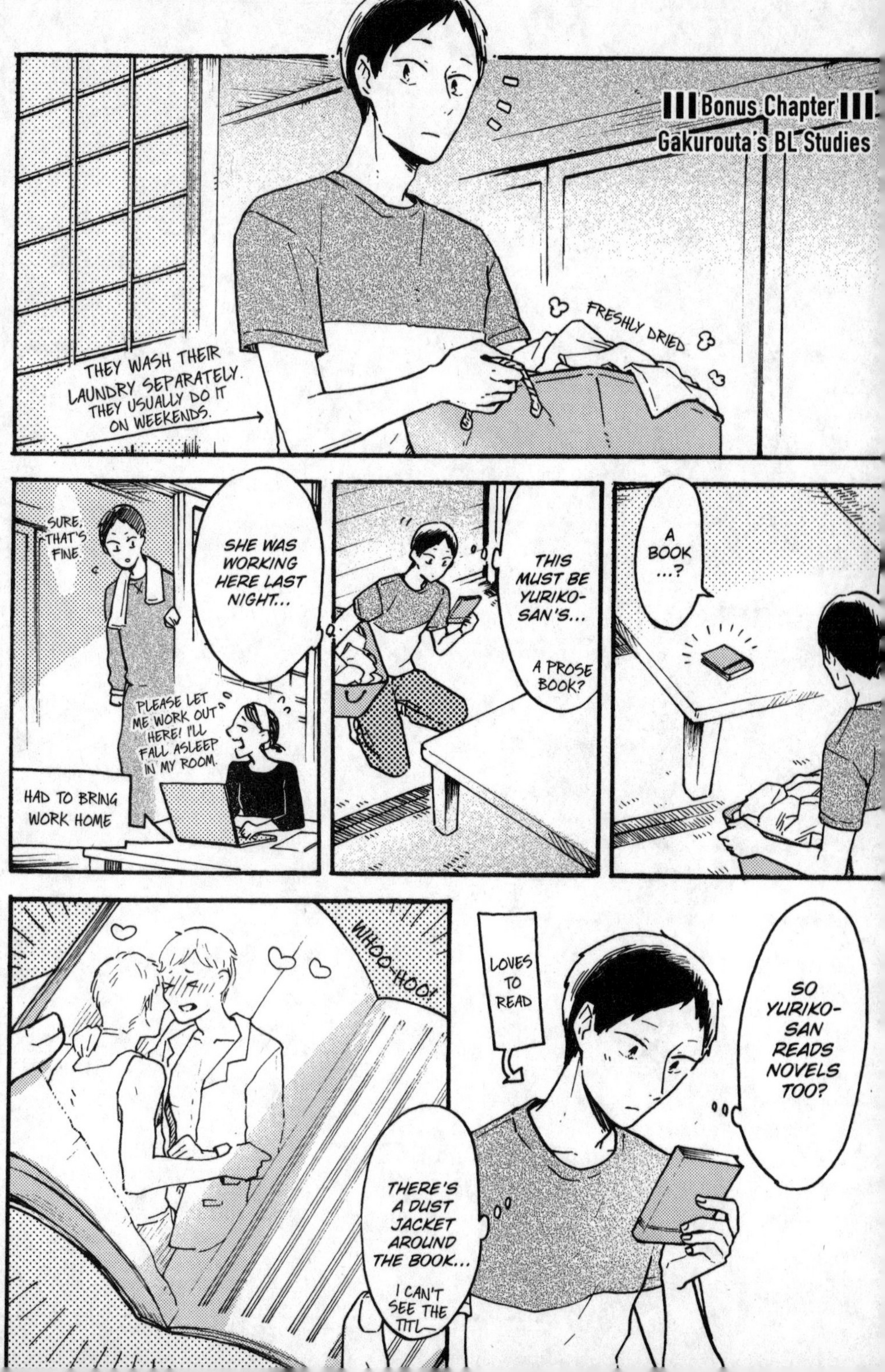
Bonus Chapter
Gakurouta's BL Studies
FRESHLY DRIED
THEY WASH THEIR LAUNDRY SEPARATELY. THEY USUALLY DO IT ON WEEKENDS.
A BOOK ...?
THIS MUST BE YURIKO-SAN'S...
A PROSE BOOK?
SHE WAS WORKING HERE LAST NIGHT...
SURE, THAT'S FINE.
PLEASE LET ME WORK OUT HERE! I'LL FALL ASLEEP IN MY ROOM.
HAD TO BRING WORK HOME
SO YURIKO-SAN READS NOVELS TOO?
LOVES TO READ
THERE'S A DUST JACKET AROUND THE BOOK...
I CAN'T SEE THE TITL—
WHOO-HOO!

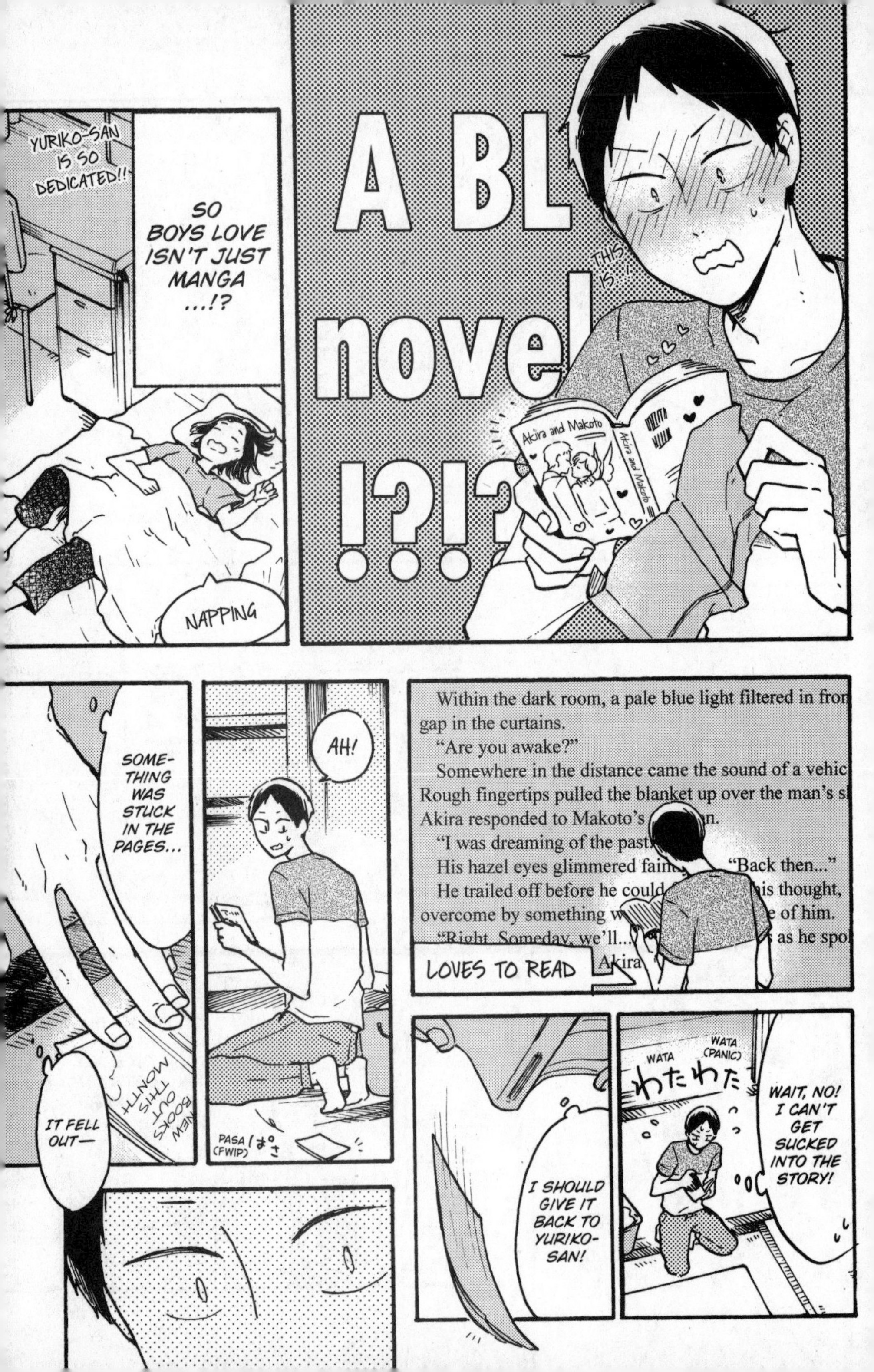
A BL novel!?!?
THIS IS...!
Akira and Makoto
Akira and Makoto
YURIKO-SAN IS SO DEDICATED!!
SO BOYS LOVE ISN'T JUST MANGA ...!?
NAPPING
Within the dark room, a pale blue light filtered in fro
gap in the curtains.
"Are you awake?"
Somewhere in the distance came the sound of a vehic
Rough fingertips pulled the blanket up over the man's s
Akira responded to Makoto's
"I was dreaming of the past
His hazel eyes glimmered fain
"Back then..."
He trailed off before he could
his thought,
overcome by something w
e of him.
as he spo
LOVES TO READ
AH!
PASA (FWIP)
ぱさ
SOME-THING WAS STUCK IN THE PAGES...
NEW BOOKS OUT THIS MONTH
IT FELL OUT—
WATA
WATA (PANIC)
わたわた
WAIT, NO! I CAN'T GET SUCKED INTO THE STORY!
I SHOULD GIVE IT BACK TO YURIKO-SAN!

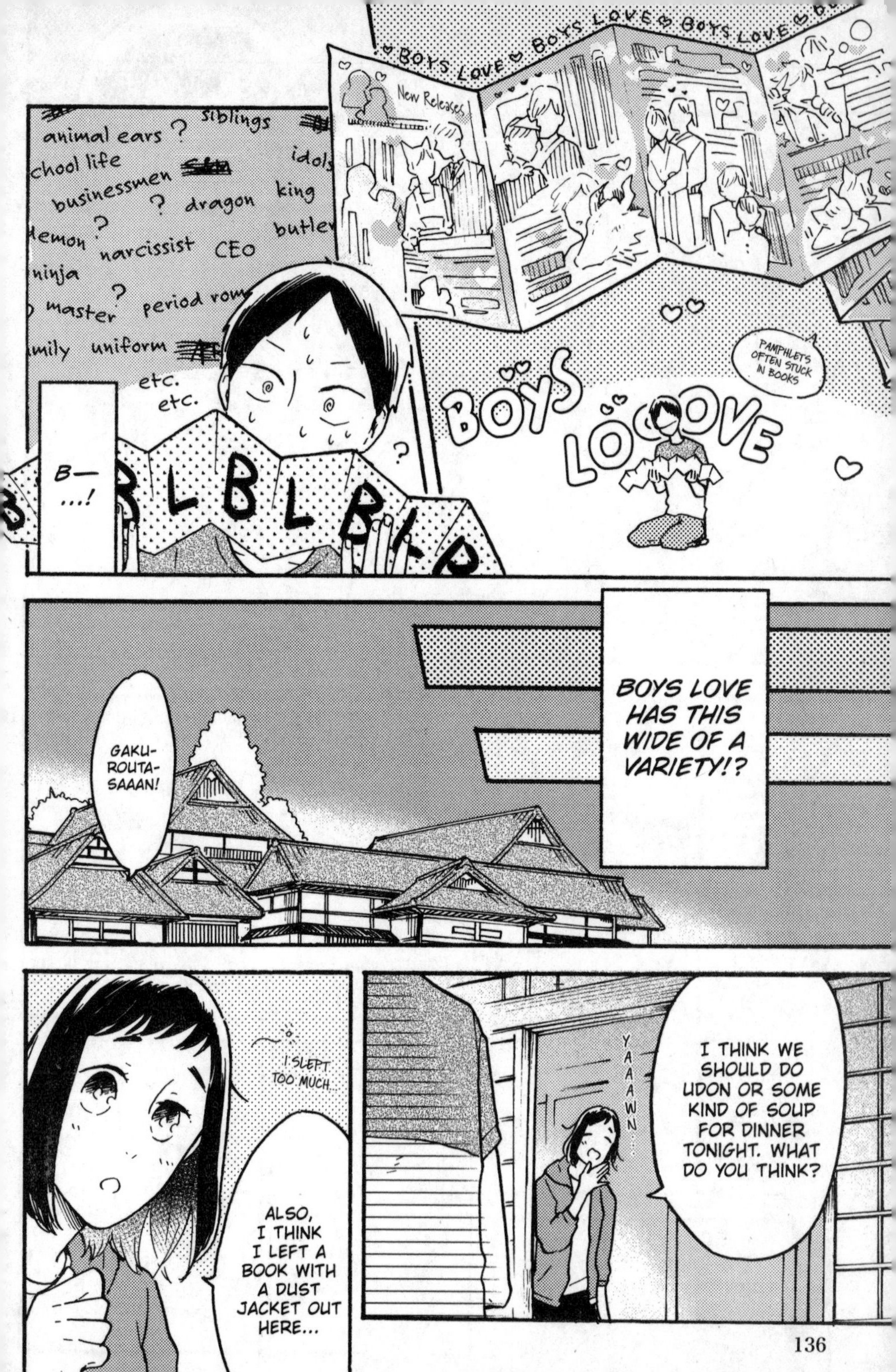
BOYS LOVE BOYS LOVE BOYS LOVE
New Releases
PAMPHLETS OFTEN STUCK IN BOOKS
BOYS LOOOVE
animal ears ? siblings
chool life idols
businessmen ? dragon king
emon ? narcissist CEO butler
ninja
? master period rom
mily uniform
etc. etc.
B— ...!
BLBLBLB
BOYS LOVE HAS THIS WIDE OF A VARIETY!?
GAKU-ROUTA-SAAAN!
YAAAAWN...
I THINK WE SHOULD DO UDON OR SOME KIND OF SOUP FOR DINNER TONIGHT. WHAT DO YOU THINK?
I SLEPT TOO MUCH...
ALSO, I THINK I LEFT A BOOK WITH A DUST JACKET OUT HERE...

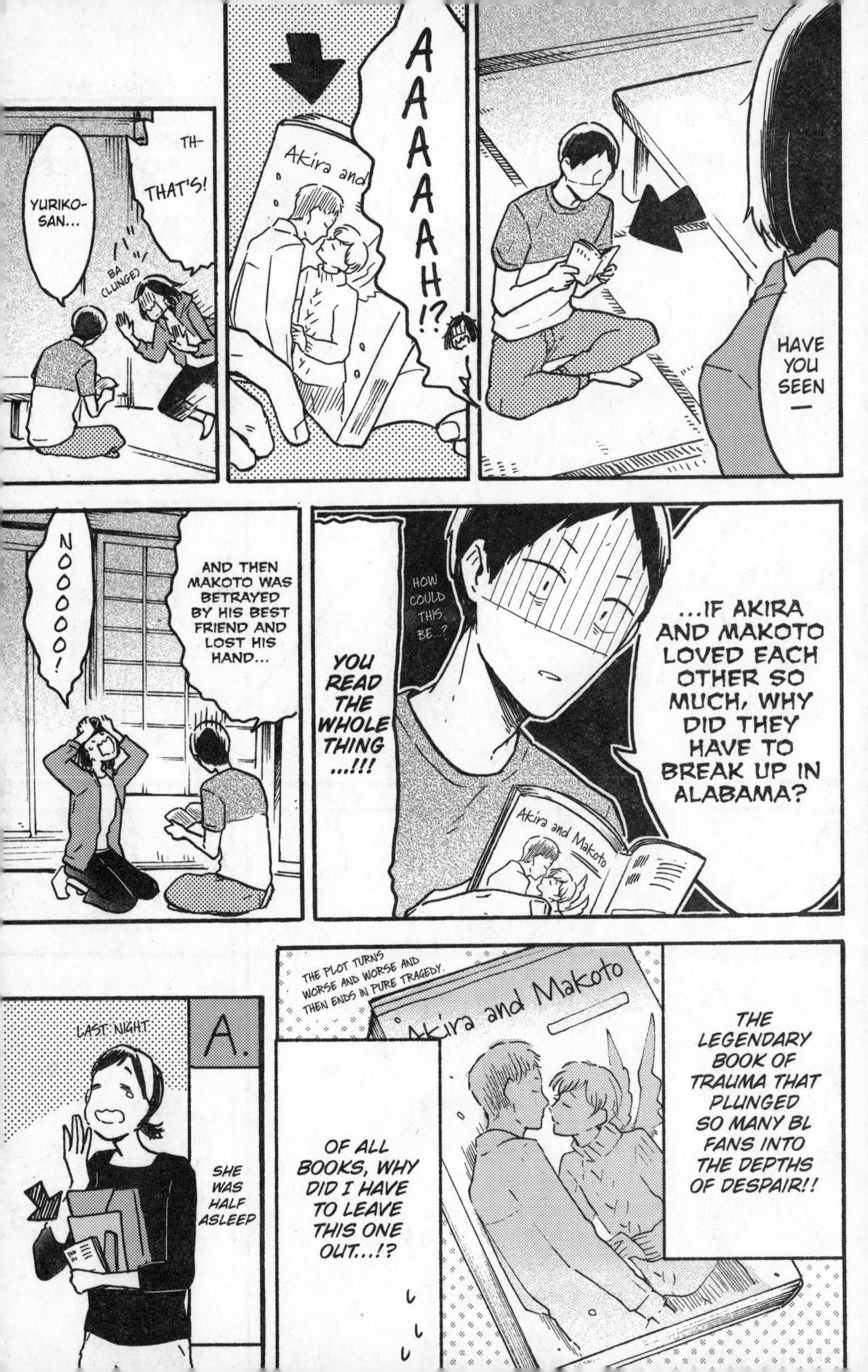
HAVE YOU SEEN —
AAAAAAH!?
Akira and
TH-
THAT'S!
YURIKO-SAN...
BA (LUNGE)
...IF AKIRA AND MAKOTO LOVED EACH OTHER SO MUCH, WHY DID THEY HAVE TO BREAK UP IN ALABAMA?
HOW COULD THIS BE...?
YOU READ THE WHOLE THING ...!!!
Akira and Makoto
AND THEN MAKOTO WAS BETRAYED BY HIS BEST FRIEND AND LOST HIS HAND...
NOOOOOO!
THE LEGENDARY BOOK OF TRAUMA THAT PLUNGED SO MANY BL FANS INTO THE DEPTHS OF DESPAIR!!
THE PLOT TURNS WORSE AND WORSE AND THEN ENDS IN PURE TRAGEDY.
Akira and Makoto
OF ALL BOOKS, WHY DID I HAVE TO LEAVE THIS ONE OUT...!?
A.
LAST NIGHT
SHE WAS HALF ASLEEP

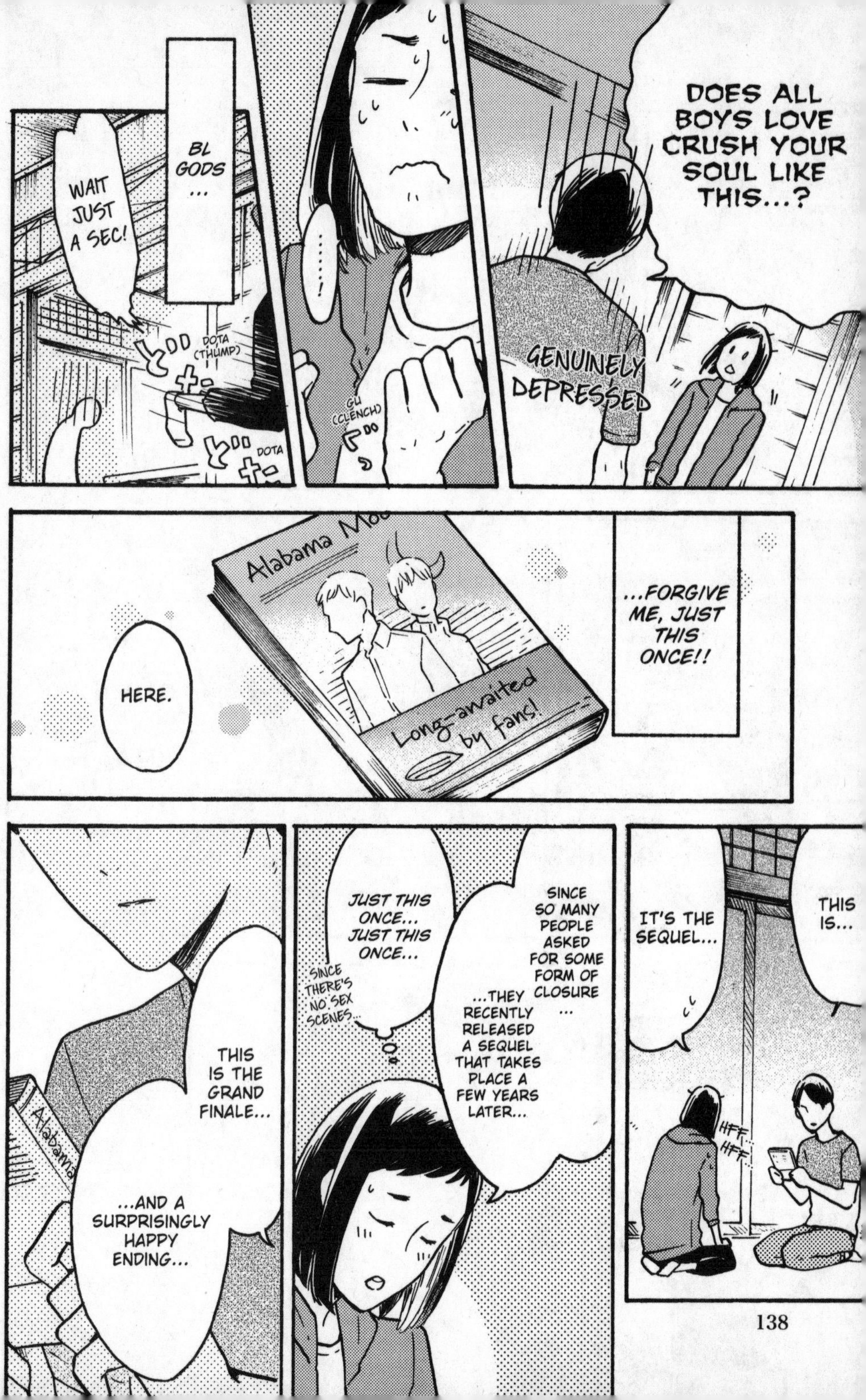
DOES ALL BOYS LOVE CRUSH YOUR SOUL LIKE THIS...?
GENUINELY DEPRESSED
...!
GU (CLENCH)
BL GODS ...
WAIT JUST A SEC!
DOTA (THUMP)
DOTA
...FORGIVE ME, JUST THIS ONCE!!
Alabama Moo
Long-awaited by fans!
HERE.
THIS IS...
IT'S THE SEQUEL...
HFF... HFF...
SINCE SO MANY PEOPLE ASKED FOR SOME FORM OF CLOSURE...
...THEY RECENTLY RELEASED A SEQUEL THAT TAKES PLACE A FEW YEARS LATER...
JUST THIS ONCE... JUST THIS ONCE...
SINCE THERE'S NO SEX SCENES...
THIS IS THE GRAND FINALE...
...AND A SURPRISINGLY HAPPY ENDING...
Alabama

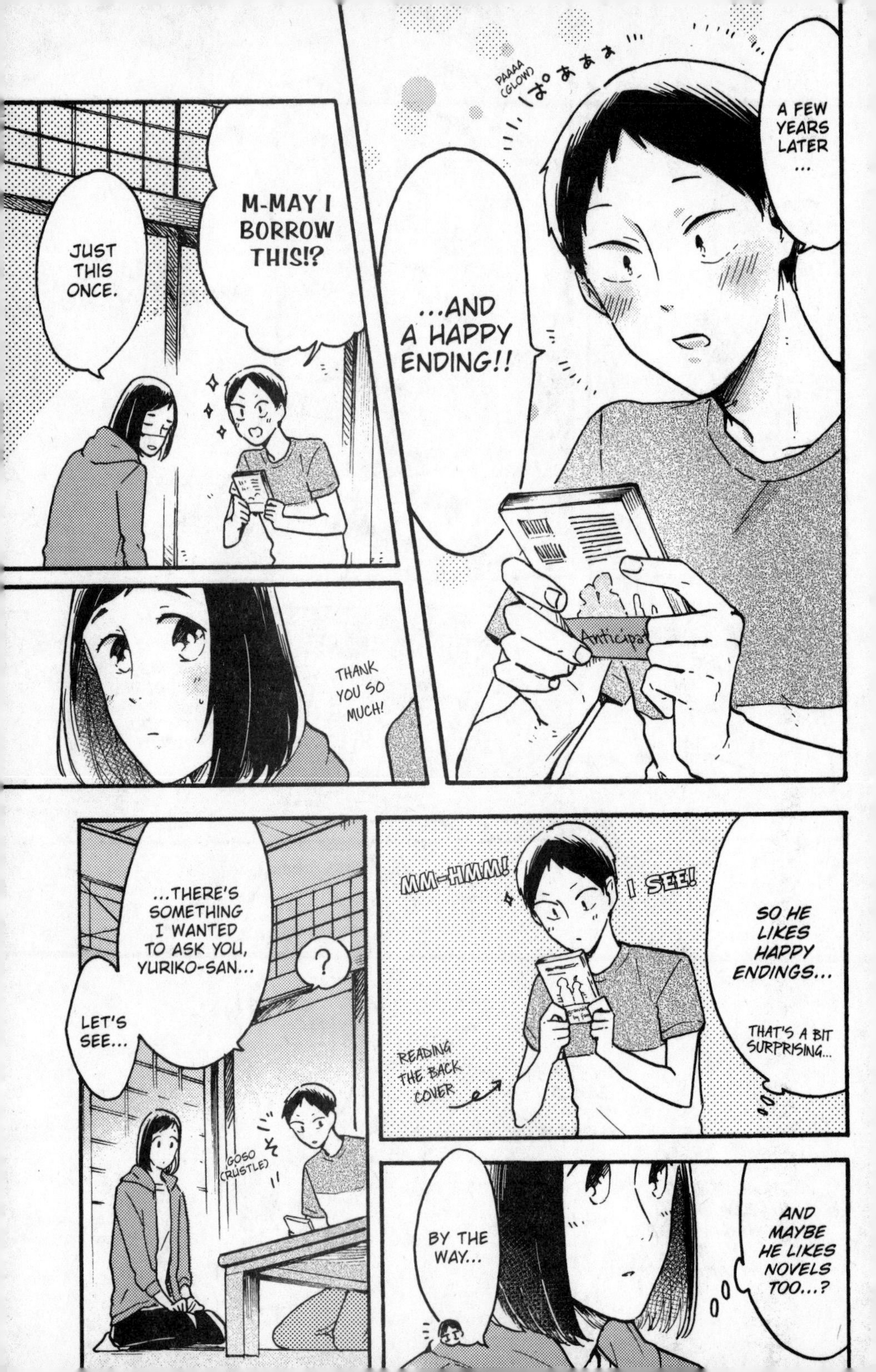
A FEW YEARS LATER ...
PAAAA (GLOW)
...AND A HAPPY ENDING!!
Anticipat
M-MAY I BORROW THIS!?
JUST THIS ONCE.
THANK YOU SO MUCH!
SO HE LIKES HAPPY ENDINGS...
THAT'S A BIT SURPRISING...
I SEE!
MM-HMM!
READING THE BACK COVER
AND MAYBE HE LIKES NOVELS TOO...?
BY THE WAY...
...THERE'S SOMETHING I WANTED TO ASK YOU, YURIKO-SAN...
?
LET'S SEE...
GOSO (RUSTLE)

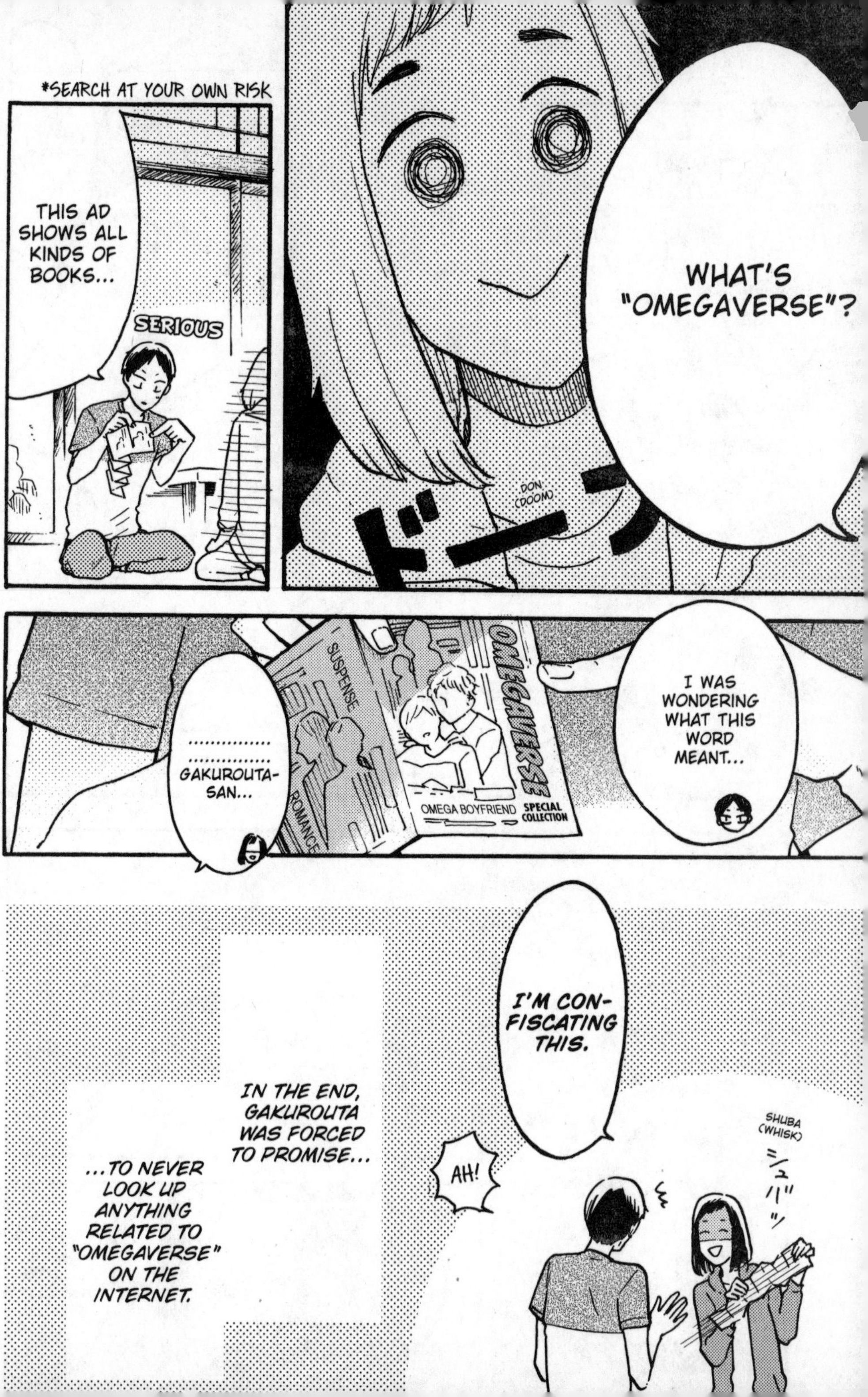
WHAT'S "OMEGAVERSE"?
DON (DOOM)
THIS AD SHOWS ALL KINDS OF BOOKS...
SERIOUS
*SEARCH AT YOUR OWN RISK
I WAS WONDERING WHAT THIS WORD MEANT...
OMEGAVERSE
OMEGA BOYFRIEND
SPECIAL COLLECTION
SUSPENSE
ROMANCE
.... GAKUROUTA-SAN...
I'M CONFISCATING THIS.
SHUBA (WHISK)
AH!
IN THE END, GAKUROUTA WAS FORCED TO PROMISE...
...TO NEVER LOOK UP ANYTHING RELATED TO "OMEGAVERSE" ON THE INTERNET.

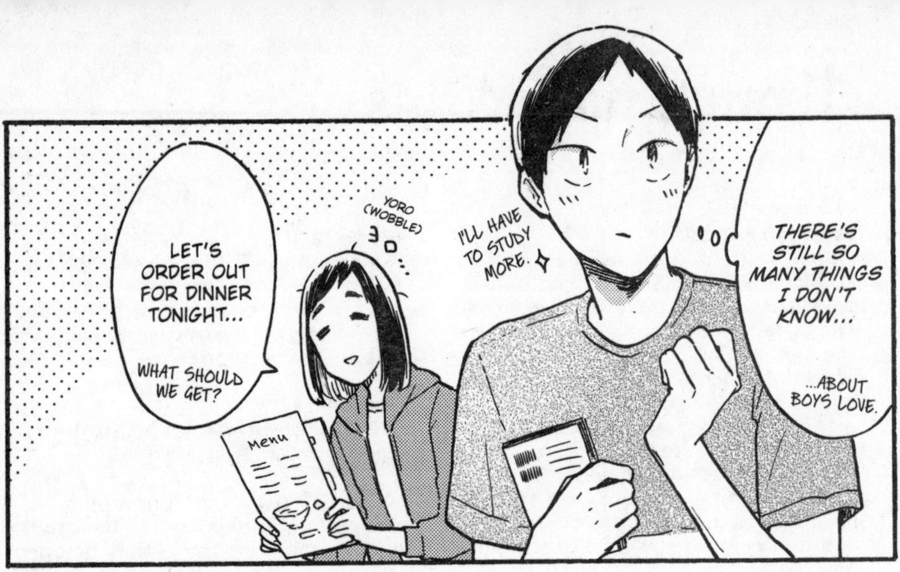
THERE'S STILL SO MANY THINGS I DON'T KNOW...
...ABOUT BOYS LOVE.
I'LL HAVE TO STUDY MORE.
YORO (WOBBLE)
LET'S ORDER OUT FOR DINNER TONIGHT...
WHAT SHOULD WE GET?
Menu

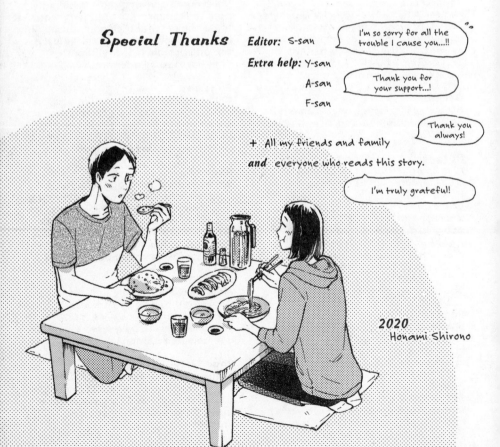

Special Thanks

Editor: S-san

I'm so sorry for all the trouble I cause you...!!

Extra help: Y-san

A-san

Thank you for your support...!

F-san

Thank you always!

\+ All my friends and family

and everyone who reads this story.

I'm truly grateful!

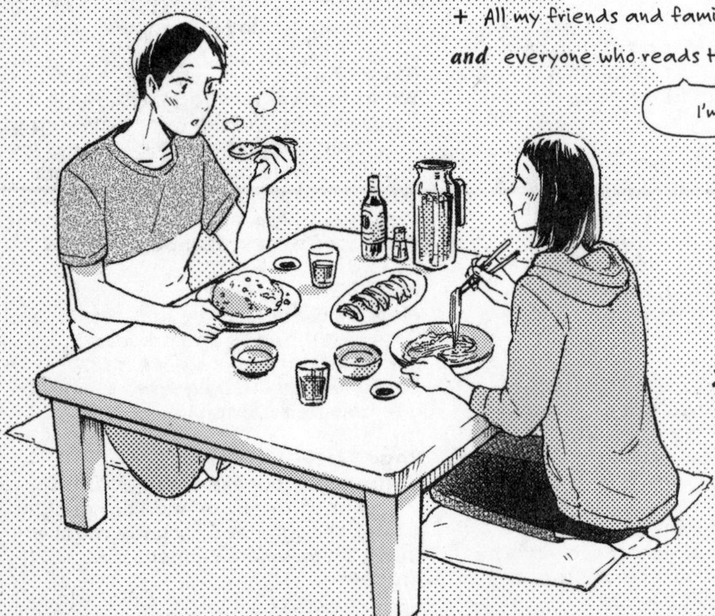

2020

Honami Shirono

Translation Notes

Common Honorifics

-san: The Japanese equivalent of Mr./Mrs./Miss. If a situation calls for politeness, this is the fail-safe honorific.

-kun: Used most often when referring to boys, this indicates affection or familiarity. Occasionally used by older men among their peers, but it may also be used by anyone referring to a person of lower standing.

-chan: An affectionate honorific indicating familiarity used mostly in reference to girls; also used in reference to cute persons or animals of either gender.

-senpai: A suffix used to address upperclassmen or more experienced coworkers.

-sensei: A respectful term for teachers, artists, or high-level professionals.

no honorific: Indicates familiarity or closeness; if used without permission or reason, addressing someone in this manner would constitute an insult.

General

BL: Stands for Boys Love, a genre that, as implied, is about romances between men.

BL fangirl: A translation of the term *fujoshi*, which refers to women who are avid consumers of BL content.

Cover

Knot: The knot pictured on the cover and title page is an Awaji knot, or *Awabi-musubi*. It's a decorative knot that can be used for auspicious occasions as pulling the ends of the string makes the knot tighter. It can also signify a long, intimate friendship.

Page 6

Shipping: Refers to when fandom members pair characters or people in fictional relationships. A shortened version of "relationshipping."

Page 9

Bottom: The subordinate partner, referred to in Japanese as the *uke*. The opposite of this would be the top, or the more dominant partner.

Page 12

Summertime: The original Japanese term here was *mugicha*, or barley tea. This is a reference to how barley tea is commonly drawn in steamy BL manga set in summertime.

Page 16

HP: Stands for "health points" and is a term commonly found in games.

OTP: OTP stands for "one true pair" or "pairing" and is used to denote the couple someone thinks truly belongs together. The Japanese term for OTP is *oshi* CP, or the coupling that one wants to push the most. OTPs are called by a nickname derived from combining both their names into one. In the case of BL, the order of their names usually denotes who the speaker thinks is the top and bottom in the relationship. They can also be referred to as "A x B."

Page 34

Christmas: While getting dumped around Christmas sucks for anyone, it's especially pertinent here because Christmas Eve in Japan is considered to be a romantic day for couples.

Page 47

Working after marriage: For a long time, working women were expected to quit their jobs and become housewives once they were married and had kids. While societal views are changing with the times, this is still the norm with more conservative companies.

Page 63

Male BL readers: Male fans are known as *fudanshi* and are less common than *fujoshi*, since most BL stories tend to be geared toward a female demographic.

Page 77

Uniforms: Japanese schoolchildren will wear uniforms for middle and high school, though not all schools require them. Uniforms for elementary schools are rarer.

Page 106

Otaku: Japanese slang term for "nerd" or "geek." *Otaku* are avid fans of something, and there are different types of *otaku*, just like there are different types of geeks. For example, computer *otaku* are extremely interested in computers. *Otaku* is used more generally for fans of manga and anime. *Fujoshi* can be considered female BL *otaku*.

Prince of Table Tennis: A parody of the sports manga *Prince of Tennis*, which gained popularity among female readers, and especially BL fans, because of its slew of pretty male characters.

Page 107

Slim book: A translation of the Japanese phrase *usui hon*, which is usually used as slang for *doujinshi*. *Doujinshi* are fan-made or self-published works somewhat similar to zines. In Japan, they have a strong reputation as erotic works, though any indie comics would also be considered *doujinshi*.

Page 110

Me and I: The Japanese title of the book is *Ore to Boku*. *Ore* and *boku* are both ways for males to refer to themselves in the first person, but *boku* is the softer and less assertive choice. Depending on who you ask, some also think of using *boku* as having less confidence in oneself while others view using *ore* as a display of arrogance.

Page 112

Shoujo manga: Manga demographically targeted to young girls and women. The specific genre it encompasses can vary greatly, but is most well known for romances.

Page 113

Shounen manga: Manga demographically targeted to young boys and men. Like *shoujo*, the specific genre it encompasses can vary greatly, but is most well known for action-packed stories with superpowers.

Page 131

Tora*ana: A reference to the Japanese e-store Toranoana, which specializes in *doujinshi*. There are also a few brick-and-mortar stores in major cities.

Doujinshi events: Conventions and events for *doujinshi* are a frequent occurrence, with the most well-known being Comiket, a massive summer convention that offers a diverse selection of goods. If an event focuses on a certain genre or topic, it's called an "only" event (i.e. BL-only or magical girl-only). This particular package of books is from one such event, and though Yuriko doesn't specify, she most likely bought them at a BL-only event.

Page 134

Dust jacket: Japanese bookstores will provide plain dust jackets made of paper with purchases, which is handy when one wants to read BL discreetly. They're also convenient for making sure covers don't get dirty.

Novel illustrations: Japanese novels with a younger or more mass appeal, known as light novels, sometimes have multiple full-page black-and-white illustrations sprinkled throughout the books.

Page 136

Mini pamphlets: Small pamphlets stuck in the middle of books are an extremely common advertisement tool used by publishers in Japan.

Page 138

Omegaverse: A popular trope set in an alternate universe where people have secondary biological genders and can be drawn to each other by pheromones. The mechanics of omegaverse mean the content is explicit more often than not.

I Want to Be a Wall

1

Honami Shirono

Translation: Emma Schumacker | Lettering: Alexis Eckerman

This book is a work of fiction. Names, characters, places, and incidents are the product of the author's imagination or are used fictitiously. Any resemblance to actual events, locales, or persons, living or dead, is coincidental.

WATASHI WA KABE NI NARITAI Vol. 1

First published in Japan in 2020 by KADOKAWA CORPORATION, Tokyo.
English translation rights arranged with KADOKAWA CORPORATION, Tokyo and Yen Press, LLC through Tuttle-Mori Agency, Inc.

Yen Press
150 West 30th Street, 19th Floor
New York, NY 10001

Visit us at yenpress.com
facebook.com/yenpress • twitter.com/yenpress
yenpress.tumblr.com • instagram.com/yenpress

First Yen Press Edition: April 2022

Yen Press is an imprint of Yen Press, LLC.
The Yen Press name and logo are trademarks of Yen Press, LLC.

The publisher is not responsible for websites (or their content) that are not owned by the publisher.

Library of Congress Control Number: 2021953400

ISBNs: 978-1-9753-3896-1 (paperback)
978-1-9753-3897-8 (ebook)

10 9 8 7 6 5 4 3 2 1

WOR

Printed in the United States of America